Give Me Tomorrow

BOOKS BY PATRICK K. O'DONNELL

Beyond Valor

Into the Rising Sun

Operatives, Spies, and Saboteurs

We Were One

The Brenner Assignment

They Dared Return

GIVE ME
TOMORROW

THE KOREAN WAR'S GREATEST UNTOLD STORY—
THE EPIC STAND OF THE MARINES OF GEORGE COMPANY

PATRICK K. O'DONNELL

DA CAPO PRESS
A MEMBER OF THE PERSEUS BOOKS GROUP

Printed in the United States of America.

For information, address
Da Capo Press, 11 Cambridge Center, Cambridge, MA 02142.

Design and production by Eclipse Publishing Services
Set in 11.5 point Bembo
Maps by Cristoph Robinson

Cataloging-in-Publication data for this book is available from the Library of Congress.

ISBN: 978-0-306-81801-1
Library of Congress Control Number: 2010929248

Published by Da Capo Press
A Member of the Perseus Books Group
www.dacapopress.com

Da Capo Press books are available at special discounts for bulk purchases in the U.S. by corporations, institutions, and other organizations. For more information, please contact the Special Markets Department at the Perseus Books Group, 2300 Chestnut Street, Suite 200, Philadelphia, PA 19103, or call (800) 810-4145, ext. 5000, or e-mail special.markets@perseusbooks.com.

10 9 8 7 6 5 4

To my "cute-o-saurus," the greatest daughter in the world, Lily

To the heroic men of George Company

To Amtrak, the greatest way to see the country
and write a book—on the rails

CONTENTS

PREFACE

*January 2005, on the flight home from the Battle of Fallujah
to Camp Pendleton, California.*

MARINES in uniform packed the commercial airliner. Most of the men
had aged well beyond their nineteen or twenty years. As I looked
to my left, I noticed that Lance Corporal Dustin Turpen★ was holding two weapons as he stared blankly down the aisle toward the
cockpit. One belonged to him, but the other contained the distinctive
203 grenade launcher. The pitted and pockmarked weapon had formerly belonged to Corporal Michael Hanks, one of Turpen's fire team
leaders. Two months earlier, in the fierce fighting at Fallujah, Hanks
took mortal wounds while clearing a small house used by the insur-
gents to launch an ambush. I had helped carry Hanks from the house
to the street, where he died of his wounds.

As the plane made its way over the Atlantic and into American
airspace, a massive cheer went up from everyone on board. A tingle
ran up my spine; it felt good to be an American. We were finally home.

★Turpen died in January 2010. He and many of the other members of First Platoon continued
to be haunted by their experiences in Iraq.

Shortly thereafter, I made my way toward the center of the plane for a soda. A Marine from another company whom I had not met approached and, somewhat angrily, asked why I, as a civilian, was wearing a Marine uniform: "It took me thirteen weeks to have the opportunity to wear this uniform. You think you earned it?"

As he said that, I looked down at my boots, which were still coated a dark brown burgundy from Mike Hank's blood.

I just looked at him, and another Marine from the unit I was with answered affirmatively for me. During the Battle of Fallujah, I wore a Marine Corps uniform while I cleared houses and fought with the troops. Why? It was a simple matter of survival. It's something I rarely discuss—a part of my life that's been airbrushed over.* Like many of the men on the plane, I too wore the thousand-yard-stare—the result of multiple near-death experiences in combat.

Nevertheless, the encounter made me uneasy, and I changed into civilian clothes onboard the plane.

The aircraft touched down, first in Maine and then later at an airbase in California. There, a bus shuttled the men of Lima Company, First Platoon, Third Battalion, First Marine Regiment (or 3/1, as they are called) and me to Camp Pendleton, California. When we arrived, all of First Platoon walked across a small bridge ringed with yellow bows. On the other side stood the families of the soldiers.

Because I had asked my family not to attend, I was completely alone. As I made my way across the bridge, I could sense people wondering who I was. It was a surreal experience.

Standing with the families were several older men wearing Marine Corps emblems—veterans from a previous war. One wore a red Marine Corps windbreaker, and another had on a red shirt with a golden embroidered eagle globe and anchor on his chest near his heart.

The veterans greeted me warmly and after a brief conversation, I asked the veterans what they thought about this generation of

---

* My book, *We Were One* (Da Capo, 2006) tells the story of the men of Lima Company First Platoon, 3/1 Marine Regiment at the battle of Fallujah, where I walked shoulder-to-shoulder with the platoon. Nearly six years have passed since the Battle of Fallujah, and on most days, my experience there feels like a dream. At other times, my memories become so vivid and dramatic that it seems as if it all happened yesterday.

Marines. One told me, "I think this might be the next great genera-tion." He was impressed by the quality of the men today and their willingness to go to Iraq and Afghanistan over and over. He then pro-ceeded to tell me that he had fought at Guadalcanal, throughout the Solomons, and was later wounded in the Pacific. He was back in action for the Korean War.

Next, he told me, "You know that 3/1 carried the George Com-pany battle guidon in Fallujah." In the November 2004 Battle of Fal-lujah, I had seen that guidon carried into the battle. It was the same flag carried by George Company through the major campaigns of the Korean War—Seoul, Inchon, Chosin, and beyond.

In one of those remarkable random acts of kindness, one of the veterans, Lieutenant Colonel Clark Henry, asked me, "Would you like a ride to the train station and lunch?" Alone and without a ride, I gladly accepted. Other veterans of George Company joined us.

As we sat down for a meal, I began telling them First Platoon's story. They listened intently. One of the men then chimed in, "You're a Marine too."

I said nothing, but felt deeply honored by the compliment.

For the past ten or fifteen years, the men of George Company have always been there for the Marines of 3/1, sending countless care pack-ages, coming to events, and feeding wounded warriors with their sup-port, both financial and emotional. Whenever the unit is deployed or returns home, these senior Marines attend to show their support. They care.

After lunch, they dropped me off at the train station. As we parted, Robert Camarillo said, "You know, George Company has a pretty interesting story also. We held off elements of an entire regiment of Chinese at East Hill of the Chosin Reservoir." I didn't know it then, but his self-effacing and offhand comment belied the fact that George Company's story closely resembled the classic tale of the epic stand of three hundred Spartans who held off the Persians.

On five separate occasions George Company (outnumbered at least ten to one) made stands against enemy regiments.

And just like that—like most of the books that I have written—the story found me.

Over the past five years, I've come to know the men of George Company. They invited me to their reunions, and they've become my friends. They have remained active in the lives of the Marines of First Platoon, as well as the Marines of 3/1. This book is a story about George Company, and a story of war and its aftermath. As one George Company Marine put it best, "The generations are all interconnected."

Prologue

THE COLD WINDS of autumn were setting in, and the leaves just beginning to turn amber and crimson. In late September 1986, thirty-six years after their first taste of combat, the men of George Company reunited.

The aging warriors circled a room in the Thayer Hotel, located a stone's throw from the U.S. Military Academy in West Point, New York. The venerable hotel had served as a temporary home to numerous dignitaries, generals, and even General Douglas MacArthur's mother, who stayed there while he attended the academy.

The castlelike ambience of the building seemed to fit the event. The handcrafted woodwork from the 1920s lent a stately air to the occasion. This chilly autumn day, it would be home to blood brothers who for the most part had not seen each other in three decades. Each man was anxious in his own way; the moment, bittersweet.

The majority of George Company hung up their uniforms at the close of the Korean War. They returned home, eighteen- and nineteen-year-olds who had grown older than their fathers. Part of the "Forgotten War," the Leathernecks never talked about their experiences to anyone. America was ambivalent about their sacrifices. Nobody understood, and unlike WWII, nobody seemed to care about the Korean War. But the invisible scars of war remained. In some cases, those wounds had grown deeper, manifesting themselves in phantasmal dreams. But in the hospitality room at the Thayer, the men rarely discussed the unpleasant side of war, even among friends.

On this day, it was all about fellowship—friendships and bonds formed in battle among men who trusted and loved one another. "It was like heaven," recalled one George Company Marine, "seeing my friends for the first time" since the war.

Bonds of friendship held George Company together, a spirit that had remained unbroken. That friendship, combined with excellent leadership, had allowed the men to accomplish the impossible, making several epic stands that had changed the course of history.

As the senior warriors circled the hospitality room, a ghost from the past entered—a forgotten warrior from the forgotten war. A balding, gray-haired man, whose bearing seemed vaguely familiar, approached one of the Marines. "Have you talked to Rocco Zullo?" he asked.

"No. Rocco was killed on the road to Hagaru in November 1950."

"No, he wasn't," responded the man, sternly.

Another Marine overheard the conversation: "Why, he's dead!"

"He's not dead."

The confident figure then added with an unmistakable bellowing voice, "You're talking to Rocco Zullo."

Most of the men in the room were dumbfounded. First Sergeant Rocco Zullo had been killed on November 29, 1950. Or so they thought.*

Overcome by emotion, one Marine fought back tears as he flashed back to one of the most difficult nights of his life.

---

* Some members of George Company knew Zullo survived the war, including a few in the room at the reunion, but most of the company thought the first sergeant perished on November 29, 1950.

The Road to Hagaru-ri, Task Force Drysdale, November 29, 1950

"Get your fucking guinea ass up here, and go find me some ammo!" The beefy, six-foot-three first sergeant barked at a nearby Marine.

Dozens of gnomelike, parka-clad Chinese soldiers darted around the trucks in front of him. *Christ! Chinese are all around,* he thought, as he scanned ten or fifteen yards to the left and right.

Out of the corner of his eye, First Sergeant Zullo saw a Chinese sapper pitch a satchel charge under one of the Marines' trucks, engulfing the two-and-a-half-ton vehicle in a massive fireball. The cacophony of enemy bugles and whistles could not drown out the deadly, high-pitched scream of an incoming mortar round. Small arms fire and explosions rocked the area, throwing up a blanket of smoke that settled over the valley. The stench of cordite permeated the air.

A streaking flare lit up the evening sky, highlighting the snow that was blowing in sideways, pelting the men's faces. Half a dozen enemy rounds perforated the soft metal skin of the 6x6 truck as Zullo worked his way into the ring mount of the .50 caliber machine gun. He frantically pulled back on the belt to clear the jam. With the temperature hovering near −20, any exposed flesh would stick to metal. Ice coated the men's beards and mustaches, and snow caked their gear and helmets.

Zullo pulled back the bolt on the .50 and threaded the copper and steel belt into the chamber. A hastily wrapped bandage covered a fresh bullet wound on his left wrist, and crimson seeped through the left shoulder of his parka where he'd taken shrapnel. He adjusted the head space on the weapon and began firing on the Chinese with projectiles that could cut a man in half.

Zullo provided covering fire as Marines rushed to recover a fallen man. He stayed on the gun for hours as the trucks pushed forward through one Chinese roadblock after another, while he administered a steady drumbeat of death.

Finally, the Marines and what was left of the convoy of trucks and tanks cleared the last enemy roadblock. Still manning the .50, the World War II veteran of the Pacific campaign spotted a beautiful sight: tents and the working lights from the airfield under construction in Hagaru-ri. *We made it*, he thought.

Abruptly, several individuals clad in Marine uniforms emerged from the tents and approached the convoy. Zullo turned to George Company's commanding officer. "Captain, what's our next move?"

Right at that moment, small arms fire erupted from the tents, and the muzzle flashes illuminated Chinese faces cloaked by Marine green. Machine gun and rifle bullets tore through Zullo's side, leaving a hole the size of a grapefruit. Blood gushed from his guts like a geyser.

Two of his men covered the first sergeant's broken body, forming a shield of flesh and bone. They loaded him back on a truck where he faded in out of consciousness as his fellow Marines worked to save his life. As what was left of the tattered Marine convoy rolled through the gates of Hagaru-ri, one Marine who'd been tending to his wounds looked up. "I can't find a pulse," he said.

Three subdued men struggled to control their emotions as they carefully lifted the fallen first sergeant into the makeshift morgue. The dead lay stacked inside the standard-issue tent like cordwood. With no room inside, the three gently placed Zullo's body outside near a corner, away from the others. Dejected, they rejoined their brothers who were still staggering into Hagaru-ri.

After his body had rested in the house of the dead for hours, word finally trickled down to the men. Zullo was dead.

The "Minutemen of 1950"

August 1950, Tent Camp 2, Camp Pendleton, California

A LONG LINE of privates and other enlisted Marines stretched out the door of the weather-beaten Quonset hut. The line included Americans from all over the country and all walks of life. Men who had been stockbrokers, reporters, and factory workers just a day before abruptly found themselves in uniform. They stood scattered among veterans of World War II and regular Marines. The speed of their assembly led one observer to dub them the "Minutemen of 1950."

Suddenly, a cocksure sergeant jumped to the front of the line and made his way to the olive-drab government-issue desk. A booming voice greeted the interloper: "I don't give a shit who you are. Get fuckin' back in line!"

Trembling, the sergeant stared at First Sergeant Zullo, who had a presence and stature that only years of combat could weld. As the sergeant turned to go back to the end of the line, he met the eyes of Private Tom Powers, a burly Irishman from Brooklyn, and said sheepishly, "You're next."

Powers's legs shook as he approached the first sergeant's desk. *This guy is absolutely terrifying*, thought Powers.

The square-jawed first sergeant then asked Powers matter of factly, "MOS?" In military jargon, MOS means "military occupation specialty."

Powers looked up at the sergeant and mumbled, "Wireman."

Zullo shot back, "Well, you're in the machine guns now."

The private had never actually touched a machine gun in his life.

Next, Bruce Farr, a lanky Southerner, approached Zullo's desk.

"MOS?" boomed the first sergeant once again.

Farr responded, "I have three."

"I'm not a mind reader. Tell 'em to me."

Farr, a man known to "talk your ear off," rattled off his three MOSs in a tangy Tennessee accent. The first sergeant then barked, "You're in the machine guns." Zullo fit men into positions like a master stone cutter building a medieval cathedral, but in the summer of 1950, he wasn't building a house of worship—he was building George Company.

The summer of 1950 was filled with baseball, barbecues, and family reunions, and Nat King Cole's "Mona Lisa" dominated the airwaves. The tranquility was shattered at dawn on June 25, 1950, when more than ten divisions of the North Korean People's Army (NKPA) rumbled across the 38th Parallel in Korea. Armed with 234 stout Russian T-34 tanks,★ the 231,000 North Koreans launched a blitzkrieg-like attack that led to the complete capture of Seoul in three days. The routed Republic of South Korea's (ROK) Army retreated south to the tip of the Korean peninsula and the port of Pusan.

★ The Soviets cheaply and efficiently manufactured the T-34, arguably the greatest tank of WWII and the first main battle tank ever produced, in large numbers. In fact, it became the most produced tank of the war. It boasted frontal armor of 45 mm and a robust main gun. Although lacking in creature comforts, the tank was known for its speed and reliability, as well as its maneuverability. It saw service in many armies long after World War II.

President Harry S. Truman acted swiftly, ordering the under-strength Twenty-Fourth Infantry Division into the fray to slow the North Korean offensive while other units readied for active duty. At the same time, the United Nations quickly passed a resolution supporting the defense of South Korea. The Soviets would surely have vetoed the resolution had they not been boycotting the Security Council for its refusal to admit communist China to the UN.

America, prosperous and victorious from World War II, had largely shed most of its military might and had turned its attention to the business of building cars, homes, and factories. In an effort to reduce America's massive budgetary deficit from the war, the budget ax had chopped away 92 percent of U.S. armed forces, reducing the nation's military might from a wartime strength of 12 million men to barely a million. Although American leaders worried that the invasion of South Korea might be just an opening gambit in a larger over-arching Soviet and Communist offensive that could eventually spread to Europe, Taiwan, and Southeast Asia, they were hard-pressed to find spare units to deal with the North Korean invasion. The only readily available combat units were understrength infantry divisions that were now taking part in the occupation of Japan.

The United Nations placed its forces under the command of the legendary American General Douglas MacArthur. The hero of the Pacific War rushed the Twenty-Fourth Infantry Division to South Korea to stem the NKPA onslaught. Led by the fearless Major General William F. Dean, the Twenty-Fourth fought bravely against over-whelming odds near the strategic city of Taejon. Equipped with obso-lete 2.36-inch bazookas★ that largely bounced off the Russian-made T-34s, even at close range, the Twenty-Fourth was mauled and forced to fall back. As the Twenty-Fourth made its stand against the onslaught, even the division's commanding general got into the action. Personally leading a bazooka team to stem the Korean hordes, fighting shoulder to shoulder with enlisted men, he quipped, "Perhaps we could do something about a couple of tanks."

★ 3.5-inch bazookas could stop a T-34 cold, but tragically were not issued to the unit for a variety of reasons, including supply problems.

Although his actions seemed heroic, Dean should have been commanding rather than fighting. Later, he became the highest-ranking American captured during the war. However, the Twenty-Fourth's stand did help slow the North Korean advance and allowed time for the skeleton occupation divisions stationed in Japan to reinforce the shrinking pocket known as the Pusan Perimeter.

Getting combat-ready men into Pusan seemed an impossible task. The Marine Corps and other armed forces were starved for warm bodies. After the war, the newly created Department of Defense, with its second Secretary Louis Johnson, had ruthlessly pursued budget cuts. Johnson's key priorities had included deep cuts in military spending and "making heads roll."

Johnson was in lockstep with President Truman's policies, which were motivated by his fiscal conservatism and his determination to bring down the massive deficit created by World War II. A former World War I artillery captain, Truman often quipped that he knew more about military strategy than the "dumb, spendthrift" brass in the military. As a result, America was dangerously unprepared for the Korean War. The decrease in manpower was even more severe for the U.S. Marine Corps, which at its height in World War II had consisted of six complete Marine divisions or 1 million Leathernecks. Making matters worse, Truman disdainfully viewed the Marine Corps as superfluous, calling it "a police force for the Navy." With a mere 75,000 men, the Corps, which hadn't lost a battle in 175 years, faced the danger of extinction.

In Korea, after several weeks of desperate fighting on the ever-shrinking Pusan Perimeter, America's vastly outnumbered forces faced slaughter by superior numbers of North Korean troops. Outnumbered, facing eleven NKPA divisions, the forces seemed likely to withdraw in a Dunkirk-like fashion.

MacArthur's general in charge of the perimeter was Lieutenant General Walton H. Walker, otherwise known as "Johnny" or "Bulldog." During World War II, Walker had commanded the corps that spearheaded General George S. Patton's advance across Western Europe. Now facing superior numbers and realizing he didn't have enough men to hold the defense in depth, Walker utilized a strategy of small counterattacks against the North Korean onslaught in an attempt to buy space and time.

In the midst of the desperate struggle to hold the Pusan Perimeter, MacArthur was boldly planning a large-scale counterstrike. But he would need more men. One of his first requests to the Joint Chiefs included the immediate deployment of a Marine brigade. Not long after the request was granted, MacArthur insisted to Marine Corps General Lemuel Shepherd, "If I had the First Marine Division, I would make a landing here at Inchon and reverse the war."

After receiving approval from the Joint Chiefs to reassemble the First Marine Division, the Corps prepared for the call to arms. A shell of its former self, the Corps consisted of just two understrength regiments—the Fifth Marines, based at Camp Pendleton, California, and the Sixth Marines, at Camp Lejeune, North Carolina—along with a Marine Aircraft wing. Estimating that it would take months to bring the division up to its wartime strength, the Corps scoured the United States for able-bodied Marines, including reservists.

After men, the Marines needed equipment. Fortunately, unlike other service branches, they had mothballed large amounts of equipment in the desert of Barstow, California. Four hundred civilians immediately went to work reconditioning jeeps, trucks, and amphibious tractors. Weapons warehoused since World War II were stripped of their protective Cosmoline coating and readied for service.

As the First Division was being brought up to strength, Pusan couldn't wait: the situation grew more desperate every day. To prevent an imminent collapse, the United States hurriedly sent in the Fifth Marines. Known as the First Provisional Marine Brigade, the Marines were used to plug holes in the perimeter that Marine Brigadier General Edward Craig described as a leaky dike. "We'll be used to plug holes as they open. . . . We're a brigade—a fire brigade—and we'll be in costly fighting against a numerically superior enemy. Marines have never yet lost a battle, and this brigade isn't going to be the first to set such a precedent," said Craig. Once ashore, the fire brigade plugged holes in the line and hurled back several Korean offensives.

Back in the United States, the First Marines rushed to get warm bodies to fill out their ranks and join their brothers in the Fifth Marines. In that chaotic summer, George Company was born.

Originally A Company, First Battalion, Sixth Marines, the unit became George Company, Third Battalion, First Marines. Formerly based in Camp Lejeune, the threadbare company commanded by Captain George Westover with First Sergeant Rocco Zullo took a four-day journey across country by train to Camp Pendleton.

Westover, an enlisted man turned Mustang officer who had fought throughout the Pacific, including the bloody hell of Iwo Jima, was officially the commanding officer of George Company. The tall and charismatic Westover was a fine officer. But in the minds of the men, First Sergeant Zullo was the heart and soul of George Company. "We waited till he said 'go.' He ran the company," recalled one Marine.

Born on December 17, 1917, Zullo hailed from Claremont, New Hampshire. The son of a lumberjack, he learned how to handle an ax and a crosscut saw at an early age, building up his muscles. In those years, during the twenties and the Great Depression, "We all worked as youngsters," remembered the now ninety-two-year-young Marine.

At sixteen, he lied about his age and joined the Civilian Conservation Corps. There, he learned how to blast stone, use a sledgehammer, and build things. During this time, he also became a prize fighter, winning his first bout in Conway, New Hampshire, by beating the reigning middleweight champion.

Following in his father's footsteps, Zullo joined the Marine Corps in the late 1930s. "I love the Marine Corps, and I always wanted to be a Marine," he recalled. Zullo quickly rose to the rank of corporal and then sergeant. He also continued boxing. While stationed on board the USS *Pennsylvania*, he was once asked by his senior NCO to fight on board the battleship USS *West Virginia* in a competition for the Iron Man trophy.

"Roc, we need a heavyweight in the fight."

A champion middleweight, Zullo wondered, "How am I going to make weight?"

"Don't worry about that. We'll take care of it."

During weigh-in, the boxers were required to jump on the scale and drop their shorts, but Zullo's handlers had a way to beat the system. They placed several heavy mercury balls inside his socks. As he stepped on the scale, it instantly went from 165 pounds to 190, enough to qualify him as a heavyweight. During the match, which consisted of three, three-minute rounds, I "knocked the hell out of the heavyweight," recalled the first sergeant 58 years later.

On June 7, 1941, the Japanese attacked Pearl Harbor, sinking a number of ships, including the USS *West Virginia*. At the time, Zullo was participating in a malaria training camp, far removed from the front lines. He reported to his commanding officer, "Colonel, I heard the USS *West Virginia* has been sunk. I'm a fighting man and want to get out of this duty."

"I understand," the officer replied.

Zullo transferred to C Company, Fifth Marines, a unit that became the very spear-tip of America's offensive against Japan, the invasion at Guadalcanal in the summer of 1942. Rising quickly through the ranks, Zullo became platoon sergeant in a weapons company and later achieved the rank of gunnery sergeant. Though Zullo was only twenty-four years old, the teenagers fighting under him considered him "the old man."

On the island of Guadalcanal, C Company led the initial assault leg. Their battles for the dark and bloody Matanikau River marked some of the first defeats for the Fifth Marine Division and the fiercest fighting for the unit. During the battles on Guadalcanal, the odds were mostly even, but along the Matanikau, the Marines were outnumbered. Nevertheless, the Japanese had run into some tough eighteen- and nineteen-year-old Americans. "We thought the Japanese were supermen. They had taken Singapore with an understrength force and captured the Philippines and most of the Pacific. We were all ready to go; we were ready to fight," Zullo recalled. After Zullo and the

Marines found out how the Japanese treated prisoners, "We were going to fight to the last man; there was no surrender."

On October 26, 1942, along the dark, enemy-infested waters of the Matanikau, Zullo had his most bitter taste of combat: "As we came upon a ridge, I saw all of our men coming back wounded and bleeding. Almost all of the lieutenants and officers were killed. I turned to the last lieutenant—there was no one else left—and said, 'For God's sakes, be careful.'"

The Japanese attacked from both sides of the ridge. After a few minutes, one of the Marines came up to Zullo and said, "Gunnery Sergeant, the lieutenant is dead."

"What do you mean? I just talked to him a couple of minutes ago," replied Zullo.

"He's dead. Machine-gun fire," answered the Marine.

As Zullo moved up toward the top of the ridge, he heard several Marines in the unit cry out, "Every man for himself."

Zullo barked back, "There will be no God damn such thing in C Company. We came here as a unit, and we'll leave here as a unit." Under Zullo's intrepid leadership, C Company held the line that night.

Shortly thereafter, Zullo once again received a promotion, this time to first sergeant. Fearing the promotion would lead to administrative work and a desk job rather than front-line duties, Zullo initially declined the opportunity. His then–first sergeant said something to him that he would retain for the rest of his life: "Remember, if you are the first sergeant, you are the first soldier of this company."

Soon, the Fifth Marines were relieved of their duties on Guadalcanal. Sickly and wounded from fighting in Guadalcanal's disease- and enemy-infested jungles, they readied for another bloody island assault: Peleliu, an island in the Palau island group. Zullo sadly reflected, "All the men were very sickly and suffered from malaria, dengue fever, and other ailments related to combat. I lost two of my best friends." In September 1944, the Fifth Marines assaulted the heavily defended Japanese island of Peleliu, where Zullo led the way once again, attacking the airfield, the main objective on the island.

"Every aperture on the cliff in front of us opened fire," he continued. Through the maelstrom of machine gun fire, mortar shells, and artillery, Zullo's C Company of the Fifth Marines advanced. Zullo screamed out to his men, "Follow me!" as they formed a skirmish line and moved toward the hill. They continued forward, repulsing several Japanese counterattacks.

Desperately short of men, C Company received reinforcements, about a dozen men. "Stay right here," Zullo admonished his reinforced unit.

Suddenly, a Japanese shell hit a coconut tree behind Zullo. "The shell took off the face of my runner and the lieutenant," he recalled. Once again, Zullo found himself wounded and in charge. The shell had also drilled a quarter-size hole through his shoulder. "I put my large index finger in the wound in my shoulder, and I continued to direct my men until I was relieved."

Badly wounded, the first sergeant nevertheless walked to the aid station without assistance. Although he received a Silver Star for his actions, the injury sufficed to take him out of the remainder of the Pacific War. He rejoined the unit several months later.

In 1950, the regular Marine Corps, including George Company, was made up of a special breed of men, America's elite. The Green Berets had not yet been formed, and America's first special operations forces from the wartime Office of Strategic Services (OSS) had disbanded shortly after World War II. The U.S. Army Rangers had nearly suffered the same fate as the OSS, but existed now only as a shell of its former self. The Marine Corps, with its Spartanlike ethos, effectively assumed the role of America's premier light infantry force. With a proud tradition of battle, the Leathernecks maintained a Jesuit-like zeal for fighting war. The Marine Corps served as the battle-ax of the military; when something had to be destroyed or killed, they sent in the Marines.

After arriving at Camp Pendleton during the first week of August 1950, the regular Marines of George Company were joined by fifty reservists and roughly fifty Marines from "guard units," including some spit-and-polish Marines who had been garrisoned at 8th and I Streets in Washington, DC.

They hailed from all parts of America. Some were veterans of World War II, while others had no combat experience at all and had never even been to boot camp. These men had been given only the most rudimentary training in drills that were conducted at what was jokingly called "a summer camp." "At summer camp, it was a lot of fun, kind of like the Boy Scouts. Then we got to find out what wearing that uniform was really all about," remarked one reservist. Arguably, they had the least amount of training of any Marines to put on the uniform. Citizens one day, the men suddenly found themselves in Marine Corps uniforms the next.★

The regular Marines who greeted them at Camp Pendleton were "not too happy" to have untrained reservists. "We found out real quickly there was a price to pay to be a regular Marine," recalled one Marine. A lot of the regulars looked at the reservists with disdain or pity. "These guys don't know shit from Shinola," said one of the Marines. He wasn't far wrong: a lot of the men had no idea how to throw a grenade or even how to clean their rifles.

A large contingent of reservists hailed from the San Francisco Bay Area. One of the reservists, plucked out of his job as a reporter for the *San Francisco Examiner*, was Robert H. Hallawell. Noted for his youthful look and brilliant mind, "he would always spit out the right answer" to even the most obscure questions, recalled Farr. While attending Northwestern University, Hallawell had met an older Marine, a veteran of World War II. The Marine's character and presence inspired the young undergrad so much that he knew he "wanted to be a Marine." After college, Hallawell put his education to use as a reporter, while spending a summer as a reservist in the Marine Corps. Bobby Hallawell had had a privileged upbringing. "I don't mean to brag, but I come from a very wealthy family. I want to mix with ordinary people," he remarked to a fellow Marine at camp.

★ Fifty years later, the Marine Corps, in an official ceremony during a George Company re-union in San Diego, would officially graduate many of the reservists from boot camp.

Zullo assigned Hallawell to the machine gun platoon. Even in 1950, the machine gun, which had performed so well in World War II, still had a reputation as one of the deadliest infantry weapons on the battlefield. In the platoon, the men operated the Browning M1919A4 light machine gun, which could fire approximately 400–500 rounds per minute.*

Ideally, each section consisted of two squads, which included two light .30 caliber machine guns. Each squad included a squad leader, a gunner, assistant gunner, and seven ammunition carriers who toted two to four boxes of .30 caliber ammunition.

Men assigned to the same squad often developed close friend-ships—for many of them, bonds that would last as long as sixty-five years, and more. One of Hallawell's friends, Bruce Farr, had been a resident of Tennessee from the age of six months. The tall, lanky Farr came from a proud military tradition stretching back to an ancestor who had served as a surgeon in the Confederate Army. An uncle who served as a Devil Dog rifleman in the Sixth Marine Regiment and liked to recount tales from the epic battles of World War I had inspired Farr to join the Marines.

Another volunteer was Bob Harbula. Originally from Pittsburgh, Harbula had followed the footsteps of his brother into the Corps. While he was stationed in Washington, the movie *The Sands of Iwo Jima* debuted in the spring of 1950, and the muscular Marine became an usher for the show, escorting senators and other dignitaries to watch some of the initial viewings. Harbula watched the show six times in two days and remembers thinking to himself, *I need a war.*† That same summer, the gung-ho Marine saw a posting on a bulletin board calling for volunteers to sign up for a special raider unit. His brother had always told him never to volunteer for anything, but Harbula did. He was among the would-be raider volunteers who were later trans-ferred to Camp Pendleton to become part of George Company and other front-line units.

---

* The gun weighed about 31 pounds, while the tripod added another 19 pounds. Boxes of ammo holding 250 rounds weighed approximately 15 pounds each.
† His views on war would later be tempered after experiencing it for himself.

Fred Hems, another fellow machine gunner, also came from a military family, though his family history seemed much less inspiring. Hems's father Bobby had joined the British Army Blackwatch Division during World War I and came home shell-shocked. Years after the war, Bobby would still hit the ground any time he heard fireworks or other explosions.

Despite their father's experience, Fred Hems and his twin brother Ellsworth, or E.C., both joined the U.S. Marines within a couple months of each other. Although they were initially assigned to different units, Fred petitioned to move from the mortar section to the machine guns with his brother. The commanding officer granted the petition, but required the two brothers to serve in different platoons. Otherwise, the two brothers from Bristol, Pennsylvania, were inseparable and "always together."

Like Hallawell and Farr, Hems also had a friend within his platoon: Tom Powers, who had a wild side. "I had been in and out of more brigs during my time in the Marine Corps and had a rap sheet like Jesse James," remembered Powers, who had been in the Marine Corps for several years and still retained the lowly rank of private. Powers's Irish grandmother, who kept him supplied with whiskey throughout the war, would often remark, "You have the devil within ya, boy."

Another friend of Hems and Powers seemed almost exactly the opposite of Powers. Red Nash was a 6-foot 4-inch, slim, quiet, good-looking Marine with reddish-brown hair. Nash picked up the name Red in the service. According to his sister, "he was a great older brother," but had a devilish side and "loved to tease." He graduated from Scottsbluff High School, Nebraska, in May 1948, and joined the Marines the same month. After basic training, he served as a guard in Washington, DC, and later was aboard the USS *Tarawa*, an aircraft carrier, until the summer of 1950.

During the hot summer of 1950, the gaggle of reservists and regular Marines that would make up George Company came together at Camp Pendleton and found themselves sleeping on an empty parade ground. The next morning, they were marched to Tent

Camp 2 in a remote area that had not been utilized since World War II. Inside recently reclaimed Quonset huts, the staff NCOs would arrange the men of George Company into platoons, squads, and fire teams.★

In a weather-beaten, dilapidated Quonset hut that the sun had faded to a burnt tan, Zullo boomed at his platoon sergeants, "Who do you want?" Zullo looked around at his fellow platoon sergeants and instructed them to pick the enlisted men who would make up the squads and rifle teams within their platoons. Though he knew very little about any of the men, Platoon Sergeant Gerald Tillman, the "ultimate Confederate Warrior," confidently strode into the center of the Quonset hut and selected his men. "I want this guy, this guy, and this guy."

Most of the platoon sergeants, including Gene Lilly and William Binaxas, were veterans of the Pacific War: Tillman, however, had had no combat experience. But the southerner had earned Zullo's respect with his talents as a natural warrior.

The semblance of a company began to take shape as the men were marched deeper into Tent Camp 2 to begin their training.

"We were all standing in a line, and I was following Tillman. It was a very confusing scene as we started to march. Someone asks, 'Where are we going?' "Third Battalion." 'Third Battalion what?' 'Third Battalion First Marines, 3/1.'"

The men found themselves part of the legendary First Marines, led by one of the most famous Marines ever to wear the uniform:

★ Typical Marine Corps unit organization and strength are as follows:
    Division 15,000+
    Regiment 5,000+
    Battalion 1,000+
    Company 200+
    Platoon 46
    Squad 13
    Fire team 4
  The number of personnel is subject to change based on the unit's mission.

Colonel Lewis "Chesty" Puller. Known for his guts and bulldog features, by the end of his career, Puller had earned a staggering five Navy Crosses. Like the ancient world's greatest warrior, Hannibal, Puller shared the hardships of his men and was renowned for honoring them, especially the enlisted. Under Puller's leadership, the regiment included three battalions: 1/1, 2/1, and 3/1. Three rifle companies made up each battalion. 3/1 consisted of How, Item, and George, along with a Headquarters and Supply or H&S Company.

First Platoon's leader was Lieutenant Richard E. Carey, who had risen from the rank of private first class (PFC) to lieutenant and eventually became lieutenant general, one of two officers from George Company to do so. From humble roots, Carey hailed from Columbus, Ohio, where he achieved local notoriety as a star high school athlete and wrestler. He enlisted in the V-5 Program in 1945, but the war ended and there wasn't a need for pilots. He took a discharge and went into the Marines in 1946. In 1948, he attended officer training school and graduated sixth in his class, second in the leadership portion of the class, with stiff competition, including many sergeant majors and other experienced Marines from WWII.

After a botched training class where many of the officers had fallen asleep, General Shepherd called Carey's class "the worst training class the Marine Corps has ever had." After the Battle of Chosin Reservoir, Shepherd would recant his words.★

At the heart of any Marine platoon is the rifleman, armed with the potent eight-shot, semiautomatic M1 Garand. In Marine Corps' terms, the rifleman was designated "0311." One such 0311 was Richard Hock from Milwaukee, Wisconsin. The gung-ho son of a Marine, Hock talked his mother into signing for him so that he could enlist at the age of seventeen. Hock and other 0311s made up the bulk of George Company.

After all the men were assigned, George Company, roughly two hundred at full strength, consisted of three rifle platoons (First, Second, and Third), a machine gun platoon, a mortar platoon (which later

---

★ Shepherd later changed his mind, saying, "I was dead wrong. Tell your classmates this was the best group of lieutenants that ever hit the Corps."

contained a forward observer team), and company headquarters personnel. The machine gun platoon was further divided into three sections, each assigned to one of the rifle platoons. Later, an assault section, consisting of men armed with 3.5-inch rocket launchers more commonly known as bazookas, along with demolition specialists, rounded out the company.

Zullo and the rest of George Company's officers and non-commissioned officers (NCOs) had their work cut out for them. They had to take scores of men who had very little training and meld them with the veterans. With the compressed training schedule, conditioning became a priority. Captain Westover and Rocco Zullo whipped the men into shape. They were receiving "people from all over the country," remembered one Marine, "There was a little bit of rifle range training, but it was mostly just climbing hills." The men got into good physical condition, but not before a couple of men were "almost bitten by rattlesnakes," recalled Hock.

With just three weeks to transform from ordinary citizens into warriors, the men regularly hiked in full gear across Camp Pendleton. They also spent time getting outfitted with the proper ammunition for their weapons, batteries for their radios, and other odds and ends they would need all too soon.

Along with the immense task of physical training came a tremendous amount of administrative work for Zullo. "Throughout this period, we were getting all kinds of people: MPs, cooks, bakers, warm bodies from all over the United States," recalled Westover. Zullo was there to "adjust their MOS" and form the men into a company. Men with physical disabilities and other factors that prevented them from serving had to be culled from the ranks. Vaccinations had to be administered; medical records had to be updated.

One trivial administrative issue involved getting every man covered by National Life Insurance. First Sergeant Zullo had a signature way of dealing with such issues.

Rap! Rap! Zullo's meaty hand knocked on the tent pole of the tent that Westover was using as George Company's Command Post. The burly Italian approached Westover, who was sitting behind a desk finishing paperwork. He had two Marines "suspended from his arms, almost holding them there," recalled Westover. The two Marines had resisted all efforts to sign up for National Life Insurance, which would have been docked from their monthly pay.

Zullo then said, "Tell the captain what you decided to do."

The men stammered quickly, "We decided to take out National Life Insurance policies."

The problem was solved. Zullo didn't pussyfoot around.

By the last week of August, compressing as much training in as possible, the men of George Company and the First Marines began loading onto transports destined for Japan and, ultimately, the Korean War.

◄ 2 ►

The Great Gamble

August 23, 1950, 5:30 p.m., Sixth Floor of the Dai-Ichi, Tokyo, Japan

STANDING IN FRONT of a large map of Korea, General Douglas MacArthur bit down on his signature corncob pipe. On the afternoon of August 23, MacArthur and U.S. commanders in the Far East gathered to discuss reversing the tide in Korea. The Pusan Perimeter was barely holding and about to break open at any moment.

With a sense of fate and destiny, MacArthur put on his greatest theatrical performance. Moving with instinct and intuition, he brushed aside all arguments against a landing at Inchon. With the presence of a movie actor, he spoke in a slow voice with "deep resonance." For the past hour, the Navy had briefed MacArthur on the near-impossibility of an amphibious landing at Inchon. There were only three possible dates for a landing, September 15 and 17 and October 11, when the tides would be high enough to allow a landing craft to put men ashore. Otherwise, they would be trapped in mud. A seawall also gave the defenders a tactical advantage. Additionally, the offshore island of Wolmi-Do guarded the approaches to the harbor

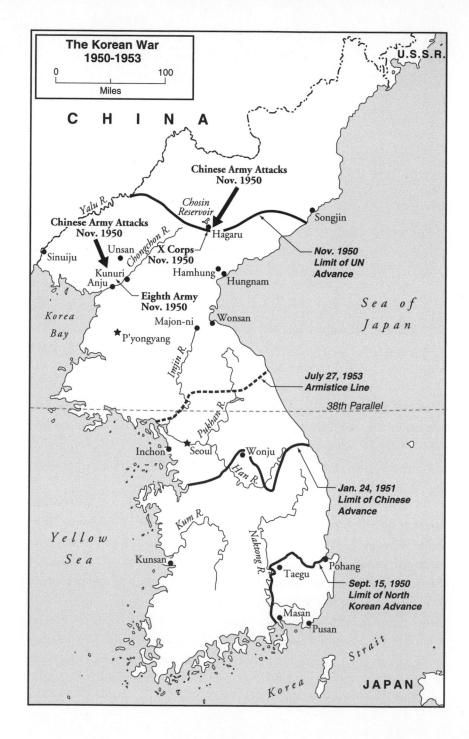

The Korean War
1950–1953

0   100
Miles

U.S.S.R.

C H I N A

Chinese Army Attacks
Nov. 1950

Yalu R.

Chosin
Reservoir

Songjin

Chinese Army Attacks
Nov. 1950

Unsan

Chongchon R.

Hagaru

Sinuiju

X Corps
Nov. 1950

Nov. 1950
Limit of UN
Advance

Kunuri
Anju

Hamhung

Hungnam

Eighth Army
Nov. 1950

Korea
Bay

Majon-ni

Wonsan

Sea of
Japan

P'yongyang

Imjin R.

July 27, 1953
Armistice Line

38th Parallel

Pukhan R.

Inchon   Seoul   Wonju

Han R.

Jan. 24, 1951
Limit of Chinese
Advance

Kum R.

Yellow
Sea

Naktong R.

Kunsan

Pohang

Taegu

Sept. 15, 1950
Limit of North
Korean Advance

Masan

Pusan

Strait

Korea

JAPAN

and would have to be seized hours before any landing, diminishing the element of surprise. Finally, the right tide occurred in the early evening, leaving less than three hours of daylight to make the assault on the beachhead. They also assumed that the enemy would sow the harbor with magnetic mines.

Summing up the massive challenges, Rear Admiral James H. Doyle concluded the briefing by saying, "The best that I can say is that Inchon is not impossible." Prior amphibious assaults during WWII also weighed heavily on the U.S. military. Inchon had shades of the fateful Anzio landing in January 1944, when an understrength Allied force hit the beach and was quickly ringed by German reinforcements and nearly annihilated. Inchon would also be launched with scant resources, but unlike Anzio, the First Marine Division would spearhead the assault.

MacArthur looked directly at Admiral Doyle and other members of the Navy brass and said, "Admiral, in all my years of military service, that is the finest briefing I have ever received. Commander, you have taught me all I have ever dreamed of knowing about tides. Do you know, in World War I, they got our divisions to Europe through submarine-infested seas. I have a deep admiration for the Navy from the humiliation of Bataan, the Navy brought us back." With a tear in his eye, MacArthur continued, "I never thought the day would come when the Navy would be unable to support the Army in its operations."

MacArthur then explained the big picture and insisted that Communist aggression would have to be stopped in Korea: "It is plenty apparent that here in Asia is where the Communist conspirators have elected to make their play for global conquest. The test is not in Berlin or Vienna, in London, Paris, or Washington. It is here and now— it is along the Naktong River in Korea."

A military historian, the great commander impressed the group with his expansive knowledge of military history. Going back in time to the winter of 1759, MacArthur discussed General Wolfe's possible assault on Quebec, which was dismissed by nearly all his staff as impossible. Yet it succeeded.

Based on Wolfe's great gamble at Quebec, where the odds were nearly insurmountable, MacArthur reasoned that the very implausibility of his plan would lead to its triumph: "The very arguments you have made as to the impracticalities involved would tend to ensure for me the element of surprise. For the enemy commander would reason that no one would be so brash as to make such an attempt."

Pulling his corncob pipe out of his mouth, MacArthur hammered home his point, "I can almost hear the ticking of the second hand of destiny. We must act now, or we will die. . . . We shall land at Inchon, and I shall crush them."

MacArthur's forty-five-minute extemporaneous oration had changed the minds of everyone in the room. Chief of Naval Operations Vice Admiral Turner Joy said, "General, the Navy will get you to Inchon."

Voyage

You know, Dick, I'm not gonna make it home." With his piercing blue eyes, Second Lieutenant James Beeler looked straight at First Platoon Leader Dick Carey as the George Company officers finished up a friendly game of cribbage. The All-American football player from the U.S. Naval Academy knew he was going to die. A premonition of his own death ominously ate away at him.

"Oh, come on. You're going to make it," Carey said, as he quickly tried to diffuse the situation. Beeler shook his head. "You're a damn good Marine," Carey interjected.

"Dick, I'm not going to come home," replied Beeler. Beeler somehow had a window into the future.

The nasty, tan keel of the 9,676-ton USNS *General Simon B. Buckner* cut through the emerald green waters of the Pacific. The *Buckner* seemed to fit George Company, as many of the men in George were from the South. Even the transport's namesake fit: he was the first and last southern general to surrender a Confederate Army during the Civil War. George Company filled most of the ship, along with other Marines heading toward Korea.

Also playing cribbage and bunking with Beeler and Carey was Second Lieutenant Spencer Jarrnigan, who commanded Second Platoon, a solid Marine officer who wasn't lacking in courage. Described as "sickly looking" and very skinny, with red hair, he seemed to be in a constant state of depression from a tragic automobile accident that had occurred several years before. Other people in the car had died, but he had survived. On several occasions, the men observed that his head was always down. Unlike his Marine brothers who punctuated most sentences with profanity, Jarrnigan was appalled by it. He would repeatedly say, "I don't care what you say, but don't say 'mother fucking' or you're going to get in trouble." Nearly every officer in the room had a death sentence hanging over his head, but only Beeler knew his future.

Below decks, the Leathernecks prepared. The reservists and other untried Marines gravitated to the combat veterans. The men flocked around the seasoned NCOs. Many of the eighteen- and nineteen-year-old reservists surrounded the experienced NCOs who had been through combat and asked them to describe the indescribable—what was combat like and how could they survive it?

The machine gun section worked especially hard to prepare. Many of its members were reservists, including Corporal Tom Enos. Of Portuguese extraction, Enos hailed from the Fresno, California, area and was learning on the job. Despite his inexperience, Enos never flinched, even after being warned by First Sergeant Zullo, "Being a machine gunner is yours to lose."

Schooled by the WWII veterans, Enos and his fellow machine gunners trained at a breakneck pace. "Training was rigorous. We were blindfolded, put in a dark room, and forced to assemble every one of our weapons in the dark," recalled the Marine from Fresno.

Fred and E.C. Hems taught the machine gunners how to assemble and disassemble the gun, "backwards, forwards, sideways, and upside down," recalled Mert GoodEagle. Machine gunners were handed parts in the dark and forced to assemble their weapons or go to the proper parts box to find it. During this so-called "snap-in" train-ing, Marines would have to name the part and the number. "Some-times, they would throw in a different part just to throw us off," recalled Bruce Farr.

The men learned every aspect of the .30 caliber medium machine gun. The other George Company Marines also learned to assemble and disassemble their M1 Garands and occasionally the M1911 pistol. Each four-man fire team within a thirteen-man squad was issued a Browning Automatic Rifle (BAR) M1918A2 for additional firepower. The BAR had an effective range of five hundred yards and could fire a little over five hundred rounds per minute.

In addition to training, the men also attempted to establish their sea legs. "I went by rail most of the way," joked GoodEagle. He and the rest of George Company spent a good amount of time on the ship's rail, heaving their guts over the side from bouts of seasickness.

A stocky Pawnee Indian from Ardmore, Oklahoma, GoodEagle was one of the few Native Americans at the heart of George Company. As an ammo bearer within the machine gun section, GoodEagle lugged around several fifteen-pound, olive-drab metal boxes of machine gun ammunition. Each box contained a belt of between 250 and 275 rounds of .30 caliber ammunition for the Browning M1919A4 machine gun. Following in the tradition of the Pawnee tribe and his father, a bareback rider and Indian dancer for the Pawnee Bill Rodeo Show, GoodEagle hoped to obtain his warrior's feather.

For many of the men, including the veterans, the boredom was nerve-racking. They wanted to get it over with or understand what they were about to face. On board, the men had time to kill. Friend-ships were born. GoodEagle, Farr, Hallowell, Harbula, and many other members sowed the seeds for a lifelong friendship.

Jack Daniels, however, adhered to a different principle and generally shied away from friendship, based on the simple adage from a veteran at boot camp: "Don't make any friends, because you're going to lose them." Daniels, an ammo bearer who would eventually become a machine gunner, hailed from a small town about thirty-two miles from Myrtle Beach, which contained only a post office and a service station. With a slow and deliberate manner and a tangy southern drawl, Daniels came from a large family of sharecroppers. To get to boot camp, he had had to hitchhike to Florence, South Carolina, take a bus to Columbia and another bus to Paris Island.

After more than a week on the water, the *Buckner* cruised to Kobe, Japan, where the men disembarked and made their way to the former Japanese Naval Base at Camp Otsu. At the base, they had hardly any time for training. "I tried to get the men in as good physical conditioning as possible," recalled George Westover. Westover, along with the other officers and Zullo, had the men climb the surrounding mountains with full packs and gear.

One man who always seemed to be at the back of the pack was Private Ralph Whitney. "Many of the men picked on him," recalled Farr. I felt sorry for him." With a demeanor described years later by some Marines as "like Gomer Pyle," he struggled to keep up. Despite some of his shortcomings, Whitney had a talent for photography and took official photos of the unit during training exercises.

The men were crammed into the small rooms of Otsu's barracks, normally eight to ten men per room. "We took anything that wasn't nailed down," recalled Dick Hock. "Sheets, blankets, soap, anything that the Army didn't really need, we would take."

There was no liberty, but someone found a small hole in a fence behind the barracks. At night, George Company would slither through the hole to make their way to the nearby town. We called it "rice paddy liberty," recalled Hock.

The small town contained several local watering holes that catered to the men. Often, they traded sheets, blankets, and other nonessential items for money to buy booze in a barter system. Hock recalled one woman who acted as a middleman: "We found a woman who was married to an army sergeant who had been deployed. We used her as a saleswoman to sell blankets, soap, and towels. We traded the stuff to her, and she gave us money for drinking."

Miraculously, every morning at reveille, the men stood in formation for roll call. "Half the company had a hangover," recalled Hock.

On or around September 8, George Company loaded into an LST (Landing Ship, Tank). Each man made his way into the cramped bowels of the grimy ship, stowed his gear, and claimed one of the scarce racks, otherwise known as a bed, a place to sleep.

The forward observer team, recently detached from the Eleventh Marines, was an artillery unit organic to the First Marines. Artillery observers were trained eyes that could radio in the exact coordinates of enemy targets and call in a deadly storm of steel from the Eleventh Marines' howitzers. The six-man team was led by First Lieutenant Dalton Hilscher from Texas. The team included Carlos Banks, Richard J. Jewel, Stanley J. Walerski, and PFC James Harrison, an orphan from Atlanta, Georgia. A product of the South, Harrison never shed his heritage and carried a small Confederate flag on his knapsack at all times and also played a small harmonica, his favorite tune being "Dixie." Harrison seemed fearless and often oblivious to imminent risk.

The unit's top NCO was Clark G. Henry, an Irishman from Galway. At age thirteen, he had traveled alone from Ireland to the United States to work on his grandfather's farm. When World War II broke out, the five-foot-nine, 119-pound Henry had lied about his age to the Marine Corps, which was desperate for young recruits. Starting at the Solomon Islands, Henry fought throughout the Pacific and was later wounded while serving as a naval gunfire observer. Prior to Korea, he was assigned to the Eleventh Marines Dog Battery and was a sergeant of the forward observer section. Known for his piercing blue eyes, pragmatism, and keen mind, Henry effectively led the forward observer team, which also acted as a scout section.

Even as the ship was docked in Japan, Marines had somehow found a way to create their own liberty. That night, the forward observer team, led by Henry, struck out into the streets of the local town. Making their way through winding back alleys, the men found what they were looking for. A shaky building built of bamboo, no more than two stories high, that had curtains that doubled as doors. The makeshift bar complimented the crude building, but its main draw was that it was also a bordello. The men made their way through the seedy structure. They were greeted by a group of Army MPs. The Marines held the Army MPs and, for that matter, all Army personnel—known pejoratively as doggies—with disdain. One of the MPs snapped at Henry, "You're not welcome in this bar." Apparently, the MPs were trying to protect their turf, recalled Henry.

A verbal melee ensued. Smokey Somers, a friend of Henry and a fellow forward observer, but attached to How Company, decided he had had enough and landed a punch on one of the MPs' faces. The Marines and the MPs launched into a full-scale barroom brawl. The Marines were victorious, but they wisely chose to escape and fight another day. The men fled through the back alleys and made their way to the ship. They were greeted by Lieutenant Dalton Hilscher, who was dipping a tablespoon into a five-gallon container of ice cream as he waited for his men on the gangplank of the LST.

"Where have you been?" he barked at Henry. No sooner had he questioned Henry than several huffing and puffing MPs arrived on the scene. Dipping the spoon back into the ice cream, the lieutenant confidently greeted them.

"These men were in a brawl with us," barked one of the MPs.

Hilscher calmly parried the accusation, "Can't be these guys. They've been sitting here eating ice cream with me for the last hour."

Several hours later, the gull-grey prow of the LST cut its way through the emerald coastal waters of Korea. It headed south toward Pusan, where it would round the tip of the Korean peninsula before turning north again toward one of the only large harbors in South Korea, Inchon.

The captain of the Japanese crew, a former navy chief in the Imperial Navy, had two subordinates, including a radioman. Communication between Westover and the Japanese captain remained a challenge throughout the voyage. Hand signals, gestures, and pointing at charts and maps replaced a translator. Neither could speak both English and Japanese.

After two days at sea, the men faced the worst possible scenario: a typhoon. The flat-bottomed boat would ride up the crest of a wave and then crash back down, creating massive seasickness throughout George Company, even affecting the veterans who had long-established sea legs. Everyone was doubled over and seasick.

On September 15, George Company finally arrived several miles outside Inchon. The LST was just one ship in an armada of more than a hundred that were about to conduct one of the most audacious amphibious landings in history. A day or so before the invasion, the men assembled above decks, nailing together scaling ladders out of two-by-fours. These ladders would supplement some aluminum scaling ladders that they had brought from Japan.

As the ships made their way toward the landing area, the men were briefed on their objective. They would be part of the first wave on Blue Beach. The "brief for the Inchon landing was just that—brief. There wasn't really much of one," recalled Westover. The men and officers received hardly any details. The landing was so rushed that the only maps available were at 1/50,000th scale and were largely strategic. Later, after the landing, they were supplied with better maps.

For hours, the heavy guns of the invasion fleet, along with aircraft and rockets, pounded the Korean defenses. The sound of the explosions shook the earth. Joe Sagan, a six-foot-one PFC from Yonkers, New York,★ watched the shore bombardment. He turned to his right and noticed that his fire team leader, a veteran of WWII, who had fought

---

★ Sagan joined the Marine Corps at the tail end of 1945 and later played an extra in the movie *The Sands of Iwo Jima*.

in Guam and the other bloody battles of the Pacific, had "completely lost it." Screaming and yelling, the Marine was restrained below decks. Sagan's sergeant then turned to him and said, "Joe, you're the BAR-man now."

Shortly after, the men boarded LVTs (Landing Vehicle Tracked) or AmTracs and made their way into the war.

Inchon

SMOKE COMBINED with the sickening odor of cordite filled the air as the LVT pushed into a cloud of manmade darkness. A gust of wind dispersed the smoke, and the men gazed on a panorama that looked like a Hollywood movie: Corsairs dropped napalm-filled canisters, while a nearby ship fired scores of rockets on the intended landing area. Splashes of light froth erupted as bullets and shells hit the water.

"Hey, they're shooting at us!" a green reservist remarked incredulously as he poked his head above the metal hull of the amtrac.

"Keep your fucking head down!" a sergeant barked.

The crackle of small arms fire pierced the din of battle over the low drone of the LVT's motor working overtime to cut through the gray-blue waves. Tick! Tick! Tick! Tick!

A machine gun zeroed in on the LVT carrying machine gunner Jack Daniels: "The bullets bounced off the armor like hailstones; several mortars landed in the water nearby," he recalled.

As the beachhead approached, one Marine nervously turned to a veteran and asked, "How do I load my M1?" The reservists were arguably some of the most poorly trained men the Corps had ever turned out, but their spirit often made up for their lack of training.

But at its core, George Company was built around veteran NCOs and officers like Zullo. Despite the incoming rounds and comments from the newbies, Zullo was "like a sphinx"—unflappable. For a split second, Zullo's mind briefly flashed back to amphibious assaults on Guadalcanal and Peleliu, places he had barely survived. Suddenly, a splash of foam from a near-miss snapped Zullo's mind back to the present, as the LVTs turned closer to the beach, and a large seawall appeared in front of them.

"Ready the ladders!"

The amtracs bearing George Company bobbed up and down as the men steadied the rickety two-by-four ladders they had constructed days earlier. Those from First Platoon nudged the seawall. Bob Harbula leaned his ladder against the wall and began the nerve-racking climb up. Crack! A bullet passed near his ear. The ammunition bearer slowly climbed each rung of the ladder; he was weighed down with over a hundred pounds of extra gear: two cans of machine gun ammunition on his back on a plastic track tray, two more cans suspended from a harness around his neck, plus grenades, his carbine, and personal gear. Step by step, he made his way to the top of the ladder. Cracking his hand across the seawall, he smashed his watch as he vaulted over it.

The other members of George Company weren't far behind Harbula, but a barbed-wire fence impeded further movement off the seawall. Someone yelled, "Bring up the cutters!"

Corporal Albert Barnes* quickly began cutting the wire so the rest of the Marines could get past the wall. Barnes feverishly snipped each strand.

Thud!

A sniper round struck Barnes in the jugular. He instantly bled to death and "turned gray."

---

* Barnes was a Southern boy, and all he kept talking about was a mule called "Old Blue." All he wanted to do was follow behind Old Blue and plow his fields. That was his goal after getting through the war.

"This was a wake-up call," remembered Harbula. "We were in a dangerous place, in a war. You always remember the first of anything—the first time someone is killed or the first time you kill someone. It stays with you for the rest of your life."

Without hesitating, Lieutenant Carey, platoon leader of the First Platoon, grabbed the cutters and began quickly snipping his way through the wire. A round drilled a hole through Carey's pack as he cut the final strand. "I don't know why I didn't hand the cutters to someone who was stronger and a hell of a lot faster, but we broke through," he later said.

Passing through the wire, First Platoon had to cross a road. Small arms fire peppered the dirt thoroughfare. One of the squad leaders barked to everyone, "Get down!"

"Everyone hugged the ground but PFC Ralph Murphy, a 'wise guy' from Brooklyn. He didn't get along with the sergeant," recalled PFC Frank McNeive, also a native of Brooklyn and a four-year veteran of the Marine Corps, who would later rise to the rank of sergeant major. Murphy stood up and advanced across the road, but was soon killed by a sniper's bullet that struck him right between the eyes.*

"The sniper's up in the stack!" someone yelled.

Based on the trajectory of the rounds that struck Barnes and Murphy, the men of George Company surmised that the sniper could only be in one location—a hole barely large enough to expose the man's head and shoulders near the top of a smokestack that jutted out of the Inchon skyline like a bayonet. Placing his rifle into the hole, the sniper enjoyed a complete line of sight on the entire beachhead.

Tom Enos's machine gun section, attached to Second Platoon, was ordered to ready their machine guns and aim for the stack. "They had us zero in on the hole. We shot a few tracers and put quite a few rounds in. It silenced the sniper," recalled Enos.†

---

* His family received a letter from Murphy that was postmarked on September 17, which led his family to believe he was still alive, even after they received official notification from the Marine Corps that his death had occurred on September 15, 1950. The Corps conducted an official inquiry into the incident.

† Several other members of George Company mentioned they also fired on the stack, so it is not known who actually silenced the sniper.

Even before the men hit the beach, it had started drizzling, and clouds eclipsed the sun. The combination of fog and smoke from the explosions created a haunting, confusing atmosphere. Some units landed in the wrong places. Timing had to be perfect, and the tide and waves just right or the entire invasion force would be trapped in the mud of the harbor and easily picked off by North Koreans defending the beachhead. With no time for rehearsals, the landing was not as crisp as previous Marine landings in the Pacific. Nevertheless, the Leathernecks and MacArthur maintained the crucial element of war: surprise.

Other parts of George Company found a break in the wall and made a dry landing, while some LVTs went up a drainage ditch. The Third Machine Gun section, attached to Third Platoon, went up the ditch. "Keep your head down! Keep your head down!" Sergeant Fred Garcia, Third Machine Section leader, barked to his men.

"He [Garcia] was around at all times. We followed him around like a duckling follows its mother," recalled Tom Powers. Powers recalled that Garcia was a family man, battle-tested yet cautious, Garcia put his men first. A quiet, reserved man, Garcia never swore. Also religious, he wore a "miraculous medal" around his neck.

Many of the men in George Company carried similar religious medals for their protective powers. Powers was festooned with dozens of Catholic scapular medals around his neck, along with his grandmother's rosary beads and dog tags. Besides religious medals, the Irishman also came "well lubricated"; his field pack contained five bottles of whiskey that he covertly shared with his section.

"I took over the same system that she used with my grandfather during World War I. She would bake a loaf of bread, then turn it over, cut part of it down the middle and hollow it out so there was just enough room for a fifth. I was always well equipped with Jamison," remembered Powers.

After moving off the beachhead, Carey's First Platoon broke through and moved toward the high ground, known as "Radio Hill"—First Platoon's D-Day objective. The small hill lay on the left flank of the battalion. As Carey's platoon stormed the hill, the ships in the harbor "spotted movement on top of Radio Hill." The hill erupted in a mass of earth and dust as naval shells struck its side. The friendly fire was about to turn deadly.

Several men were wounded badly. Hock remembered the horror of seeing a Marine's arm "hanging by a thread." He was cradling one arm with the other and was clearly in shock.

Carey immediately got on the platoon's radio and screamed, "You sons-of-bitches, stop firing! We're friendlies on the hill! Cease fire!"

"It was one of the most rapid reactions I've ever seen. They stopped firing, but not before several of my men were badly wounded," recalled Carey.

After the friendly fire incident, the men dug in for the night, each platoon circling the wagons "like pioneers heading West." Carey reflected, "That night, we remained in the foxholes, and I'll never forget how damn cold it was. I shook all night."

Known as "the loners of First Platoon," GoodEagle, Farr, and Hallawell would typically share the same foxhole. They had gone to radio school together and became very close friends. First machine gunner Ralph Whitney, also a loner, disappeared from the unit that night, not being able to keep up with the rest of the machine gun section, but he reappeared at daybreak.

That night, George Company was told to consider anything in front of their foxholes the enemy, unless the password "*Lucky Strike*" was given. "We heard movement in front of our position," recalled Daniels. "The man in front of me yelled out 'Lucky!' There was no response. Several shots rang out from the Marines' M1 Garands. A moaning voice responded, 'I'm Lieutenant 'so-and-so,' clearly in pain." It was another case of friendly fire for George Company, and it certainly wouldn't be their last. The wounded officer was treated and evacuated from the battlefield.

As dawn broke, George Company, along with the rest of the First Marine Regiment, began expanding the beachhead to reduce the possibility of a North Korean counterattack. Battalion command gave

First Platoon its own separate mission to secure some high ground on George Company's flank. That morning, September 16 (D+1), as Carey's platoon moved out toward their objective, the First Machine Gun Section was hit by North Korean machine gun fire. The heavy small arms fire was coming from a wooded area on the side of a hill. Turning to his right hand, Carey ordered Sergeant Tillman to conduct a classic double-envelopment. Tillman, a dashing figure who wore double-buckle combat boots, was the type of person who "everyone liked" and was also one of the youngest sergeants in the Marine Corps. "I left one squad as a base of fire to contain the center, while Sergeant Tillman and his squad moved to the left and I moved with Sergeant Gene Lilly and his squad to the right."

With bayonets fixed, Tillman and Carey both threw smoke grenades into the open field.

The platoon charged forward into a cloud of grey smoke. The move was so well executed that they surprised an entrenched enemy platoon. Remarkably, in the midst of the battle, Carey faced his counterpart, the lieutenant leading the North Korean platoon. Stunned, the North Korean officer dropped his pistol and threw his hands up in the air. As he raised his hands, "The North Korean made a sudden move I thought was initially threatening," recalled Carey. Carey squeezed the trigger on his .45 and the North Korean went down.

Carey thought to himself, *I just killed a man who was surrendering.*

Luckily, the officer was still alive. "The round I fired hit his pistol belt buckle and knocked him to the ground," recalled Carey. First Platoon then took the enemy platoon and its commander as prisoners.

It was a classic case in which the Marines' training and leadership paid off. The Marines were able to defeat the North Koreans without taking a single casualty. The Marines had outmaneuvered and out-fought their foe—something they would repeat in coming days.

As George Company pushed forward, they moved up a road that passed through a defile or cut. Several North Korean soldiers waited on top of the defile as most of First Platoon walked by. When the machine gun section approached the chokepoint, a grenade landed in the middle of the road with a thud and detonated, wounding several Marines.

Standing nearby was G. Pendas, a First Platoon guide whose role included managing "everything from beans, bullets, and bandages" and making sure they got to the men. A New York City native, Pendas enlisted in the Corps in 1947. With only fourteen days left in his initial enlistment when the Korean War broke out, he re-enlisted in order to serve. Armed with a Springfield Star gauge 1903 rifle with an x8 power scope, Pendas, later known as "Peepsight" for his keen eye, doubled as the platoon's sniper.

He recalls a memory seared in his mind forever. Two of George Company's corpsmen, who "looked no older than high school sopho-mores," rushed to help the wounded men. As one of the corpsmen, Stanley Martin, reached the wounded Marines, the North Koreans hurled a second grenade, which landed only four feet from the corps-man. Martin pulled the wounded Marine into his chest and turned his body to absorb the blast. Boom! The grenade went off. Pendas remembers: "Stanley Martin got wounded in the buttocks, and here comes Doc Anderson, the other corpsman. We have three or four wounded, and he pulls down Martin's trousers and started patching him up. Martin never quit working on the wounded man, trying to save his life even after he was wounded. I'll never forget it—it was the bravest thing I've ever seen."

Shortly thereafter, several Marines climbed to the top of the de-file, flanked the enemy, and took out the North Koreans.

Second and Third Platoons also received enemy contact that day and humped a lot of difficult miles. Most of the men were exhausted from going up and down hills, over rugged terrain, and fighting the enemy.

Fortunately for George Company, the tempo of combat settled down by the evening of D+1, and the First and Fifth Marines secured the Inchon beachhead. Massive quantities of men and material were pouring through. Fear of a North Korean counterattack subsided, as the men prepared for the eighteen-mile fight to Seoul.

◄ 5 ►

Tank!

A WAVE OF CRIMSON and orange napalm coated and torched the five thirty-ton North Korean T-34/85s, burning them to a crisp. The ammonia-like after-effects of the flaming jellied gas bombs assaulted the men's nostrils. "I smelled the dead burning. Have you ever smelled burning flesh? It is something you will never forget," remembered Jack Daniels. He and many of the other men gagged from the acrid odor that hung over the battlefield. "These are the things that you try to forget. I spent sixty years trying to forget these sights and smells, and I got pretty good about forgetting."

To speed up the assault on Seoul, the First Marine Regiment, including George Company, rode on top of M26 Pershing tanks. The bulky silhouettes of the tanks made them giant targets, drawing small arms fire from the North Koreans. "Tanks draw fire," recalled Bob Harbula sardonically.

Strikingly, the North Koreans frittered away some of their precious armor in a vain attempt to thwart the Marine heavy metal

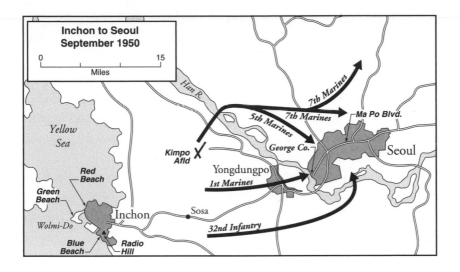

advance. Dick Hock recalled that a T-34 attempted to engage the Marine column perched on the side of a hill. A squadron of Marine Corps Corsairs strafed the tanks. One plane went into a dive, releasing a five-hundred-pound general-purpose bomb on the tank. "That Corsair never came out of the dive," crashing on the side of the road near the tank. "The biggest part of the tank remaining was the bogey wheel—everything else was destroyed."

The pilot of the plane, Captain William F. Simpson, would be one of many casualties of the day. "There were burnt bodies everywhere. They were trying to get out of the tank as their skin was burnt and bubbled like potato chips. Many of them were still burning," remembered Tom Enos.

The Marine tank column passed near the burned-out hulks "rolling over several bodies" on its advance toward Seoul, recalled BAR-man Joe Sagan. Near the village of Mahang-ri, the column again came under attack from intense machine gun fire and snipers. To deal with the threat, the men dismounted from the tanks and fired on the enemy positions. After dispatching the enemy, the column paused briefly. During the breather from combat, Lieutenant Carey and several members of First Platoon noticed a stovepipe that appeared to be moving. He quickly realized it was the barrel of a T-34 tank. Carey and his men feverishly banged on the cupola of the M26 and yelled: "Tank, nine o'clock! Tank, nine o'clock!"

The tank commander quickly traversed the turret of the Pershing and aimed his 90 mm at the enemy tank, which was hidden beside a thatched-roof house. Carey and the four men in his platoon riding the tank scrambled off, but as the turret turned, it snapped the wooden stock of one of the men's BAR.

For a few seconds, there was a Mexican standoff. Both tanks faced each other at a range of thirty yards. A shot from either tank would be deadly. "Our M26 fired at point-blank range, and I caught the muzzle blast in my ear," recalled Hock. The Pershing's 90 lit up the T-34 as it exploded and set the nearby house on fire. "Why didn't he fire? I will never know," reflected Carey. "It's mystery to me. But once again, I guess the Lord was taking care of us."

Another North Korean tank, disguised as a haystack, fled the battlefield. "I'll never forget seeing a haystack move at twenty-five miles per hour," recalled Hock.

After the close call with the T-34, the tank column moved forward. As the column made its way around a bend in the road, they were suddenly surprised to see a North Korean officer riding in a motorcycle sidecar. Both parties seemed equally surprised at finding each other. Carey recalled the drama: "The entire column fired, riddling the motorcycle and its riders with bullets and turning them into a bloody pulp." The engine kept running, and the riderless vehicle careened into a ditch.

During the push forward toward Seoul, Tom Powers recalled another bizarre incident when George Company and the enemy seemed to bump into each other. A North Korean soldier ran across the road. Powers and the entire convoy opened up on him. As his rifle discharged next to Sergeant Garcia's ear, an annoyed Garcia turned to Powers with a "dirty look." Every bullet had missed the North Korean soldier. As he made his way across the road and up a hill, the North Korean elegantly tipped his hat toward George Company and descended the hill to safety.

The gas-guzzling M26s were soon running on empty. The tank platoon commander requested refueling. Shortly thereafter, trucks appeared on the road, and the Marines began refueling the tanks with fifty-five-gallon drums of fuel. Fuel barrels lined the side of the road, and the Marines hastily jammed hoses into the fuel ports to feed the thirsty tanks. They feverishly turned hand cranks to pump the fuel to the vehicles. Suddenly, mortar rounds screamed, and George Company was peppered with machine gun fire. "Things were getting really hairy and the tank in front of us backed into a fifty-five-gallon drum, crushing it like a beer can," remembered Hock.

Mortar rounds bracketed the tanks, giving the initial impression of friendly fire.

Westover grabbed the headset from his radio operator and barked to his mortar officer, "Are those your short rounds?"

The officer blurted out, "Those aren't our short rounds, sir. They're North Korean rounds."

A North Korean antitank gun then opened up, damaging one of the lead tanks. The Marines blasted the gun.

A tank recovery vehicle lumbered over to the disabled tank. Unfortunately, the North Koreans hit the Marine recovery vehicle as well, damaging it beyond repair. Both vehicles now blocked further progress up the road.

Suddenly, a squad of North Korean soldiers descended on the tank and attempted to knock it out with grenades.

Westover ordered George Company to dismount on the side of the road and flank the North Koreans by gaining the high ground. Hock remembered a mortar round dropping between the legs of one of his fellow Marines, severing both limbs. Remarkably, the Marine was still lucid. In a state of shock, he blurted out, "They dropped a mortar between my legs!" as a corpsman applied a tourniquet to stop the bleeding.

As George Company and the tanks were clearing out the resistance, they moved further down the road and took fire from a small farmhouse.

Zullo went into action and barked, "Throw a grenade!"

A young Marine within the company did as instructed, but the grenade landed short—right between Zullo's feet.

"The man was absolutely fearless," recalled Powers. With one fluid motion, Zullo kicked the grenade into the door like a "soccer ball," using the side of his foot. A split-second later, the grenade detonated, killing the North Koreans inside.

"I think the First Sergeant's mad at me," the young Marine who threw the grenade sheepishly commented.

Several of the Marines then looked at the teenaged Leatherneck and sternly admonished, "You better go over there and apologize to the First Sergeant."

The young Marine followed instructions and scampered over to Zullo. "He came over to the First Sergeant with two grenades held by the pins on his backpack harness," Powers laughingly recalled.

Zullo looked down at the young kid with a glance of horror and laughter and, noticing the grenades dangling on the chest harness, yelped, "He's trying to kill me! He's trying to kill me!"

Kidding aside, the Marine was squared away, and the grenades were secured.

Zullo seemed ever-present. Sergeant Henry recalled, "I don't mean to get vulgar, but Zullo was like flies on shit. He was all over the place. Whenever there was a fight, Zullo was there."

The firefight continued as George Company cleared several adobelike houses. Carey recalled Tillman turning to him and tapping him on the shoulder. "Look who's coming up the road!" he said incredulously.

In a scene straight from a movie, General Douglas MacArthur confidently walked straight up the center of the road, "bullets flying around him." Carey was dumbfounded. As MacArthur walked up to his position, Carey pulled him behind the building. "The general fell over" and stared at the lieutenant, quickly snapping, "What the hell do you think you're doing, Lieutenant?"

"I'm just trying to keep you from getting killed," Carey snapped back. MacArthur glared at Carey with icy presence and said, "There isn't a bullet made that can kill me."

By this time, MacArthur felt invincible. Inchon was proving to be his masterstroke and was unfolding in a way that was beyond his wildest dreams. The landing had been a lance deep into the side of North Korea, choking off supply lines to the south in Pusan. The Eighth Army was finally breaking out, and the North Korean army was in full flight and shambles.

MacArthur's staff later escorted the general out of harm's way, and George Company pressed forward. They fought their way toward Seoul for several days, heading toward the heavily defended village Yongdungpo.

Yongdungpo

A DENSE, HEAVY FOG covered the rice paddies as George Company advanced in column. Suddenly, a spectral figure burst though the mist. Sergeant Henry watched in horror as a South Korean father ran past him carrying the broken body of his daughter: "Blood was all over the place. The anguish in his face has been seared in my mind's eye for over fifty years."

Both father and daughter were screaming and crying. A George Company corpsman tried to offer assistance to the wounded girl. The ten-year-old girl's arm was dangling by a thread and required amputation. "Our corpsman cut off her arm with a knife," recalled Dick Hock. The Navy medic then tenderly bandaged the young girl's arm. The father was in a state of shock.

Despite the horrors of war, Hock didn't lose his humanity. "I dug a shallow grave for it, and I buried her tiny arm," recalled Hock tearfully.

On the foggy morning of September 21, George Company penetrated the outskirts of Yongdungpo. Located between the Kalchon and Han rivers, Yongdungpo lay directly on the path to Seoul, about two miles distant. The suburb of Seoul consisted of flat, open ground, filled with rice paddies, locks, and dikes, and rows of buildings that faced the South Korean capital. A key communications hub, the industrialized town also contained crucial railroad and highway bridges, which linked it to Seoul.

"If Yongdungpo is lost, Seoul will fall," the North Korean leadership acceded in various conferences. They assigned an entire North Korean regiment to Yongdungpo. George Company marched into a buzz saw.

Initially, George Company set out marching in a column instead of a skirmish line because of the open nature of the ground. After advancing about three-quarters of a mile without any casualties, the platoons then formed into a skirmish line as they came under sniper fire. Returning fire, the company killed several North Korean soldiers.

As they entered Yongdungpo, a Corsair came in and began a strafing run. Furrows of .50 caliber bullets cut through the soft dirt of the paddies. The men dove for cover. Someone quickly pulled out George Company's red marker panels. Luckily, the pilot recognized in time that they were friendly troops and waggled his wings in recognition.

As the Marines resumed their march forward, numerous South Korean civilians continued to spring up along the way, informing Westover that the North Koreans were dug in and waiting. Sensing a trap, George Company requested permission to halt and asked for additional instructions. The battalion radioed back that they should stay in place.

As First Squad in First Platoon rounded a corner to dig in further, Hock remembered practically bumping into two Korean soldiers armed with M1 Garands. "The men didn't look menacing as they lowered their weapons," recalled Hock. "We thought they might be ROKs."

"Go get Sergeant Binaxas!" someone yelled.

"Binaxas spoke a little Japanese, and First Squad thought he might be able to communicate with them. Both North Koreans had their weapons at 'parade rest.'" Binaxas, known affectionately as "the Greek god" for his prowess with women or less affectionately as "the God-damned Greek," rounded the corner and barked, "Put down your rifles!"

Suddenly, with a flick of a wrist, one of the North Koreans lifted his weapon and "fired from the hip." A gaping wound appeared in Binaxas's stomach, as he crumpled over writhing in pain: "He aged twenty years in twenty seconds."

In the confusion, both North Koreans took off running. The squad fired at the fleeing North Koreans, but they seemed to escape into some buildings.*

Face flush with horror, Sergeant Tillman informed the remaining members of First Platoon, "Binaxas is KIA."

Hock reflected on the moment fifty-nine years later. "Nothing is so screwed up as combat. Binaxas was a good man—a World War II vet and very colorful."

By midday, headquarters ordered George Company to resume its advance. Westover instructed Third Platoon, reinforced with a section of light machine guns, to head for a water gate that controlled passage from a canal to the Kalchon River. "There was a dike on either side of this canal that came into a river, which ran directly across our line of attack," remembered Westover. In order to reach the rusted-steel water gate, Third Platoon would have to cross the canal between the two dikes and expose themselves on top of the dike—the perfect position for an ambush.

As expected, the North Koreans were dug in along the dikes. Moving forward toward the water gate, Third Platoon encountered heavy fire. The men dropped to their knees as the earthen dike in front of them erupted.

As Third Platoon crawled to the top of the earthworks, a barrage of machine gun bullets struck one Marine in the head. For over half an hour, the Third Platoon commander, Lieutenant Jarrnigan, boldly attempted to position his machine guns in a place where they could

---

* Several of the men later recalled that these men were recaptured, while others simply remember the men fleeing.

return fire. Jarrnigan fearlessly moved to the top of the dike. He placed his field glasses to his eyes and scanned the area. A second later, he lowered them. "I saw the bullet take off half his face," recalled Mert GoodEagle.

Jarrnigan had been in a tragic automobile accident and "always seemed depressed. He seemed to want to die. All of us were convinced that moving over the dike the way he did was a suicide mission, but what were we going to do? If you didn't follow orders, you would be labeled a coward or would be up for a court martial," recalled Hems. "It was reckless. Why did he do it? I think he wanted to die."

After Jarrnigan went down, another Marine PFC jumped up on the dike and heroically started firing his BAR. Raking the North Korean position and killing several of them, he drained his twenty-round clip and began changing it out as machine gun bullets ripped into his left side. Someone yelled, "Corpsman up!" But within a matter of minutes, the Marine died.

As the earth around his position exploded with enemy machine gun fire, the gunner working with Fred Hems carefully traversed his machine gun, sending bullets arcing toward the incoming fire. An enemy round interrupted his fire. Striking the Browning M1919A4 and bending the top of the receiver into an S-shape, it exploded the cartridges inside the machine gun's chamber. Another bullet struck the gunner's hand. "Blood spots from the powder burns covered my face," recalled Hems. Despite the searing powder burns on his face, Hems took over for the gunner and worked to put the damaged gun back into action.

Pinned down, Third Platoon faced obliteration. To extricate his trapped platoon, Westover decided to outflank the North Koreans and send First Platoon and Second Platoon out on the endangered platoon's flanks. He also called in an air strike and utilized the forward observation team to put artillery fire on the target. The napalm was particularly deadly, as Westover recalls: "I remember seeing the sticky, searing gas-jelly coat their bodies. As they were trying to get it off, they were smearing it all over their bodies, burning their flesh from their bones."

After the air strikes and artillery fire, Second and First Platoons blasted their way forward in an attempt to relieve the Third Platoon near the water gate.

First Platoon's objective for the day was to reach a highway that paralleled the Han River. "I couldn't raise George Westover [on the radio], and I remembered our objective was to reach the highway, so I made my decision," recalled Lieutenant Carey. "We had to move through several dikes, which provided us cover. Then we were about five hundred yards from our objective. At this point, there were about five hundred yards of open field, with no cover."

Carey had a very difficult mission. Across the open field, there were several warehouse buildings that contained dug-in North Koreans. First Platoon would have to cross the field in broad daylight, exposed to withering fire. "I planned to make the attack with two squads forward and one to the rear. We formed a line of skirmishers. The squad leaders would use fire team rushes, with covering fire from the third squad," remembered Carey.

"Fix bayonets!" Sergeant Tillman yelled as the men inserted steel on the ends of their M1s. He repeated the famous line from Gunnery Sergeant Daniel J. Daly, WWI Marine hero at Belleau Wood: "Come on, you sons of bitches! Do you want to live forever?"

The men surged forward.

The Marines hit their stride and covered nearly two hundred yards at a dead sprint. The Leathernecks met intense fire, evidenced by enemy muzzle flashes from the building. Carey's squad was pinned down. *We're in serious trouble*, thought Carey. "I knew if we didn't move forward, we would be dead in the open ground. I was on the right flank, while Tillman was on the left," he recalled.

A natural leader and tactician, Tillman changed his direction of advance, drawing the enemy fire off Carey's squad. Carey then shouted at his men, "Move it! Move it!"

Several First Platoon Marines went down. "It could have been from the covering fire," recalled Hock. "But I'm not sure." Nevertheless, Tillman remained cool under fire "in utter disregard for his own safety" as he led his squad forward on the assault. Carey later praised him saying, "Tillman acted decisively. I'm certain I would have lost a third of my platoon, had he not been there."*

Eventually First Platoon reached the buildings and fired on the North Koreans. Several fled as the squads descended on the buildings.

After driving the North Koreans out of the warehouse, Carey's platoon moved to their objective—the highway—as the sun began to set. First Platoon dug in along the highway, which paralleled the Han River, and Second Platoon covered the flank of Third Platoon, freeing it from the deadly North Korean crossfire. The platoons then advanced toward the Han. Eventually, the remainder of George Company joined First Platoon along the thoroughfare and dug in.

Hock found it remarkably easy to burrow through the soft dirt. His entrenching tool soon hit flesh and bone, the bloated corpse of a decomposing body resting in a fresh grave. The body seemed to be moving. "It was covered with maggots, which seemed to be moving the clothing. We got chicken and rice in our C-Rations. After that I would never eat them again," recalled Hock.

The North Koreans were only yards away that night. "Our supply of grenades was low, so we made IED-type explosives using C-2 that we packed with nails and detonated with blasting caps as we threw them at the enemy," recalled Carey.

During a lull in the fighting, members of George Company stumbled upon a gold mine.

"Skipper, we found a brewery," someone informed Westover.

With a nod and a smile, Westover told his Jeep driver, "Let's go."

Westover and other members of the company descended on a squat, red-brick building. A massive wooden gate blocked their progress until one of the men climbed over the wall and unlocked it. They were in.

The men converged on the 3,000-gallon vats of unprocessed "green" beer like mad dogs attacking a meat shop. Not waiting for the slow flow of the taps, the men snipped "the clear measurement tubes on the side of the tanks." A green elixir spilled onto the stone

---

* Tillman received the Silver Star for his actions that day.

floor of the brewery. After several days of combat, everyone wanted some of the brew. "It was warm and green," recalled Mert GoodEagle.

After days of bloody combat, "We wanted it. Warm, green beer— there was nothin' like it," Tom Powers recalled with a smile, fifty-seven years later.

Some of the men were a little more cautious. George Company had its share of teetotalers, and some wisely turned away after "we found a dead North Korean in one of the large vats," recalled one Marine.

The men used their helmets as beer steins and filled jerry cans with the partially fermented elixir. The men quickly became buzzed. Within two hours, though, things took a turn for the worse. "It seemed like we had shits for a week," recalled Bob Harbula. Men lined up in makeshift latrines as they rid their bodies of the ale.

Luckily, George Company didn't have to enter intense combat right away. Waiting for DUKWs* to transport them across the river into Seoul, they remained in their positions along the highway and exchanged fire with the North Koreans, who were prepared to fight to the death in South Korea's capital.

---

* GMC-manufactured, six-wheeled amphibious trucks.

Seoul

Bᴏᴏᴍ! Sᴘʟᴀsʜ!

Boom! Splash!

The amphibious vehicle swerved to avoid the incoming North Korean mortar fire, while nervous Marines clenched their weapons and prayed that none of the rounds would hit the DUKWs.

Orace Edwards, a tall teetotaler from Texas who was a rifleman with First Platoon, remembered, "Our DUKW operator moved the rudder back and forth to zigzag the vehicle, making an *S* pattern in order to avoid the enemy mortars that were hitting the zigzag pattern where we weren't. I sat on the seat and looked at mortar shells hitting the water, wondering if one of them was going to get lucky—and hoping it wouldn't."

Earlier in the day, George Company had boarded trucks and moved down toward the Han River. There they had clambered into the DUKWs. After ten minutes of successfully dodging the incoming mortar fire, the line of DUKWs hit dry land on the other side of the river. Without suffering a single casualty, the men disembarked, offloaded their gear, and quickly headed for the high ground. They dug in and spent a relatively uneventful night before the main assault on Seoul.

After Inchon, Kim Il Sung had heavily reinforced Seoul with 20,000 troops, including 5,000 battle-tested men from the Twenty-Fifth Brigade who had fought in Mao's army. Despite the impressive number of troops Kim had brought into the city, his strategy included a major flaw: he wasted many of his precious T-34 tanks by sending them to counterattack the Marines in a piecemeal fashion. George Company had witnessed one such incident on the second day of the landing.

Nevertheless, the North Koreans held Seoul firmly and were digging in. A modern city with a prewar population of over 1 million, Seoul was one of Asia's large cities, complete with modern stone buildings, a power grid, and a trolley system.

By September 24, two Marine regiments, the Fifth and the First, had entered the city's perimeter, along with a regiment of Seventh Division and the 187th Airborne Regimental Combat Team. Colonel Chesty Puller's First Marines would go up through the heart of the city.

Rather than enveloping Seoul, the Marines and MacArthur argued that they would have to take it block by block. That decision would result in tragic carnage. Before the development of smart bombs and other precision-guided munitions, the UN Allies would have to apply overwhelming artillery and air power in a massive fashion against the dug-in North Korean resistance.★

At 0200 on the morning of September 25, the First Marines began their attack on Seoul.

As the lead company for 3/1, George spearheaded the advance. They soon encountered their first obstacle—a railroad embankment

---

★ As R. W. Thompson from *The Daily Telegraph* wrote, "The slightest resistance brought down a deluge of destruction, blotting out the area."

that lay across their path. Second Platoon went under the railroad underpass. They "started getting murdered," remembers George's sniper "Peepsight" Pendas, and took a lot of casualties.

Orace Edwards recalls, "As we were going up the rise in the field, gunfire opened up on us, and the Second Platoon took the brunt of the attack with a lot of casualties."

With Lieutenant Beeler's Second Platoon and Third Platoon pinned down, First Platoon, including "Peepsight" Pendas, was tasked with breaking the enemy's hold with a flanking maneuver. As the platoon, led by Carey and Tillman, moved over the top of the railroad embankment, they went through an open field, where they got into a violent firefight. Pendas recalls, "There was a machine gun on top of the plateau peppering us pretty bad. We couldn't move over to Second Platoon. It seemed simple to me, if I could get around the flank of the machine gun, I could throw a grenade. I took my 03 and ran around the plateau, which seemed like winding goat trails and small ravines. All of the sudden on the path, up pops a guy with a white shirt who had hair eight inches long straight like wire. He had a rifle. He fired at me, no more than fifty feet away. I was in a small depression. The bullet hit right in front of me. Debris and a portion of the road hit me right in the face—right between the eyes."

Pendas thought, *I know I'm dead.* The bullet "knocked the feet from right underneath me. I knew I was shot. Reaching up behind the back of my head, I was feeling around for a hole. The war had ended for me for about thirty-five seconds as I was trying to find out if I was alive. There was a lot of blood but no hole."

As time stood still for Pendas, the North Korean would pop out of the hole, fire his bolt-action rifle for no more than two seconds, and then pop back into the hole, reload, and pop up again. Peepsight had trouble zeroing in on the man. The North Korean was a difficult target, so Pendas zeroed in with his telescope. As he saw the top of the North Korean's head, he pulled the trigger. The round hit him in the chest. Pendas then crept up toward the machine gun nest and "pulled the pin on a grenade and let the spoon fly" killing the enemy machine gun crew.

Sergeant Tillman then shouted, "Come on, we're pulling back."

"See if you can help this man!" shouted Lieutenant Carey. Machine gunner Calvin New had been hit in the mouth with a bullet. Dick Hock recalls, "New was choking on his own blood and drowning; he was bleeding like an open fire hydrant."

Pendas dressed his wounds and "with the strength that only adrenaline can provide," put New in a fireman's carry, and brought him off the field of battle. Several Marines then placed New in a poncho and took him to the rear.★

First Platoon pushed across the field, through a bean patch, and flanked the enemy troops firing on Second and Third Platoon.

George Company then began the advance up the main thoroughfare in Seoul, Ma Po Boulevard. One of the few thoroughfares in the city wide enough to accommodate tanks, the road cut through the heart of Seoul. Knowing that Ma Po would form the axis of the attack, the North Koreans had prepared roadblocks, bunkers, and other defensive positions along the gauntlet that George Company would have to pass through.

Meanwhile, to the south in the Pusan Perimeter, General Walker's Eighth Army was breaking out after a very slow start. Walker faced the difficult task of reducing several fortified mountain strongpoints before his men could advance.

For nearly a week, the North Koreans had wisely refused to tell their troops about the Inchon landing and how the Americans were cutting off their lines of communication from the rear. Finally, by September 19, the news finally filtered down to the rank-and-file North Koreans. Feeling doomed, many of Kim Il Sung's troops panicked and began the long retreat north. Hot on the heels of the retreating troops, Walker ordered his men to "pursue and destroy the enemy."

★ Thirty-five years later Pendas was reunited with New at the home of Harrell Roberts. New somewhat begrudgingly said, "You son of a bitch you broke my neck when you put me down." Pendas was awarded the Bronze Star for taking out the machine gun nest.

Urban Holocaust

CORPSMAN UP! Corpsman up!"

One of George Company's corpsmen dashed through the fire and moved to the mortally wounded Marine.

"I couldn't save him! I couldn't save him!" screamed the corpsman as he continued to press down on the bloody neck of "his best friend" whose lifeless body lay in the back of a Jeep, his brain oozing out the back of his shattered skull. No one could remove his blood-drenched hands still clutching the dead man's jugular.

Minutes earlier, "a North Korean woman armed with a rifle had fired the fatal shot from a second-story house," remembered Fred Hems. Her first shot took the Marine's helmet right off his head. Rather than reaching for cover, he grabbed his helmet, and as he was putting it on his head, the second round shattered his skull.

Navy corpsmen attached to George Company—some of the most heroic individuals on the battlefield—placed their lives at great risk as they attempted to treat the wounded. But for this George Company man, it was too much.

"The medic just cracked up. It was too much for him to see his friend's brains hanging out," recalled Hems.

During the firefight, George Company had lost about four or five people in short order. The gore of the battlefield overwhelmed the corpsman's senses and brain in a short time. The human brain can only process so much trauma. In battle, each individual finds his own way of coping or cracks. After he lost his best friend, the corpsman had to be taken to the rear.

George Company had to fight its way through the heart of Seoul. Ma Po Boulevard was lined with the burned-out gray hulks of churches and office buildings. With no room for maneuver, the men went straight up the gut, into a gauntlet of fire "so thick you could see the bullets."

Astride each side of the road, George Company fought beside M26 tanks that supported them for most of the day. As the Marines fought up the boulevard, they faced hundreds of dug-in North Koreans. Armed with antitank guns and machine guns, the North Koreans bravely fought to the death. The narrow streets and houses made flanking attacks nearly impossible: everything in front of the barricades became a kill zone.

As the Marines advanced, North Koreans hiding in houses sprayed them with burp guns and then quickly melted away into the smoking ruins of Seoul.

"As we were going up Ma Po Boulevard, a sergeant—I can't remember his name—pushed me into a doorway because we were taking a lot of fire from the hill. As we stepped through the threshold, I heard a thud. When I turned around, I saw the sergeant had fallen to the ground. He had taken a round in the head," said Tom Powers. He thought to himself: *He's a World War II vet and had a wife at home. These guys always try to take care of us.* "He had just saved my life. I think I purposely blocked his name from my memory for fifty-nine years because it was so painful," remembered Powers.

Under the intense fire, George Company casualties mounted hour by hour. And in early afternoon, several men went down simultaneously, including another member of First Platoon. Spotting the wounded man, Lieutenant Carey went to his aid, putting him in a fire-man's carry to bring him to the rear. Blood from the wounded man's body coated the young lieutenant's uniform. In the heat of battle, the charismatic officer didn't notice the crimson on his clothing.

During a slight pause in the fighting, First Platoon took a much–needed breather.

"Are you hit?" Westover asked Carey.

"No, I just carried off one of my men. I'm not hit," responded Carey, noticing his blood-soaked uniform for the first time.

Sitting on some rubble, Carey found himself "shooting the bull" with Sergeant Gene Lilly. Lilly, a WWII vet who had taken so many of the reservists, including Orace Edwards, under his wing, also asked Carey about his blood-stained clothes.

Whizz!

A sniper round landed right between the two men.

"We gotta move!" snapped Carey to Lilly.

As Carey moved to the safety of cover, Lilly passed right into the space Carey had been occupying. Another sniper shot rang out. With a thud, a round penetrated Lilly's heart. A devout Mormon, the sergeant seemed to stand up, arms and hands reaching straight up into the sky.

"Mother of God," he gasped.

Lilly's lifeless body then fell to the ground. Under fire, Carey scrambled over to Lilly's body and checked for a pulse.

"He's dead."

The platoon jumped back in action as M26 tanks from Baker Company began blasting the pockets of resistance, silencing machine gun fire. "When the tank's 90 fired, the muzzle blast would knock the plywood and plaster off the fronts of the buildings," recalled Dick Hock.

As the rest of George Company pushed down the road with the tanks, Lilly's lifeless body remained alone on the side of the road, waiting for retrieval by the Graves Registration Unit.

Suddenly, he moved.

Using the tanks for cover, one of the corpsmen went back to check the body. The medic soon returned, shaking his head. "Just nerves," he said. "Lilly's dead."

The afternoon began to turn into evening, and fire became more and more intense. North Koreans pinned down George Company in front of a barricade made of logs, barbed wire, and sandbags. On the right-hand side of the street stood a stone elementary school several stories high with a rock retaining wall, which the North Koreans used as a weapons and ammunition cache. Several abandoned 120 mm mortars lay silent in the courtyard. A bend in the road to the right revealed another enemy roadblock, about fifty yards away.

As First Platoon passed over a small bridge, they were immediately hit by a torrent of small arms fire and an antitank gun. Dozens of North Koreans opened up on George Company.

Whoosh!

A round "cut a Marine in half," remembered Hock.

With First Platoon in the lead, they were followed up by Tom Enos's Second Platoon. "I remember the after-effects. One of the Marines was hit by an 85 mm round. It hit him in the chest, tore him apart. He was a radioman, and the radio was torn off his back and disintegrated. I just looked at it and kept going. This is the stuff I never talked about after the war."

"With the curve in the road, there was such heavy fire," recalled Hock. One of George Company's advance teams out in the vanguard soon became pinned down. Luckily, the men found a nearby shell hole as they sought cover. The rest of Carey's platoon clambered behind the other roadblock and began to return fire on the North Koreans in an attempt to relieve the beleaguered four-man fire team. The firefight went on for well over thirty minutes with no letup. Soon, battalion ordered Westover to pull back from the curve in the road to the protection of the stone wall and hill. Citing the iron rule of the Marine Corps to leave no man behind to the enemy, Westover informed the battalion that he needed to extricate his cutoff fire team.

The George Company men came up with several novel solutions. First, they attempted to pierce a nearby building wall with rockets so that they could reach the trapped men and pull them out. Once a small hole was created, two blocks of TNT were used to make it wide enough for a Marine to slither through. As the riflemen went through the hole for the rescue mission, they were cut down immediately by small arms fire. The first two men had holes drilled through their heads as they emerged from the other side of the aperture.

Next, the forward observer team called up mortars to lay in smoke, but the wind caused it to drift too far. With smoke mortars in short supply, a solution came in the form of incendiary grenades. As Hock recalled: "Someone threw out the grenades as far as they could. We used the smoke to cover the withdrawal."

Through the smokescreen, Hock and the other Marine sprinted down the street and extricated the fire team, including two badly injured comrades. Their fellow Marines placed the wounded men in fireman's carries and sprinted down the street under heavy fire, miraculously avoiding further wounds.

After the melee, another problem surfaced. On the eastern edge of the intersection near the schoolhouse lay a sewage canal. A South Korean civilian, acting as an interpreter, reported to Westover that dozens of North Korean soldiers were hiding in the culvert. Westover turned to Zullo: "First Sergeant, how about taking care of that." (Throughout the melee, Zullo had been "all over place and wherever there was a fight," barking orders, recalled Dale McKenna.)

Zullo nodded and sprang into action. He carefully maneuvered down into the drainage ditch. Next he ordered a machine gun set up on one end of the culvert and ordered his men, "Don't fire until I tell you too."

Zullo then ordered a small group of riflemen and a BAR-man to the other opening in the culvert. "I made it clear if the enemy fired no one would come out of the culvert alive," he recalled.

Zullo wanted to take the North Koreans alive. Using an interpreter, Zullo attempted to coax the North Koreans into surrendering.

The First Sergeant knew they might be able to provide valuable intelligence. But "someone got trigger happy and fired into the tunnel," recalled Hems.

"Now they're not going to come out," Zullo lamented. He gave the order: "Kill 'em all."

Hems began firing the .30 caliber machine gun into the darkness. The BAR-man and the other men with Zullo followed suit. The incident ended when Zullo went down toward the drainage ditch alone and pitched two grenades into the darkness. Placing his carbine on full automatic, he emptied a thirty-round clip of ammunition into the dark tunnel. A Marine foolishly tried to place his head into the ditch. Zullo barked, "You stupid son of a bitch. Do you want to die?"

Hems recalled, " I felt bad about it. It was the first time I killed someone at close range. I think about it all the time, killing human beings. And I didn't like to shoot them. As I think about it now, I was only a teenager."

Not all of the Marines agreed with Hems. "Later, Hems would recap what happened that day, internalize things. It got to be too much sometimes. I'll never forget telling him one day to shut the fuck up!" recalled Powers.

The effects of the incident—both physical and mental—remained for days. "My boondockers were coated with green shit. People avoided me because of the stench," recalled Powers, who had waded into the raw sewage to feed belts of ammo to Hems's gun.

A handful of Marines had destroyed an entire enemy platoon, over forty men. Later, Zullo explained, "I wanted to take them prisoner, but we had to annihilate them once they didn't come out. Otherwise, they would have hit us from the rear. Nice guys don't win wars."

North Korean Counterattack

TANKS! TANKS! TANKS!" First Lieutenant Dalton Hilscher barked over the forward observer team's SCR–300 radio, which Carlos Banks carried. "The fire team began to call in mortar and artillery fire directly in front of us. The noise was tremendous," recalled Banks.

Shortly after 8 p.m. on the evening of September 25, the First Marine Division headquarters received a jarring message: "You will push your attack *now*, to the limit of your objective . . . in order to ensure maximum destruction of enemy forces." Major General Oliver Prince Smith, a thirty-three-year veteran of the Corps, sometimes called "professor" for his studious looks and deliberate manner, stared at the order with near-disbelief. Knowing the North Koreans had been heavily defending the city block by block, he realized a night attack without proper preparation could be costly for his men and bordered on suicide. The men would be going into the heart of enemy defenses after being exhausted from a full day's battle.

Smith requested a confirmation and received a firm response: "The order went out exactly as General Almond dictated it and is to be executed without delay." Also relayed in the message was Almond's information that elements of the North Korean army were retreating from Seoul.

General Edward Mallory "Ned" Almond was MacArthur's chief of staff for the Far East and commander of X Corps, making him Smith's superior officer. Ambitious and driven, during WWII, Almond had served as the major general in command of the Ninety-Second Infantry Division, an African-American unit that fought in Italy. Initially an outsider to MacArthur's chain of command and not part of the "Bataan Gang" that MacArthur utilized during the Pacific War, Almond ingratiated himself with MacArthur, who had appointed him chief of staff.

It seemed to Smith that Almond had become obsessed with capturing the city in time for MacArthur's manufactured deadline of September 25, exactly three months from the day the North Koreans launched their invasion. His order roiled an already tempestuous relationship. With only ten months separating them in age, Almond condescendingly referred to Smith as "Son." Known for his aggressive nature, Almond was called "Ned the Dread," which referred to his "power, brusque manner, and sometimes arbitrary actions."

General Lemuel Shepherd, commanding general of Fleet Marine Force Pacific, summed up the relationship this way: "He [Almond] and O.P. [Smith] just didn't get along, from the very first. They are two entirely different personalities.... O.P. [was] a very cautious individual, a fine staff officer who considered every contingency before taking action. On the other hand, Almond was aggressive and anxious for X Corps to push ahead faster than Smith thought his division should." Smith's deliberate nature would later save the First Marine division from destruction.

Reluctantly, Smith accepted Almond's orders. Phoning his regimental commanders, Smith told them, "I want you to coordinate your attack carefully. Don't try to advance too rapidly. Take it slow, and stay on the main avenues you can identify at night. I'm ordering a fifteen-minute artillery preparation before you jump off."

Colonel Puller knew he was sending his men, including George Company, into a meat grinder and delayed the attack until 0200 because preparation was "inadequate." Doing the best he could for his men, Puller ordered two fifteen-minute artillery bombardments to plaster the area in front of the assault. In fact, the Marines never made their attack. The North Koreans struck first.

At 1:53 a.m., hundreds of North Korean troops and a column of T-34 tanks and self-propelled guns barreled down on George Company's position behind the roadblock. "You could hear the clanking of the T-34's steel tracks as they rumbled down the street," Dick Hock remembered.

Whoosh!

Suddenly, the main gun on one of the T-34s cracked. An 85 mm round went down the street at a blazing 800 meters per second. The armor-piercing projectile flew into a house being used as George Company's Command Post. Boring a hole through the wall and decapitating a battalion radio operator, it exited through the rear wall and "landed unexploded on a Marine's shelter half several yards behind the command post."

Voices shouted as the tanks made their way down the block: "Friendlies coming in! Friendlies coming in!" Stationed in front of the George Company roadblock, the First Machine Gun Section had a front-row view of the approaching enemy.

"I could hear a tank coming up closer as I started to run down the street back toward the roadblock," First Platoon Rifleman Orace Edwards remembered. "Automatic weapons spat and sparks from bullets hit the street surface around my feet. That made me run faster."

Ammo bearer Bob Harbula was taking turns with the machine gunner manning a gun. "All of the sudden, Edwards, this six-foot-two Marine, landed directly on top of my head," recalled Harbula.

"Hey, I'm on your fucking side," Harbula snapped. Despite the maelstrom, both men briefly laughed, breaking the unfolding tension.

Positioned on the left-hand side of the road, which was bisected by two trolley tracks, Hock leaned against a telephone pole behind the barricade, with his M1 rifle pointed directly at the oncoming tank. Suddenly, a Marine he didn't know dove behind the barrier. The Marine shouted, "Does anybody have any M1 ammo?"

"I never wanted to be caught unprepared, so I always carried extra bandoliers of ammunition. I moved away from the pole and back to my pack laying on the ground a few yards behind the barrier," remembered Hock. While Hock scrounged for the ammunition, the young Marine took over the rifleman's old position behind the telephone pole and fired the remaining rounds in his M1 at the oncoming tank.

"As I was reaching for the extra bandolier, the T-34 fired another round," remembered Hock. The armor-piercing round went through the center of the telephone pole, taking off part of the other Marine's head. Dirt and pieces of sandbag flew everywhere, and the round threw the Marine's body back several yards from the pole. The dead man's helmet landed several feet from his body. "I reached for him, but I knew he was dead," recalled Hock. "Everyone opened up on the tank, lighting it up like the Fourth of July."

Nearby, Sergeant James Hancock, armed with a 3.5-inch rocket launcher, told the Marine next to him, "Son, if you load, I'll fire."

Wham!

The tank fired a second round, and its heavy steel tracks clanked closer to the barricades. Earlier in the day, an engineer unit with the assistance of George Company had laid antitank mines in a random pattern in front of the roadblock. Remarkably, the tank threaded its way through the minefield without hitting one.

Ominously, the thirty-ton behemoth bore down on the First Platoon, its coaxial machine gun spewing out lead like a garden hose watering a lawn. While the tank undoubtedly readied another round in its main gun, Hancock squeezed the trigger on the bazooka, hitting the tank in its barrel and halting its movement. Hancock's teammate feverishly loaded another round and tapped him on the shoulder. The Marine bazooka-man squeezed the trigger again, hitting the tank in the turret.

Pelted by the bazooka rounds and small arms fire, the tank backed up and hit a mine, throwing its right track. "It backed up in an arc and came to a stop on the side of the street next to a schoolyard wall," remembered Hock.

Behind the lead T-34, three other North Korean tanks and a self-propelled gun rumbled down the boulevard, along with a battalion of infantry troops pushing several antitank guns. Harbula and the other members of the First Machine Gun section, along with the rest of the members of First Platoon, opened up with everything they had on the incoming North Korean assault. One of the machine gun barrels burned out because of the massive volume of fire. Hock recalled that the gunner had to twist the rounds on the belt "to stop it from firing and jam the gun because it wouldn't stop firing." The gun was literally firing itself.

"We were on the phone all night," recalled forward observer and radio operator Banks. A storm of steel greeted the North Koreans.

In the maelstrom, a small George Company patrol, led by Corporal Chuck Collins of the Second Platoon, was trapped behind the lines. With a mission to make contact with the Fifth Marines, Collins's small squad of men made their way through the North Korean positions. When suddenly confronted by scores of enemy troops that were making the counterattack, Collins heroically ordered his men to filter back to George Company lines, in an attempt to hold off the North Koreans while his men escaped. Evading North Korean patrols and, more miraculously, thousands of incoming Allied rounds, Collins slipped through the next morning in a clever manner. He found women's civilian clothing and reported back to George Company in drag.

As the first fingers of crimson crept over the blown and blasted bits of George Company's roadblock, the attack finally subsided. During the night, the forward observer team had assisted in calling in thousands of artillery rounds, making it even larger than some of the artillery bombardments at Guadalcanal. The Eleventh Marines laid on one of the largest artillery barrages of the war up until that time.

That morning when the melee was over, Hock covered the fallen Marine next to him with a poncho. Two stretcher bearers soon came to carry away the dead man. As they were positioning the body, "his brains slid out," recalled one of the Marines nearby.

Fifty-nine years later, Hock lamented, "He changed positions with me and saved my life."

Retrograde

As DAWN BROKE on the morning of September 26, the faint sound of "Dixie" could be heard over the crackle of machine-gun fire and the thud of mortar rounds. Barely eighteen, Jimmy Harrison played a small silver harmonica as the men milled around the tanks and prepared to jump off. Harrison was "fearless" and "liked to get into trouble," recalled Carlos Banks, a team member from the forward observer team.

The men could see the hulking outline of the disabled T-34. Several burned-out hulks of tanks and self-propelled guns trailed behind it. The broken bodies of hundreds of men lay in the wreckage of bombed-out buildings along Ma Po Boulevard, directly in front of George Company's positions. Four battalions of artillery, along with machine guns, rifle fire, small arms, and bazookas from George Company had crushed the North Korean counterattack.

Dick Hock recalled poking around the North Korean equipment: "I remember looking inside of the hatches and seeing the burnt-out bodies of the North Koreans still sitting in their seats."

By this time, all three of George Company's platoons had fallen far under their initial strength. Many of the men who had come ashore at Inchon were dead or wounded. Tom Powers remembered Third Platoon as having less than fifteen men standing from its original complement of forty-two.

Encountering minimal resistance, George Company pushed through the rubble of Seoul. The entire block in front of them lay pulverized. Downed electrical wires littered the street, along with the gray, burned-out buildings. This portion of Seoul had largely been flattened into an urban holocaust. Feral dogs and cats moved around the area. "Our objective was to cross over an area where the two streetcar tracks intersected. As we were making our way up the street, we came across a massive white wall. We had no idea what was on the other side of it," recalled Captain Westover.

To find out what was inside, a squad formed "a human pyramid." One man used the pyramid to scale over the wall, went down the other side, and opened a massive gate. "We had stumbled upon the royal palace of Duk Soo. There was no one inside." As other units of the First Marine Regiment arrived, the palace was quickly converted into Colonel Chesty Puller's regimental headquarters. George Company fanned out around the ancient building.

The North Koreans fell back in full retreat as the First Marine Division began occupying most of Seoul. To cover their retreat, the North Koreans launched several counterattacks and continued resisting the UN troops. George Company cleaned up pockets of resistance and attempted to trap Koreans fleeing to the north. Meanwhile, General Walker's Eighth Army advanced quickly up the spine of South Korea, pursuing, killing, and capturing large numbers of the enemy.

As George Company probed deeper into the city, they stumbled on a prison where they encountered grisly atrocities committed by the North Koreans. Fred Hems recalled seeing several of the prisoners, their hands bound behind their backs with wire and bullet holes drilled into the backs of their skulls.

During the advance, the Third Platoon entered a schoolhouse used as a makeshift hospital to treat Seoul's civilian population, which had suffered heavily during the battle. As they crossed the threshold, they entered a cavernous room that resembled a Civil War hospital on the set of *Gone with the Wind*. Civilian and Navy doctors frantically treated the wounded. "There was blood all over the place. People were screaming and hollering. The doctors' aprons were soaked in crimson," recalled Powers. Nearby stood several fifty-five-gallon drums filled with "bloody, amputated arms and legs."

At this time, the unit also encountered elements of the South Korean security services. "We didn't know who they really were. We just saw some guys in uniforms with armbands who claimed that they were security forces," recalled Clark Henry.

The FO team had been using a South Korean civilian to help carry equipment. "He was a burly guy and very friendly to us," remembered Henry. Suddenly, the uniformed guys showed up and took him away, claiming he was a spy. "They took him around a corner, and a shot rang out," recalled Henry.

Tom Powers recalled a similar incident. He stood in the middle of a street where all of the buildings were burned-out shells, a stark reminder of the battle. Westover was standing next to Powers when two men from the "security service" appeared and started grilling a civilian whom they accused of being a spy. When he wouldn't answer their questions, one of the security officers, armed with a Russian carbine and "pigsticker" bayonet, jabbed the rodlike dirk in the man's eye. The civilian buckled over screaming. "I lost it," recalled Powers, as he "butt-stroked" the security officer in the back of the head with his M1.

On the previous day, as George Company had been advancing up Ma Po Boulevard in its heaviest fighting so far, X Corps Commander Edward Almond had announced that Seoul had been liberated. As in so many wars in the past, when the generals announced something secured, it was hardly the case for the men doing the fighting on the ground. MacArthur had hoped to hold the liberation ceremony on September 25, but the North Koreans weren't cooperating, and resistance continued through September 29. Several counterattacks were repelled, even though George Company was in a reserve position and had not been in any firefights.

A ceremony turning Seoul over to the South Koreans and President Syngman Rhee was scheduled for the morning of September 29. A portion of security on the parade route became the duty of 3/1. However, the Marines who had captured Seoul were ordered to stay out of sight while performing their duty. After spilling their blood to capture the city, some felt the order was a slap in the face. When Chesty Puller arrived at the airport to greet MacArthur and other dignitaries, an Army MP tried to turn his Jeep away, saying the airport was restricted only to "staff guard." The MP caved in only after Puller growled, "Drive over that SOB if he doesn't move."

MacArthur and Rhee drove to the royal palace. Lieutenant Carey recalled, "The general's motorcade passed near our position. He looked over at me and remembered the day I had grabbed him. He looked over at me and said, 'How's it going, lieutenant?'"

In one of his finest moments, MacArthur opened the ceremony with a brief address: "Three months to the day after the North Koreans launched their attack south of the thirty-eighth parallel, the combat troops of X Corps recaptured the capital city of Seoul. . . . By 1400 hours, 25 September, the military defenses of Seoul were broken." In a dignified manner, MacArthur turned toward Rhee:

> Mr. President, by the grace of a merciful Providence, our forces fighting under the standard of that greatest hope and inspiration of mankind, the United Nations, has liberated this ancient city of South Korea. . . . On behalf of the United Nations command, I'm happy to restore to you, Mr. President, the seat of your government, that from it you may better fulfill your constitutional responsibilities.

MacArthur then bowed his head as tears flowed from his face and said the Lord's Prayer.

Nevertheless, the announcement seemed in keeping with MacArthur's manufactured time line of three months to the day for the liberation. The rumble of artillery and small arms fire punctuated his words. Several shards of broken glass hit the floor from the damaged skylight above the ceremony. After MacArthur completed his words, Rhee, also overcome with emotion, said, "We love you as the savior of our race. How can I ever explain to you my own gratitude and that of the Korean people?"

On September 27, President Truman authorized MacArthur to pursue operations north of the 38th Parallel. Specifically, the Joint Chiefs of Staff's direct orders to MacArthur were the following:

> Your military objective is the destruction of the North Korean armed forces. In obtaining this objective, you are authorized to conduct military operations, including amphibious and airborne landings or ground operations north of the 38th Parallel in Korea, provided at the time of such operations there has been no entry into North Korea by major Soviet or Chinese Communist forces, no announcement of intended entry, nor a threat to counter our operations in North Korea. Under no circumstances, however, will your forces cross the Manchurian or U.S.S.R. borders of Korea and, as a matter of policy, no non-Korean ground forces will be used in the Northwest provinces bordering the Soviet Union or in the area along the Manchurian border. Furthermore, support of your operations north or south of the 38th Parallel will not include air or naval action against Manchuria or U.S.S.R. territories.

Cut off and in danger of destruction, North Korea's armies were in full retreat north. By the end of September, Seoul was firmly in UN hands, and by the first of October, South Korean units had pushed across the parallel. Encountering limited resistance, Walker's Eighth Army advanced north. MacArthur had additional plans for X Corps.

After the ceremony, George Company moved to defensive positions around the northern position of the city. The men passed through the ruins of Seoul, which was returning to daily life.

"I found a barbershop," recalled Hock. North Koreans still occupied some buildings, and there was always a fear of sniper fire. "Hock, come on, let's get a haircut," said one of his fellow Marines. "I'll cover you if you cover me."

Hock did exactly that, and the men were able to amble into the barbershop and find a seat. Inside were several elderly gentlemen in stovepipe top hats. One man, who looked like he was 110 years old, asked in perfect English, "Where are you from?"

Hock was stunned. "Wisconsin," he answered.

The man responded matter of factly, "I graduated from the University of Minnesota."

With a smile, he then asked Hock, "Do you miss the cheese?"

The Marines received haircuts and then went about their duties.

On their excursions through the city, the men also spied a bank. Tom Powers remembered, "We found the vault, and one of the men put C-4 explosives on the door. The plastic blew the door off and money was lying all over the floor." The men descended on the bills like locusts. The money was completely worthless, consisting of North Korean banknotes. "I still have one of them, which has burn marks on its edges," recalled Powers.

The men also found additional loot at a plant that manufactured swords. "Everyone had a sword. We were pulling them out of barrels and putting them in our packs. We were feeling pretty cocky," recalled Bob Harbula.

In the final week of September, George Company was ordered back to the Inchon beachhead. On their way back, the men got a welcome treat. A trailer with hot showers awaited them. Before they entered, they tossed their torn and filthy uniforms into a pile. Victorious, the men cleaned off weeks of dirt, grime, and blood as they enjoyed the warm water that hit their bodies.

As they filtered out of the showers, they were issued a fresh pair of dungarees. They formed up and marched toward a pontoon bridge that spanned the Han River. They encountered a company of doggies. Interservice rivalry immediately bubbled to the surface as both groups traded insults. Someone yelled, "Jarheads!" Powers then snapped, "What's the blue line down the middle of your patch stand for? It separates the horse shit from the chicken shit."

The men were from the First Cavalry Division and wore the First Cav patch of a horse separated by a blue line. The insults continued to fly as the fracas suddenly spiraled out of control. A Marine dropped a live grenade onto the pontoon bridge that the Army was crossing. The grenade began smoking. Several of the Army personnel hastily dove into the water. The grenade exploded with a tiny pop. Someone in George Company had dropped the grenade and removed all of the powder from its pineapple casing. Army officers immediately began barking, "Who's in charge of this outfit?"

MPs were screaming, "Who threw the grenade? Who threw the grenade?"

No one spoke a word as Captain Westover and First Sergeant Zullo appeared on the scene.

The MPs frantically searched for the perpetrator, but no one uttered a word. George Company proceeded across the bridge toward the beachhead.

Wonsan

Bᴏʙʙʏ Hᴀʟʟᴀᴡᴇʟʟ briefly glanced down at his watch, one of the only working timepieces worn by a fighting member of George Company, and then looked to his right and left. Many of his comrades from Pendleton were gone—killed or wounded at Inchon or in the house-to-house fighting in Seoul. First Sergeant Zullo's piercing voice broke through his moment of reflection. "Get the men into formation," he barked to his NCOs.

George Company assembled by platoon, the men standing shoulder-to-shoulder in their thinned ranks. For the last few days, the remnants of George had been living in a bombed-out factory that was only partially covered by rusted, corrugated iron skin. They were about to board LSTs and leave Seoul.

Earlier, hiding his deep disappointment at leaving the men he had commanded for the past two months, company commander George Westover had introduced his successor to his officers before quietly slipping away. "I had a great affinity for these men," he would say later.

George Company's new commander, Captain Carl Sitter, ambled to the front of the group and was greeted by a thousand-yard blank stare repeated on scores of haggard Marines' faces—what was left of George Company. He addressed the group with no fanfare or bluster, just a few unmemorable words acknowledging the change of command.

Unlike Westover, Sitter's outward appearance didn't impress the men. One Marine thought with a smirk, *This dumpy, pear-shaped guy from H and S Company is going to lead us?* Another later quipped, "We didn't think much of him. We were riflemen, and we heard he was from Headquarters Company." When he first saw Sitter, Harbula thought, *This isn't the typical spit-and-polish officer. This guy looks frumpy.*

The men of George Company didn't realize that Sitter was a Mustang, initially an NCO before becoming an officer. A seasoned combat veteran, Sitter had been involved in several major campaigns during the bloody battles in the Pacific, earning the Silver Star. Sitter also received a Purple Heart for wounds suffered on Eniwetok, located in the Marshall Islands.

In the summer of 1950, an out-of shape Sitter had almost been left behind as the First Marine Regiment boarded ships for Korea. Despite an impressive combat record in World War II, the captain, who "began having weight problems" as he grew older, was not considered regimental timber. To remedy the situation, pudgy Captain Sitter reported directly to regimental commander Chesty Puller.

"I want to go over. I want to fight," he told Puller.

Puller then turned to an officer under his command, "What slot do we have for a captain?"

All of the officers' billets were filled at the time, with the exception of the Regimental Special Services Officer, a slot normally reserved for a first lieutenant. Sitter graciously took the demotion, which included the inglorious duty of inventorying basketballs, softball bats, footballs, and athletic supporters. Sitter had gotten his wish and was finally in the regiment, on a ship heading toward the war and his destiny.

Once the First Marines had docked in Kobe, thousands of men from the regiment disembarked, and their equipment was offloaded onto the Japanese docks, including Sitter's special service gear. Ironically, a massive typhoon hit Japan then and blew the equipment into the water. Sitter reported back to Puller, "Sir, we have no more special services gear."

In a gruff manner, Puller barked back, "Damn it, Carl, we came here to fight, not play."

That was effectively the end of Sitter's career as a special services officer. Shortly after landing at Inchon, he was made a liaison officer for the Fifth Marines. After the capture of Seoul, Sitter was transferred back to the First Marines, where he later joined George Company.

As Sitter finished addressing the Marines and he assumed command, his destiny became intertwined with theirs. While few of the men knew their fate, forty years later, an article in *The Leatherneck* would ask an interesting question: "Would history have been altered if Col. Louis B. Puller had answered 'No'?" The men of George Company and Sitter would soon find out.

Shortly after Sitter's brief change-of-command speech, the Marines formed up and marched to Inchon, where they boarded the LST, once again ironically commanded by the Japanese, their former enemy. Just five years earlier, the two had fought savagely during the bitter battles for control of the Pacific.

Each man made his way into the cramped bowels of the grimy ship, stowed his gear, and claimed one of the scarce racks. Within an hour, the gull-grey prow of the LST cut its way through the emerald coastal waters of Korea. It headed south toward Pusan, where it would round the tip of the Korean peninsula before turning north again toward one of the only large harbors in North Korea, Wonsan.

After the spectacular success of the Inchon landing and the recapture of Seoul, combined with the U.S. Eighth Army's breakout from the Pusan Perimeter, the shattered North Korean People's Army was on the run. Sensing that the enemy was mortally wounded, MacArthur raced toward the Yalu River, North Korea's border with China.

With the recapture of Seoul, X Corps, commanded by Major General Almond, which included the First Marine Division under Major General Smith, was to be loaded onto ships. They would steam around the North Korean peninsula and land in the eastern port of Wonsan. Simultaneously, the Eighth Army was advancing up the west coast of Korea toward the Yalu, led by Lieutenant General Walker.

MacArthur split his command, a violation of the sacrosanct rule of command.

Wonsan was one of the few open ports on the eastern side of the peninsula. The plan called for X Corps to land at Wonsan and drive northwest to the Yalu. The Seventh Marine Regimental Combat team would advance north from Wonsan to a larger city known as Hungnam. There they would continue to advance toward the Manchurian border 135 miles away across some of the most rugged terrain in North Korea, including the jagged and barren Taebaek Mountains, which have been compared to a smaller, less picturesque version of the American Appalachians.

A single road connected X Corps objectives. Starting in Hamhung, the road went to Koto-ri through the nearly impassable Funchilin Pass. From Koto-ri, the next major hamlet was known as Hagaru-ri. The road, ingloriously dubbed the Main Supply Route—in Marine lingo MSR—connected the small towns and passed a large body of water, which, on the aging Japanese maps the Marines used, was labeled the Chosin Reservoir. (North Koreans and South Koreans referred to the area as the Changjin Reservoir.)

Just as six years earlier in Operation Market Garden, a single road would determine the fate of the campaign and maybe even the entire war.

From their first operation at Inchon, the tension continued to fester between Smith and General Almond. After the war, Almond described the relationship this way: "I got the impression initially (and it was fortified consistently later) that General Smith always had excuses for not performing at the required time, the tasks he was requested to do." Smith had reason to advance the First Marine division north cautiously toward the Yalu River and the Eighth Army. The Marines were going over some of the most impassable terrain in North Korea, which presented numerous supply and logistics problems. Additionally, his flanks were exposed to a counterattack by North Korean and Chinese forces.

Almond was there to push and prod X Corps. He cast sound, battlefield-tested tactics aside for a speedy advance north. Ominously, X Corps's flanks were dangerously exposed.

Smith's First Marine Division was divided into three regimental combat teams, RCT-5, RCT-7, and RCT-1. RCT-1 included Third Battalion First Marines and George Company.

Life on board the ship became monotonous and boring. To kill time, the men played cards, smoked, traded stories. Bruce Farr remembered, "We were just anxious. We just wanted to get off the ship and get on land."

For the Marines, food became a big topic. The men lived on a steady diet of canned corned beef and canned pears for nearly a week. Sixty years later, some men still won't touch a canned pear. Tom Enos recalled that being placed on guard duty was a "big deal," because it meant being able to raid the storeroom of canned cheese, which worked wonders on the soldiers' digestive tracts. Fresh water was also scarce. The men showered only once on the entire trip. Combined with the cheese, the men's bowels created a ripe stench.

On October 26, the LST arrived off Wonsan harbor. However, it steamed back and forth along the Korean coast, while mine sweepers cleared underwater mines. The unforeseen threat delayed the operation. The Marines of First Division boarded LVTs and churned across the choppy, sea-green waters as they made their way toward the beach. Instead of angry machine-gun nests, mortars, and artillery, the men were greeted by Air Force and Army personnel who snidely remarked, "Ha! We got here before the Marines this time!"

Days earlier, South Korean forces had captured Wonsan and had been cleaning up isolated pockets of resistance. As George Company moved deeper into Wonsan, they observed Bob Hope's USO show entertaining the troops who had liberated the port several days earlier—rubbing further salt in the wound.

As they marched toward the battalion assembly area, George Company got to know Sitter, who marched alongside them, sometimes pulling ahead of the column. Though Sitter was out of shape and his feet quickly blistered (his socks becoming red with blood), he insisted on keeping up with his men. At an assembly area, they bivouacked in a secure area on the side of a hill outside the port. North Korean farms made a patchwork quilt around the area. After eating nothing but canned corned beef and pears for days, the men salivated at the site of a large, bloated, black-haired pig. Harbula turned to fellow machine gunner, Roy Shirey, a rusty-haired farm boy from the Deep South. The men of northern extraction liked to poke fun at Shirey, but he took it all in stride and dished it back in stride. Many of George Company's Marines hailed from Alabama and Georgia where the Civil War still raged in some people's minds. Several of the men even carried stars-and-bars confederate battle flags or forced their northern brethren within George Company to carry the banner sometimes as a light form of hazing.

Harbula quipped, "That pig would sure be good after what we've been eating for the past few days." He looked at Shirey, "Do you know how to butcher one and what part do we take?"

In his southern drawl, Shirey responded, "We'll take the tenderloin and give the hams to the tankers."

They began negotiations with the local farmer, initially without an interpreter. The men pointed to several cans of C-Rations: "We'll give you all that food for the pig."

The man seemed to agree at first. Then the negotiations broke down, and the farmer became very excited. The men couldn't understand why. Luckily, one of George Company's interpreters was brought forward, and the men now understood why the farmer had gone into a tirade.

"He wanted the pig's head," recalled Harbula.

The request was granted. The men had a pig roast.

"It was really good food; everyone had a pork chop in their mess kit. The next day we were forced to move out, and the rest of the meat was salted down, put into barrels, and given to the tankers."

With food in their bellies, the machine-gun section and the rest of George Company boarded trucks and headed west.

Majon-ni: Luck of the Draw

WE NEED A PLATOON to take prisoners back to Wonsan and pick up the company's cold weather gear and other supplies," Captain Sitter informed his three platoon commanders.

Rather than select a platoon for the mission himself, Sitter opted to let fate decide who would go back to the North Korean port. Calmly, the pudgy company commander held out his clenched fist, which contained three straws, one shorter than the other.

Lieutenant James Beeler reached over and chose a straw. The other platoon commanders followed suit and then held up the straws that they had drawn. Beeler's was short.

Beeler knew something was wrong with the ominous mission; he felt it. Nevertheless, as Tom Enos recalls, "The charismatic platoon leader accepted his fate and duty without shirking."★

★ Enos's fate was also tied to the draw. Shortly after the incident described, Beeler transferred the machine gunner from Second Platoon to First Platoon. Enos credits the administrative change with possibly saving his life.

For five days after their arrival on October 28, 1950, George Company had occupied the tiny Korean village of Majon-ni. Nestled in a valley with alpine peaks and clear mountain streams, the hamlet could, at first glance, have doubled for a town in northern Italy. But ramshackle houses, a couple of drab buildings, and, incongruously, a schoolhouse with an onion-shaped dome broke the picturesque skyline. Shortly after World War II, the Russians had moved into Majon-ni, and it became a center of political indoctrination for the North Koreans. But the tiny town also served a strategic purpose: one road connected the village to Wonsan, while two other roads led south toward Seoul and west to Pyongyang.

In a sense, Majon-ni resembled a much smaller version of Bastogne, the site of the Battle of the Bulge—all the major roads in the eastern portion of North Korea converged there. The battalion had been tasked with setting up a "defensive position at Majon-ni, destroying enemy forces, and denying them the use of this road-net." Additionally, 3/1 had to "control roads to the north, south, and west and keep the road open between Majon-ni and Wonsan." Their commanders later amended the latter order because it was mission impossible for the battalion of some nine hundred men to keep the roads open. As in northern Italy, the roads that fed Majon-ni were cut from the sides of mountains featuring sheer cliffs, gorges, and numerous hairpin turns. Tanks could barely traverse the thoroughfares, which were typically only wide enough for a single vehicle. In addition, several of the shelflike roads sliced through a 3,000-foot pass, the ideal place for a trap.

As 3/1 was moving into Majon-ni, the North Korean Fifteenth Division attempted to utilize the through roads and retreat north toward their lines. Despite the crushing blows at Inchon, the Fifteenth remained largely intact and had orders to conduct guerrilla warfare around Majon-ni. After breaking out from the Pusan Perimeter following the Inchon landings, the division was moving north, foraging for supplies and living off the land.

The battalion's rifle companies were each assigned a road: George Company had the road to Wonsan, How Company the road to Seoul, and Item Company took the road to Pyongyang. It soon became clear to the command that the battalion could not control a road net that stretched for dozens of miles.

Contact with the enemy began almost immediately upon 3/1's arrival. On November 2, a platoon of How Company, reinforced with a mortar and machine gun section, drove into an ambush in a deep gorge five miles south of Majon-ni. The Marines took several casualties but were miraculously able to escape through a wall of small arms fire coming from an unseen enemy hiding in the crags above the gorge. After another convoy was hit, the Marines dubbed the route "ambush alley."

Keeping Majon-ni supplied became a major challenge since the roads were constantly ambushed by the North Koreans. Radio communications were virtually nonexistent due to the high peaks surrounding the area. Typically, the Marines could contact their base for only a few hours at night. Majon-ni was effectively cut off from the outside world.

After drawing the unlucky straw, Beeler collected his platoon along with other personnel from headquarters. As he boarded a lead truck, Beeler carefully placed his Purple Heart medal in a manila envelope. A deep sense of foreboding overcame him. He felt *something was wrong*, and the former All-American standout wanted to make sure his parents received the medal he had been awarded for his wounds at Inchon.

The men and prisoners loaded up onto trucks, which were assembled into a convoy. It contained members of the Second Platoon, Headquarters Company, and even an attached machine gun squad from First Platoon. At Wonsan, they would load the trucks with ammunition and food to resupply 3/1 at Majon-ni. On the fateful morning of October 3, the convoy set out.

Approximately fifty Marines from Second Platoon spread out in ten trucks. The machine gun squad from First Platoon augmenting the convoy was led by Sergeant Bob Hurt and included Corporal Bob Harbula.

"I'm really not quite sure why we were chosen. But our part of the perimeter wasn't seeing any action, so we were asked to join Second Platoon that day," recalled Harbula.

The trip down the dusty mountain road to Wonsan began without event. Harbula kept eyeing the prisoners in the back of his truck. *Please try something, go ahead, so I can shoot ya*, he thought.

"We hated the North Koreans; they left a bad taste in our mouth after seeing GIs with their hands tied behind their backs, civilian women, children, even babies massacred in the hills around Seoul," he recalled.

A pathetic mass of prisoners, the "scared" North Koreans didn't make any aggressive motions. After several hours in transit, the convoy pulled into the gates at Wonsan. Second Platoon escorted the prisoners to the division POW cage, and in a workman-like fashion, the Marines loaded the GMC 6x6 olive-green trucks with crated supplies for Majon-ni.

With November had come freezing weather and icy winds. The cold cut through the men's M-43 field jackets like a knife; the jackets simply weren't enough to keep the men warm. For the most part, George Company used the "layer principle," piling one layer or field jacket on top of another. The Marines usually wore long johns, cotton T-shirts, olive drab service trousers, and a flannel shirt that was topped off by their M-43s. Harbula and the other men loaded the trucks with wooden crates of cold weather gear, including the much-desired Navy parka. The parka resembled a long, hooded trench coat. Though heavy and clumsy, the parkas kept the men warm. Inside the wooden crates, they also found mittens and gloves that had leather and fabric outer shells and interiors of knitted wool.

As one of the harshest winters on record was setting in, covering the extremities, where body heat escapes the fastest, became most important. The men received Shoe Pacs, which had a rubber sole with laced leather. For the most part, the gear was vintage WWII stock. Unfortunately, the equipment had not incorporated the lessons learned at the Battle of the Bulge. The men would come to despise the Shoe Pacs because after extensive marching, their feet would sweat. Once they stopped, the sweat would freeze, creating potential trench foot or frostbite. The theoretical workaround was that the Marines would each carry two pairs of socks so they would always have a dry pair. In combat situations, it hardly worked. Thousands of casualties would be caused by the faulty government-issued gear. Veteran members of George Company can still feel the tingles of decades-old frostbite whenever they are exposed to winter weather.

After the men loaded the last of the wooden crates and supplies, the trucks rumbled out the gates back toward Majon-ni. Second Platoon hunkered down on the truck beds as Harbula and two ammo bearers sat on the tailgate of the fourth truck as it struggled with gears, squealing up the serpentine mountain roads to Majon-ni. The road seemed to be cut right out of the mountain. A deep gorge that fell several hundred feet into the valley below ominously awaited any truck that made the slightest mistake. The drivers of the trucks now had to navigate the steep mountain incline as they slammed the trucks into second gear.

Harbula was lighting a cigarette when he looked over to his right and saw two large boulders. Suddenly, out of the corner of his eye, two shadowy figures jumped from behind the rocks. The monotony of the journey was broken by the whine and crackle of gunfire. The two enemy fighters emptied the drum magazines of their PPSh-41 submachine guns into the trucks. At nine hundred rounds per minute, the slugs ate into the soft-skinned vehicles, hitting flesh and bone. The guns were of the type that had first seen action in WWII. The Red Army dubbed them "widow makers." The Marines called them "burp guns," because of their deadly rate of fire.

As the North Koreans lit up the trucks, a massive explosion rocked the convoy. Harbula, Roy Shirey, and another Marine fell off of the tailgate in unison. Harbula rolled toward the gorge and was stopped by a small berm that prevented him from falling off into the deep valley below. In addition to breaking his deadly fall, it provided him some cover from the incoming rounds of the North Koreans. Hundreds of rifles and submachine guns then opened up on the convoy from all directions around the gorge. Moments later, Harbula saw the other two Marines lying motionless "with their eyes open, in the middle of the road." Tragically, the rusty-haired Shirey, who had butchered the pig at Wonsan, was cut down by the PPSh-41 and killed, along with the other Marine.

The first three trucks in the front of the convoy continued forward. As they went around the sharp bend in the mountain, disappearing from view, scores of rifles and machine guns opened fire from concealed positions above the road. Putting their training to use, the Marines immediately piled out of the trucks and formed a skirmish line, firing back at the enemy cleverly hidden in the crags. Time was moving in slow motion when Harbula turned to his right and noticed several North Koreans milling around in the valley below the road. Oddly, they seem detached from the other North Koreans ambushing the convoy.

Harbula took aim, lining up a North Korean in his carbine's iron sites and squeezing off several rounds. Unfortunately, the low-velocity .30 caliber bullets didn't have the power to penetrate the North Koreans' heavily padded uniforms. This was to be a recurring problem for the Marines. The solution was to aim for a head shot.

"I hit several of them, I know it, but the bullets didn't seem to have any effect," said Harbula. I thought, *What's my next move: join the skirmish line or find out what is going on with Sergeant Hurt and the machine gun?* Harbula made a split-second decision and darted toward the three trucks, which had split off from the convoy disappearing in the bend of the road to the left.★ In the search for cover, Harbula worked his way around the bend and saw several large boulders the North Koreans had moved into the road as a crude roadblock. Three trucks were stopped in front of the boulders.

Beeler screamed, "Let's get out of here!"

Seconds later, Beeler was cut down by a hail of small arms fire.

In the convoy's tail, Dick Hock didn't fare much better: "I was in the back of the truck when two guys wearing black pajamas jumped up with burp guns."

★ Since joining George Company in California, Harbula had built a friendship with Hurt, and they had spent liberty together in Japan.

Hock "cut loose" a few rounds from his M1, putting a bullet in one man's heart and knocking the other down.

"Brooks, the man next to me, was hit," remembered Hock. He and the other Marines attempted to turn the truck around.

Harbula also knew the only way out was to turn the convoy back to Wonsan. Shortly after Beeler was killed, Harbula spied four enemy soldiers standing in front of the first truck in the convoy. An eerie quiet permeated the air as the firing stopped. Moments later, Harbula made his way toward the bend using the berm along the side of the gorge as cover to conceal his movements. As he made his way to Hurt's truck, he noticed four or five dead Marines in the road. In one truck, a driver slumped over the steering wheel "shaking like a leaf." He found Hurt with a shattered shoulder, bleeding profusely from gunshot wounds. Harbula looked at the driver, whose eyes were as big as saucers: "We gotta get the hell out of here. Can you turn this truck around if I cover you with the machine gun on the back?"

The driver nodded, "I can sure try."

Harbula told the driver, "Don't move until I tap on the cab of the truck" [indicating he was ready with the machine gun].

It was a difficult maneuver, trying to turn a two-and-a-half ton truck around on a one-lane mountain road. Nearly impossible under normal circumstances, too much pressure on the accelerator or a wrong turn of the wheel would send the truck careening down the side of the mountain. Turning the vehicle around while under fire from the North Koreans was incomprehensible.

Next, Harbula made his way to the back of the 6x6 and spotted the squad's .30 caliber machine gun. He saw PFC Jack Dunne taking cover behind a wooden supply box in the truck bed.

Harbula lifted the machine gun but realized he couldn't use the weapon's built-in tripod while he was standing in the truck bed. He quickly grabbed some web gear and wrapped it around his left hand to protect himself from the heat of the gun's barrel. He made eye contact with the driver, and with a tap on the cab, he signaled him to start the tricky maneuver. He stood up, in the middle of the truck, firing the .30 caliber from the hip, spraying the North Koreans with over 275 rounds per minute like he was watering the lawn. Harbula took out the first three Korean soldiers, while the fourth dived behind a boulder.

"We kept up a steady stream of fire as the second and third trucks headed in the right direction. By this time, a lot more North Koreans showed up to join the battle, and we were drawing a lot of fire," remembered Harbula. The situation was beginning to look hopeless.

Harbula then climbed onto the truck and began firing from the tailgate. Several times, he was knocked around or fell down as the truck jolted down the road.

Finally the trucks were turned around and headed down a road that led to the bottom of the mountain gorge. The other trucks in the convoy followed suit. Suddenly, Harbula felt the truck lift up from underneath him, from some unknown force. Miraculously, he bounced from the tailgate, and in a stroke of good luck, he was able to land on solid ground as the truck plunged over the side of the gorge, rolled down a gully, and landed nose down in a stream. He later learned an enemy satchel charge had struck the truck.

The driver in front of Harbula's vehicle saw the explosion in his rearview mirror and stopped. Harbula descended into the gully where the twisted, broken remains of the 6x6 had landed. All of the men were "unconscious," including Hurt, Dunne, and the driver. Because both doors on the cab were jammed shut from the impact, he was unable to extract his fellow Marines. But determining they "weren't in danger," he quickly scrambled back up the side of the gully, and to the truck that had stopped. Harbula climbed into the truck and they raced back to Regimental HQ without further incident. At Wonsan, they requested the assistance of a rescue force. Colonel Puller himself was briefed on the ambush and took the lead, snapping, "We're going to get our boys out of there."

Hock also talked to the bulldog-faced Marine colonel. He inquired about Brooks. "Don't worry about your buddy; he'll be okay," said Puller. Puller quickly ordered stretcher bearers, corpsmen, and riflemen to assemble, and the rescue force made its way to the ambush site.

Hurt, Dunne, and the other members of the convoy were treated for their injuries and then evacuated from Wonsan to Japan, before being sent to the United States. Forty years would pass before the wounded were reunited with their George Company brothers. Beeler, however, would never reunite with his fellow Marines in this life. Not content merely to take his life, the North Koreans mutilated his body and, as a final sign of disrespect, jammed his Purple Heart into his mouth. Nine other Marines were killed in action, and fifteen were wounded.

For several weeks following the ambush, George Company manned a portion of the perimeter around Majon-ni by night and aggressively patrolled the area around the small town by day. A semblance of normalcy crept into George Company as the men began to receive mail from home. Harbula and other members of George received Dear John letters. Harbula's sweetheart hammered the point home, not once, but three times. Ammo bearer Mert GoodEagle also received an interesting piece of mail, a notice from his draft office saying that he must report immediately for the draft—in Oklahoma City. Excited, the Pawnee Indian rushed to First Sergeant Zullo's make-shift office and showed him the letter, tongue-in-cheek. Zullo looked at him with a smile and said, "You ain't getting out of here that easy."

Interrupting the normalcy, elements of the North Korean Fifteenth Division would launch probing attacks that kept the battalion on edge. One attack occurred on the morning of November 7. Booby traps and flares illuminated the night as the North Koreans attempted to breach the perimeter in front of George Company. A mysterious, heavy fog settled into the area one night "reducing visibility to almost zero" and an "intense firefight" erupted in the mist. The forward observer team was positioned along the perimeter.

"We could hear them, but we couldn't see them. They detonated several mines," said one Marine in the team.

The men then brought 81 mm mortar and artillery fire to bear on the North Korean probe. By dawn, as the fog was lifting, the enemy began withdrawing. The Marines peppered them with small arms fire while they retreated. For the next several weeks, patrolling and defending against sporadic attacks occupied much of George Company's time.

During the next several days, North Koreans surrendered in droves. On the surface, the war appeared to be winding down, as more and more prisoners began surrendering to 3/1 in Majon-ni. Later, battalion reports stated: "The prisoners caused no trouble and generally gave the impression that they were better fed and more satisfied and content as prisoners." Although cooperative, the prisoners were searched and interrogated for valuable intelligence. In all, the battalion, including George Company, took a total of 1,395 prisoners.

George Company's time at Majon-ni was short lived. On November 14, 1950, the men once again moved north.

Incredible combat footage of First Sergeant Rocco Zullo firing a 3.5-in bazooka into a Chinese bunker on the Chosin Reservoir's Telegraph Hill on November 29, 1950. Zullo's exploits on the hill and in Task Force Drysdale merit the Medal of Honor. The men of George Company have submitted affidavits to the proper authorities; however, the issue has never been resolved. *Photo courtesy of Harrell Roberts.*

First Sergeant Rocco Zullo. To a man, the men of George Company consider him to be the greatest Marine they have ever known. For over thirty-five years, most of George Company thought Zullo died of his wounds on November 29, 1950. *Photo courtesy of Rocco Zullo.*

An iconic photo of a Marine scaling the seawall at Inchon September 15, 1950. George Company was in the first wave of the assault on Blue Beach. The company later fought through the heart of Seoul. *Photo courtesy of the Marine Corps Historical Center.*

A burning T-34/85 tank, arguably one of the greatest tanks ever made. These highly regarded tanks spearheaded North Korea's invasion of South Korea in the summer of 1950. The tank's armor, reliability, and firepower made it a formidable opponent on the battlefield. *Photo courtesy of the Marine Corps Historical Center.*

Left: Combat footage of George Company attacking Telegraph Hill, November 29, 1950.
Right: "Corpsman Up!" George Company suffered numerous casualties on Telegraph Hill, including the venerable "Confederate warrior," Sergeant Gerald Tillman, pictured here suffering a mortal wound. One of the most courageous Marines in George Company, Tillman earlier won the Silver Star. *Photos courtesy of Harrell Roberts.*

Chinese commander Peng Dehuai (left) talks with North Korean leader Kim Il Sung. *Photo courtesy of The Marine Corps Historical Center.*

Private Tom Powers, machine gunner, third section. Like most of George Company, Powers fought through a year of hell. One of the more colorful characters in the company, the Irishman's grandmother often told him, "You have the devil within ya, boy." *Photo courtesy of Tom Powers.*

Private First Class Richard Hock, rifleman, First Platoon, in his dress blues in Rome, Italy, 1950. *Photo courtesy of Richard Hock.*

First Platoon machine gunner Bruce Farr holding the Browning Automatic Rifle (BAR). *Photo courtesy of Bruce Farr.*

Private First Class Robert Harbula and Royal Marine Sergeant John W. Whiting. George Company and 41 Royal Marine Commando share a special brotherhood ever since both units fought valiantly in the Chosin Reservoir. The fellowship continues, and men from both units attend each other's reunions. *Photo courtesy of Robert Harbula.*

Clark Henry (center) of George Company's forward observer team brandishing a recently "liberated" sword. *Photo courtesy of Clark Henry.*

Hellfire Valley. Destroyed trucks litter the road. The dead are covered with tarps. *Photo courtesy of Robert Boulden through Richard Hock.*

Destroyed Marine armor in Hellfire Valley. Facing nearly a division of Chinese troops, Task Force Drysdale, which included George Company, fought their way through to the town of Hagaru-ri, where against all odds they would hold the strategically important East Hill. *Photo courtesy of Robert Boulden through Richard Hock.*

The "Little Round Top of the Korean War," East Hill, which George Company
held against 10 to 1 odds or more, holding off thousands of Chinese soldiers.
Photo courtesy of Harrell Roberts.

Dramatic photo of Chinese soldiers attacking a hill in North Korea.
Photo courtesy of the Marine Corps Historical Center.

Machine gunners of the third section behind their Browning .30 caliber light machine guns. Jack Daniels is kneeling behind the gunner on the right. George Company's guns had a devastating effect on the Chinese assault. As one Marine aptly put it, "If the machine guns were firing, we knew we could hold." *Photo courtesy of Tom Powers.*

Corporal Harrell Roberts, a rifleman with George Company, received the Purple Heart for wounds sustained on East Hill. *Photo courtesy of Harrell Roberts.*

A poignant photo of Private First Class Jim Byrne taken during the spring of 1951. Byrne had just picked up an extra ammo belt, thinking it might come in handy when a photographer from the *San Francisco Chronicle* snapped the image for his hometown paper. *Photo courtesy of Jim Byrne.*

Marines begin breakout from the Chosin Reservoir, December 1950. They are surrounded and trapped by tens of thousands of Chinese troops. *Photo courtesy of the Marine Corps Historical Center.*

PFC Steve Olmsted, Korea, 1950. Known for his keen mind and charismatic leadership style, Olmsted rose to the rank of lieutenant general. *Photo courtesy of Steve Olmsted.*

Breakout from the Chosin Reservoir, December 1950. *Photo courtesy of Robert Boulden through Richard Hock.*

Penstocks, pipes that carried water to a hydroelectric power plant. The photo shows the hairpin turns and mile-high chasms the First Marine Division had to navigate to exit the Chosin Reservoir. *Photo courtesy of the Marine Corps Historical Center.*

The Chinese blew the strategically important bridge located near the penstocks, creating a yawning gap over a mile deep. In an amazing engineering feat, the Marines air-dropped spans of a bridge to traverse the gap. *Photo courtesy of the Marine Corps Historical Center.*

The frozen bodies of the fallen. The Marines fought their way out of the Chosin Reservoir with all their equipment. They did not leave their fallen comrades behind. *Photo courtesy of the Marine Corps Historical Center.*

The indomitable First Sergeant Rocco Zullo at a reunion in 1991. At 92 years young, Zullo remains the heart and soul of George Company. *Photo courtesy of Harrell Roberts.*

George Company's first reunion, West Point, NY, 1986. Reunited after not seeing each other for over 35 years, the men of George Company now get together every year to renew their bonds of fellowship and brotherhood. In November 2010 in Quantico, Virginia, they are dedicating a monument to more than 140 of their fallen comrades. *Photo courtesy of Harrell Roberts.*

Goldbricking It

YOUNG, **INEXPERIENCED**, and untested, the Second Replacement Draft ambled up the hill toward the ruins of the red brick church. The solitary Catholic church seemed forlorn and out of place in communist North Korea.

As the men made their way through the courtyard, they passed the rusted hulk of a 1938 Nash automobile. Through the arch of the church's main entrance, they could see sunlight shining through the holes in the destroyed roof. Overturned pews and other rubble littered the surroundings of the formerly proud house of worship.

In one corner of the building, the combat veterans stood in line waiting to wash their hands in an M1 steel pot. For generations, the M1 helmet has served multiple uses, including head protection, scooping, pooping, cooking, and even heating water, if clean enough. One of the men noticed that flames had left a layer of charcoal gray soot on the crown of the steel pot. Each Marine washed weeks of war from his hands, and the water became cooler and gradually turned a deep, earthy dark-brown color.

While the hand washing continued, Sergeant Tillman turned to address the greenhorns: "Put all of your gear in front of you."

Most of the replacements had trained together, friends* who formed part of a weapons company at Pendleton. They dutifully followed the order, opening their rucksacks and placing rations, knives, canteens, mess kits, and other gear in front of them. Tillman then removed any duplicate items that the replacements possessed and gave them to the needy, battle-worn veterans of the First Platoon.

"Listen up, people, open up your mess kits and give me your knife and fork. Put your spoon in your trousers. Put the bottom part of your mess kit in your parka and give me the top half. I won't have anybody making any extra noise," barked the veteran Marine NCO. He knew what it took to survive combat.

After Tillman picked the newbies clean of any unnecessary gear, First Sergeant Zullo entered the church. His commanding presence and piercing voice quickly caught the attention of the rookies. Zullo was a mountain of a man, "whose voice you could hear over a mile away," recalled Harrell Roberts, a member of the Second Replacement Draft.

Born and raised in Bainbridge, Georgia, Roberts later moved to Savannah when his father was transferred with the WPA. The tall southerner joined a USMC reserve unit in 1949 after a year of college and reported to Camp Pendleton in August. Like many of George Company's members, he had never gone to boot camp.

After their brief encounter with Zullo, the new recruits were given assignments within the platoon. Several joined the machine gun section, whose ranks had been sorely depleted. Machine gunner Corporal Harbula looked over the replacements and reflected on the chilling fact that he was the only member of his machine gun squad still left from Inchon. The majority had been killed in action or wounded.

"I was still in a state of shock from what happened at Majon-ni. Most replacements did not have all that much training, and one of

---

* Including Jim Byrne, Paul Price, Clayton Sepulveda, and Steve Olmsted, among others.

the biggest problems was that the men with the least amount of training would always bunch up. Many of these guys never saw a machine gun," commented Harbula. Although the men had learned in boot camp not to bunch up, they forgot their disciplined training and became complacent in their inexperience.

At this point, 70 percent of George Company consisted of men from the replacement drafts, replacing officers and NCOs alike. Some of the men, Marine reservists, had received the threadbare thirty days of training required. These Marines were as green as it got. *These men don't know shit from Shinola*, thought Harbula.

In order to augment the machine gun squad with veterans, Joe Rice, a quiet man who was Harbula's best friend, was transferred into the unit. Rice, approaching his mid-twenties, was considered an old man in the unit. Always dependable and someone Harbula could count on, the two best friends did their best to train the new Marines.

Besides being a bivouac area, when a rabbi showed up, the Catholic church also served as a house of worship. Sergeant Clark Henry of the forward observer team remembers Smokey Somers coming up to him.

"Sarge, this guy came all the way from division to give us a service," said Somers. "What do you want to do? I think I am the only Jewish guy in George Company." "Go to the services. We will all go to the service," responded Henry.

The all-Christian scout sniper section filtered in for service, removing their hats as they had been taught to do when entering a church. The combat rabbi turned to Smokey with a whimsical look: "Are you sure these guys are all Jewish?" "Yes, they are, Rabbi," Smokey shot back. With a smile, he responded, "Well, tell them to put their hats on."

Shortly after the service, Henry received another surprise when Private Jesus "Bob" Camarillo walked into camp. The two men had met in California before the war.★

★ They have since remained the very best of friends for nearly sixty years.

"What the hell are you doing here?" Henry asked. "I got in a fight with a staff sergeant," responded the muscular Mexican-American.

Henry just shook his head and smiled, and said, "Don't let it happen again." Camarillo officially became part of the scout sniper team.

For the next several days, George Company enjoyed light duty. The men continued to guard X Corps headquarters, located near the church ruins. As the Fifth and Seventh Marines pushed north, the First Marines remained behind in the Hungnam-Chigyong area. The First Marines faced the serious challenge of a lack of transportation. There simply were not enough trucks to move the men of George Company north. This recurring complication would lead to some ironic consequences that would have a profound impact on the war.

After several days of guard duty, the men's ticket north arrived in the form of a narrow-gauge train. In a scene ripped from the pages of a Western novel, the entire company rode atop the flat cars and gondola, along with fifty-five-gallon drums filled with aviation fuel. They stood ready to deal swiftly with any would-be fuel bandits. The riflemen and machine gun teams were distributed down both sides of the train in case any guerillas attacked, knowing that small arms fire or a direct mortar hit would ignite the train into a barreling flame. "We were very nervous sitting on gasoline barrels all day," recalled PFC Bruce Farr.

Smoke and soot spewed from the locomotive engine as the rolling gas bomb headed down the narrow-gauge rails. Men looked around, alert for threats, as they nervously chatted with one another on the ride. After an hour of uneventful travel through the drab North Korean countryside, the train pulled into a marshaling yard. First Platoon and the gunners noticed a group of combat engineers repairing the track. Standing upright against a box car were two dozen brand-new M1 Garands glistening in the rays of the early afternoon sun. Tillman saw an opportunity and asked his men, "Do you want to survey your weapons?" which means "swap out" in Marine lingo.

Several men nodded and looked at their Marine-issued M1s, their stocks pitted and worn from months of combat. Accustomed to receiving low-grade and cheap equipment, the Marines jumped at an opportunity to upgrade at the expense of their Army brethren. "Everything that came from the Army was much better, if you could snatch it or commandeer it!" recalled Roberts.

Tillman responded in a matter-of-fact tone, "If you do, take off your leather sling, and go over there and remove their canvas slings and replace your weapons with theirs."

Without hesitation, the men leaped off the train and descended on the new Garands "like starving locusts" and quickly made the exchange without the Army men even noticing.

The enlisted men in First Platoon and in the machine gun section were not the only ones "liberating" items from other units. Richard J. Jewel of the scout section clambered onto the train car carrying gear for most of his comrades. His outstretched arms were loaded down with cold-weather gear and parkas. "Jewel was an expert scrounger, and a real piece of work," recalled Henry. "Apparently, Jewel being the piece he was, found the gear in a parked boxcar in the rail yard."

Lieutenant Hilscher shot Jewel an icy stare: "Take it back!"

With his tail between his legs, Jewel returned the gear to the boxcar where he had found it. However, two recipients of Jewel's handiwork managed to hold on to their new duds: First Sergeant Zullo and Captain Sitter emerged from the boxcar next to the train sporting brand-new trench coats.

"The two looked like movie stars," recalled Roberts.

The train rumbled north, leaving the Army minus a few Garands and trench coats. Farr and his best friend Bobby Hallawell of the machine gun section soon heard the all-too-familiar clicking discharge of machine gun fire.

"When we heard the firing, we left the train like a flock of birds, and scooted, and rolled," remembered Farr.

Fred Hems and his assistant gunner also leaped from the train, setting up the machine gun on the right side of the tracks and firing several rounds. Farr, GoodEagle, Harbula, and Hallawell quickly joined them and took up defensive positions. Captain Sitter, who literally tumbled out of the train, tore a ligament in his knee but stoically refused evacuation. "All the old souls from Inchon and Seoul bailed off the train in a heartbeat," recalled Roberts.

Many of the green replacements were stunned as the train stopped in the midst of "the attack." Roberts remembers aiming his M1 blindly into the distance. Several men began to fire as if being shot at. About a hundred yards down the road, several civilians were seen diving for cover. "Nobody quite knew what they were firing at. I was not sure if we hit the civilians," remembered Roberts.

After less than a minute of gunfire, someone yelled: "Cease fire!" "Cease fire!"

The firing stopped. They soon located the source of the "attack": someone had decided to test-fire a captured enemy weapon. After everything was sorted out, Zullo ordered the men back on the train. Bitching and moaning, the men boarded as the engine steamed up and resumed its course north.

Bobby Hallawell glanced down at his watch, the only timepiece in the section. It was approximately 3 p.m.

The train pulled into a forgotten North Korean village on the afternoon of November 17, and the regiment assigned the company several unmemorable days of guard duty.

During downtime, George Company assembled into formation. Several men in the unit received medals for their heroic actions at Inchon and Seoul. Colonel Chesty Puller himself decorated the men. When he came up to Lieutenant Carey, he smiled, and as he pinned the award on his chest, he said, "Lieutenant, what are you doing here?" Puller was known for always favoring the enlisted men over officers.

Puller then turned and pinned a Silver Star on Sergeant Tillman. "I would have followed that man anywhere," recalled Jim Byrne, a reservist from San Rafael, California, who had arrived with the second reserve draft. After the ceremony, Tillman beamed with pride and later told the men, "Next, the Congresh." The men who knew him certainly thought it was possible for Tillman to earn the Congressional Medal of Honor.

Shortly after the ceremony, Lieutenant Carey was moved up to battalion headquarters and assumed command of the S-2 (Intelligence Section) shop, a role normally reserved for a major. Major Edwin Simmons said, "Dick, you've seen enough." Carey protested the promotion, but followed orders and became 3/1's S-2. The sole surviving platoon commander from Inchon, Carey was the only person alive who had witnessed Lieutenant Beeler's prediction.

Thanksgiving brought the first snowflakes. The men received turkey for the holiday, but within minutes, the bitter cold froze the trimmings to the metal trays. As the company filed toward the service area, Zullo detoured across a rice paddy dike. The fresh snow "made everything slimy." The whole company watched as Zullo's right leg slid knee-deep in the mud and excrement of the rice paddy. Harbula recalls a couple of men beginning to snicker. Ominously, the first sergeant looked over and shot the entire company an icy stare.

"He turned and looked at us, and you could have heard a pin drop. It was an ominous look," recalled Roberts. "That ominous look was all that anyone needed. We were more afraid of Zullo than the enemy!" recalled Powers. "That man ruled the roost, even our officers were afraid of him."

No one else snickered, and everyone acted like nothing had happened. Farr and the other members of George Company wolfed down their quickly freezing Thanksgiving dinner, as the snow flurries melted on their faces.

As a twenty-two-year-old, he was older than many of the eighteen- and nineteen-year-old men in the machine gun section. "I knew it was possible that we might make it to Japan by Christmas, but I knew we would not be home. I just did not believe the rumors that we'd be home by Christmas," said Farr.

As is so often the case in American military history, the rumors that the "boys will be home for Christmas" once again proved false. Chinese troops launched a massive series of attacks.

On November 28, General Douglas MacArthur issued an alarming communiqué to President Harry Truman: "We face an entirely new war."

Despite the Chinese attacks, executing according to MacArthur's original plan, X Corps continued to push further north toward the Yalu River. Once again, lack of transport would keep George Company in the rear as most of 3/1 moved north. Over the next several days, the Marines marched from one village to another. Remarkably, and reminiscent of WWII scenes, North Korean civilians raised flags and greeted George Company as they marched through the villages.

"Quite often they waved flags, or handkerchiefs. There weren't that many afraid of us. It has to be a traumatic thing to see a foreign force marching through their homeland. But they were happy to see us," recalled Farr.

George Company marched across the barren North Korean countryside, which was peppered with small huts and an occasional brick building. When First Platoon came across an abandoned schoolhouse, they set up camp. During one night in the building, four members of First Platoon played a game of Hearts. At the center of the room, several men sat around a wooden desk, with a C-Ration can filled with sand and gasoline to illuminate the room. The night wore on. The blue haze of cigarette smoke filled the tiny room. Roberts decided to call it an evening, and his place was taken by PFC Clayton Sepulveda. Meanwhile, the glow of the C-Ration can grew fainter and fainter. Eventually, the light died out. "I will get us some more gas," volunteered one of the men at the table.

The man returned with a jerry can filled with gasoline. "Don't bring that in here," barked Roberts. The man then returned with a small can of gas and began pouring the flammable liquid into the glowing red sand of the C-Ration can. Flames shot from the can and turned Sepulveda into a flaming torch, screaming in agony.* The men

---

* Since November 1950, Harrell Roberts has not played another game of Hearts.

rushed to his aid and put out the fire. Unfortunately, portions of his face were burned. Evacuated to the rear, he returned to active duty several months later.*

On the morning of November 28, 1950, the men of George Company slowly emerged from the sleeping bags. As usual, the temperature had plummeted during the night, and the bitter cold assaulted them as they emerged from the warmth of their bags. The men lined up in formation by platoon and were ordered to begin boarding trucks. With no idea where they were headed, some men passed on the lingering rumor that they were going home.

---

* Sepulveda, after recovering from his burns and returning to active duty, was shot in the chest and killed in action by a sniper in 1951.

◄ 14 ►

The Road North

S**ADDLE UP!**"

The men formed into platoons. George Company loaded itself, veterans and replacements, into the olive drab 6x6 trucks of Baker Company Second Motor Battalion.

Baker Company transported two hundred-plus men of George Company in its trucks. Some had canvas covers; others were open to the elements. It was the afternoon of November 28, and the temperature plummeted to −10 degrees and continued to drop. Puffy white cumulus clouds masked the sun, and hard snowflakes occasionally pelted the men along the winding roads north. The three dozen or so trucks in the convoy made their way along the treacherous and steep mountain roads of the Taebaeks. Bob Harbula and his buddy Joe Rice sat together, huddled in the cold with the other machine gunners for the long ride north.

"Most of my time from Majon-ni to this point was a blur. I was just numb, but I remember looking at Joe and then someone snorted out 'maybe we'll see a saber tooth tiger or dinosaurs.' The place was so desolate and barren; it had a prehistoric feel that was surreal," remembered Harbula.

As the trucks wound down the roads, riflemen Harrell Roberts remembered nervously peering over the side of his truck, seeing a sheer chasm dropping steeply several hundred feet to the valley floor below. He recalled, "I remember seeing the remains of a damaged helicopter. One of ours that didn't make it."

The convoy kept pushing north, and the persistent rumors of going home were deflating, like the air coming out of an old balloon. By now, most of the men realized they weren't going home for Christmas. They were heading north, deeper into the war zone.

The next major landmark the convoy encountered was Funchilin Pass where the convoy traversed a narrow bridge spanning a deep gorge with a 2,000-foot drop on one side. The engines whined and the gears ground as they crept along the shelflike road cut along the eight-mile pass. The road was cut into the side of a cliff and was nearly impassable. The trucks traveled mere feet from the drop-off. Since early November, the First Marine Division had sporadically engaged elements of the Chinese near Funchilin Pass. Bob Camarillo, Clark Henry's best friend, couldn't help but notice the hundreds of spent artillery and tank shells littering the road along the pass. The bridge had not been blown up by the enemy, leading Major General Smith to wonder suspiciously, "Was this the dog that had not yet barked?" Did the Chinese want to lure them past the bridge, then trap them on the other side? Smith suspected this, and the worst; however; Generals Almond and MacArthur ignored the signs.

Since Inchon and the liberation of Seoul, MacArthur had been racing toward the Yalu River, victory seemingly in his grasp. At their historic meeting, October 15, 1950, on Wake Island, MacArthur had assured Truman, "Victory was won in Korea."

However, the Chinese had clearly signaled their intention to intervene in support of North Korea. On October 3, 1950, China woke India's ambassador in the dead of night and told him, "We will intervene," if MacArthur's forces pass the 38th Parallel. The warning was a charade. Mao hoped his "warning would be ignored: thus he could go into North Korea claiming he was acting out of self-defense." If the Chinese had wanted to make their intentions known, they would have issued an official public statement through normal channels so that the press could cover it. Obsessed with victory that seemed nearly at hand, MacArthur's staff and the general himself failed to connect the dots, believing only the most optimistic intelligence assessments that reported the Chinese were not in Korea in great strength.

A small CIA station located in Japan, run by former OSS Officer William Duggan, reported that many former Nationalist Chinese troops, now members of the People's Liberation Army (PLA), still possessed their radios and were transmitting valuable intelligence on their whereabouts to Nationalist forces in Taiwan. Duggan's operatives in Taiwan relayed this information to Duggan, who clearly understood that all the messages shared a common theme: troops were heading to Manchuria and North Korea. Chillingly, at the end of October, radio contact went silent as the Chinese marshaled their troops and began crossing the border. Although the valuable intelligence came in many forms and from different sources, MacArthur's intelligence officers dismissed the information and did not relay it up the chain of command.

Victory seemed to blind MacArthur. Perhaps in a state of denial, he ignored all the signs of a Chinese invasion that had already begun. He informed President Truman that only 125,000 Chinese troops were situated along the border of North Korea and, at best, only 50,000 to 60,000 troops could have passed the Yalu River. Confidently, MacArthur stated, "They have no Air Force. Now that we have bases for our Air Force in Korea, if the Chinese tried to get down to Pyongyang, it would be the greatest slaughter in history."

In reality, between 300,000 and 400,000 Chinese soldiers had infiltrated through the mountains, traveling by night and hiding by day to avoid detection by air reconnaissance teams. Over 200,000 Chinese troops stood ready to face down the Eighth Army. Another 125,000 or more cleverly positioned themselves around the First Marine Division and X Corps. The Communists constructed a massive trap to "consume" UN troops. The bulk of the troops consisted of Americans and South Koreans, but Turkey, the U.K., Canada, Australia, France, Greece, the Netherlands, the Philippines, Belgium, New Zealand, South Africa, and Luxembourg had sent forces as well. The trap was about to be sprung.

The first signs of the massive juggernaut appeared in late October when the Chinese mauled the U.S. Eighth Cavalry Regiment and the Sixth ROK Division in a surprise attack. To avoid tipping their hand, the Chinese surreptitiously disappeared and melded back into the mountainous rock formations, masking their true numbers as they patiently waited to entrap the Eighth Army. Along the Marine front, Chinese prisoners captured in different locations were also evidence of the country's intervention. By mid-November, the Marines had engaged with the PLA in several clashes. However, the intentions and true numbers of the Chinese Red Army were still unknown. The Chinese remained essentially invisible.*

At Chinese headquarters, General Peng furrowed his brow as he leaned over the main relief model of the Chosin Reservoir (the Chinese called it the Changjin Reservoir). Born a peasant in Hunan Province, Peng Dehuai had dabbled in Communism for years. He aligned himself with Mao Zedong and emerged as a commander during the Long March. During the Chinese Civil War, Peng was twice wounded in hand-to-hand combat. Now an experienced and gifted general, Peng served as the political commander and czar of Chinese forces in Korea.

---

* In the words of historian S.L.A. Marshall, they were "a phantom which cast no shadow."

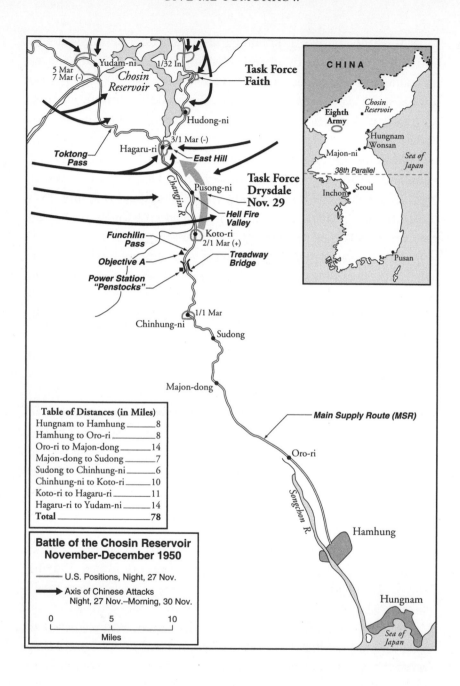

**Battle of the Chosin Reservoir
November–December 1950**

U.S. Positions, Night, 27 Nov.

Axis of Chinese Attacks
Night, 27 Nov.–Morning, 30 Nov.

Table of Distances (in Miles)	
Hungnam to Hamhung	8
Hamhung to Oro-ri	8
Oro-ri to Majon-dong	14
Majon-dong to Sudong	7
Sudong to Chinhung-ni	6
Chinhung-ni to Koto-ri	10
Koto-ri to Hagaru-ri	11
Hagaru-ri to Yudam-ni	14
Total	**78**

Units under his command were regularly destroyed and remanned with fresh bodies.

Peng's concentration was interrupted by Major General Liu Fei (pronounced loofy), who served under the command of Ninth Army Group Commander Song Shilun. "It is snowing thicker than cow shit on the reservoir," announced Liu.

Peng chuckled at the remark and shot back, "The enemy has learned nothing over the last few weeks. They continue to advance recklessly. To that extent, our first-phase offensive has been a failure."

Beads of sweat formed on his forehead. Peng leaned further over the model as the other members of his staff craned their necks in anticipation of his next words. "The Ninth Army group will encircle and exterminate the U.S. Marines around the Changjin Reservoir. Other enemy forces in that area will be mopped up along the coast. This should be possible, bearing in mind the enemy's scattered disposition across difficult country."

Also present at the meeting was the Commander of the Ninth Army Group General Song Shilun. Only forty years old, Song had worn a uniform since the age of seventeen. The graduate of Whampoa Military Academy became a master of guerrilla warfare under the tutelage of Mao's right-hand man Chou En-lai. Courageous and able, he had commanded the regiment in its famous Long March. With over 120,000 men, General Song's soldiers outnumbered the First Marine Division eight to one. Two of his field armies, the Twentieth and Twenty-Sixth were initially earmarked for the invasion of Taiwan. His forces also included the Twenty-Seventh Field Army, and each army group was beefed up with an additional division. Beginning in mid-October, Song's army marched a torturous 150 miles on foot across the Yalu through the rugged mountains to the Chosin Reservoir in just twelve days.

With China's inexhaustible supply of men, Mao planned to "grind down" the Americans. He later told Stalin that after losing 100,000 Chinese soldiers, he was "ready to persist in a long war, to spend several years consuming several hundred thousand American lives so they will back down."

Mao planned for the long war. "Don't try to win a quick victory," he added. "The enemy will not leave Korea without being eliminated in great masses."

The Chairman reminded Stalin he could seriously weaken America—for a price. Mao wanted Russia's industrial expertise, and he built a first-class army and the industrial base to support it. World domination was more than a pipe dream: with the atomic bomb capabilities he also craved, he could achieve it.

But Stalin wasn't going to give Mao what he wanted. He had no intention of building a Chinese arms industry that could eventually compete with Russia, yet he wanted Mao to do his fighting. So he gave them just enough to stay in the fight. Initially promising Mao air cover, Russia reneged and told Mao the planes would not be ready.

At the time, America did not know of the rifts between the two leaders, instead believing Communism was monolithic. In part, America was right, because "Uncle Joe" Stalin called the shots.

Spurred by Stalin, who advised, "The Chinese soldiers may be considered as volunteers and of course will be commanded by the Chinese," Mao officially authorized a name change for the PLA units entering North Korea to "Chinese People's Volunteers." Volunteers in name only, units were formed from the Northeast China Border Defense Force. On October 8, 1950, he wired Prime Minister Kim Il Sung of North Korea, "We have decided to dispatch the volunteers to help you." In keeping with the artifice, many Western commentators referred to these units as Chinese Communist Forces or CCF.

Despite the contrived veil of "volunteer" status, the PLA of 1950 remained a potent force, with nearly inexhaustible reserves. Its core had been battle-hardened from the infamous 6,000 mile Long March, which winnowed its numbers from 90,000 to 20,000, as well as years of Civil War fighting, in which they defeated superior numbers of Nationalist forces. The PLA would emerge as one of America's greatest adversaries. By 1950, the PLA consisted of survivors, men of iron, who shed creature comforts and made do with very little. Perhaps most strikingly, the PLA made no provision for the honorable discharge of its soldiers from military service. Soldiers for life, the Chinese men remained in uniform until dead, wounded, or captured.★ In many cases, soldiers were denied an honorable discharge for more nefarious reasons; Mao had a lot of people he wanted to "get rid of." In the final year of the Chinese Civil War, millions of Chiang's Nationalist troops surrendered. The war provided "the perfect chance to consign former Nationalist troops to their deaths." In the event the war did not kill the former Nationalists, "there were special execution squads in the rear to take care of anyone hanging back."

Chinese forces largely dropped rank at the platoon level and encouraged their men to criticize their comrades and even spy on each other. The men also received intense political indoctrination.

Chinese officers were professional and skilled in European battle tactics that had been modified to include Mao's strategy, as well as Sun Tzu's *The Art of War*. When the Chinese had at least a three-to-one advantage, their tactics usually included overwhelming positions with large numbers of bodies.

At times, weapons were scarce for the Chinese. Attacking in wave after wave, the first two waves of men carried weapons. The third wave, and often the fourth wave, would remain in the rear and bear only light arms in anticipation of picking up weapons from fallen comrades.

Usually, the Chinese leadership informed their men of the basic plan of attack, which rarely changed once decided. This differed significantly from the American style of warfare, where officers and NCOs would issue orders in real time on the battlefield.

Following Chinese tradition, men from the same town formed into companies, and men from the same ethnic group fought in the same unit. Battalion and regiment forces linked to the same ethnic and geographic makeup averaged about 2,200 men on paper. The regiments folded into divisions of between 8,000 and 10,000 men. A Chinese army typically mustered 30,000 troops.

★ Chinese soldiers could be discharged for old age or disease.

The typical Chinese soldier subsisted on a diet that would starve a gerbil: soy beans, rice, and millet. Winter clothing remained scarce, and after crossing the Yalu, troops received a two-piece reversible mustard-yellow-and-white uniform. Heavy cotton caps, often fur-lined, covered their heads. Gloves remained in abysmally short supply, and winter boots were nonexistent until months after China entered the war. Most troops wore canvas tennis shoes with crepe rubber soles. Their hands and feet froze in the harsh winter battles.

While Chinese artillery and tanks remained in short supply, Chinese troops carried a variety of hand-me-down weaponry from a half-dozen nations, with one of the largest stocks coming from U.S. surplus. The United States sold hundreds of millions of dollars worth of rifles, machine guns, bazookas, and other munitions to the Chinese leader at fire-sale prices. American guns now in Chinese hands were being turned against their maker.

On November 25, the Chinese struck a massive blow, using precise intelligence on the American armies. They hit the Eighth Army hard on the west coast and two days later X Corps on the east coast. Faced with obliteration, the forces retreated south in what was called "the Big Bug-out."

Remarkably, two full days *after* the Chinese offensive started, Generals Almond and MacArthur ordered an immediate offensive by the Marines to drive west and penetrate forty miles into the enemy-occupied territory. Their mission was to link up with the Eighth Army. The roads were likely impassable and the weather cruel, often dropping to −20 degrees. MacArthur still did not realize that they were severely outnumbered and that the enemy had nearly surrounded them. They were almost cut off and completely isolated. Additionally, the Eighth Army was in full retreat and at high risk of being defeated by the Chinese on the west coast. The plans bore no resemblance to the situation on the ground.

"In those days, it was like complete insanity in the Command," remarked Colonel Bill McCaffrey, a member of General Almond's X Corps headquarters.

Almond pressed the Marine and Army units under his X Corps command to relentlessly advance, suspending the reality of facing certain death. Lieutenant Colonel Don Carlos Faith, a battalion commander in the Thirty-Second Regiment, told Almond correctly, "he was facing two entire Chinese Divisions."

Almond flatly stated, "That's impossible; there are not two Divisions of Chinese in all of North Korea!"

Three and a half days after the Chinese attack, Almond still refused to acknowledge the full catastrophe falling on the American troops in North Korea: "We are still attacking and going all the way to the Yalu. Don't let a bunch of Goddamn Chinese Laundrymen stop you."

Conversely, General Song issued these orders to his troops: "Soon we will meet the American Marines in battle. We will destroy them. When they are defeated, the enemy army will collapse, and our country will be free from the threat of aggression. Kill these Marines as you would kill snakes in your homes."

Snow pelted the convoy as George Company drove north. The Marines had no inkling of the higher-level strategies and the catastrophes befalling their division. Before sunset, the trucks rolled into the North Korean hamlet of Koto-ri. Clark Henry of the forward observer section noted: "It looked like a giant circus, just a bunch of tents strewn around, trucks, and other equipment. That was Koto-ri."

Captain Sitter and the command of George Company presented themselves to the headquarters of the First Marine Regiment, led by Colonel Puller. The men were ordered to take up positions on the perimeter of the town, which meant finding a place to sleep. The lucky ones bedded down in the recesses of trucks, while other men found shelter from the elements anywhere they could.

The Road to Hell

As THE FIRST fingers of dawn snaked their way across the frozen land-scape surrounding the tiny hamlet of Koto-ri, Bruce Farr and Bobby Hallawell emerged from their makeshift foxhole. Slowly, Farr peeled back the stiff snow and frost that coated the sleeping bag like a spider web. The Marines had slept back to back, "so each of us had one eye out watching for the enemy on either side."

That night, the temperature had plummeted to −20 degrees; just waking up had its own special meaning. The fighting overnight across the neck of the Korean peninsula claimed the lives of scores of Chinese and U.S. servicemen alike. Overnight, the war had profoundly changed. Instead of being on the offensive, both X Corps and the Eighth Army found themselves in the battle of their lives, their very survival at stake.

Moments after they awoke, George's machine gunners heard familiar voices bark the orders: "Get your asses up!"

Zullo directed his noncommissioned officers to round up the men and square them into platoons. After the men were briefed on the planned assault to capture several hills outside Koto-ri, they guzzled down cups of scalding hot coffee. Even the piping hot Joe wasn't immune from the effects of the elements. It would freeze in a matter of seconds. "At 20 below zero . . . vapor was coming out of your mouth. Ice froze to our beards and moustaches. Couldn't touch any metal, [your] fingers would freeze upon touching it," recalled machine gunner Harbula.

By the morning of November 29, the Chosin Reservoir had become an insidious trap. Throughout the area, a massive Chinese army of twelve infantry divisions comprising over 120,000 men caught X Corps and the First Marine Division off guard and seemed poised to cut them off and destroy them. The Marines faced terrible odds, outnumbered roughly eight to one. Meanwhile, on the western side of Korea, the Eighth Army faced over 200,000 Chinese. In what became known as the "Big Bug-out," the Eighth had entered full retreat in the face of near-certain defeat.

Initially, the Marines had been preparing their own offensive into the western portion of North Korea. They intended to link up with the Eighth Army and move forward toward the Yalu River. The First Marine Division was spread out over several strong points that stretched from Koto-ri through Hagaru-ri (which contained the First Marine Division's headquarters) all the way to Yudam-ni in the far north.

In the north, X Corps got pounded by the Chinese. The Chinese surrounded the Fifth and Seventh Marines, and a similar fate befell Army units. Days into the Chinese offensive, Fifth Marine's Lieutenant Colonel Raymond Murray would reflect: "Once I learned we were being hit from virtually all sides in considerable strength, and knowing we were out there all by ourselves, I figured we were finished. Frankly, I thought Yudam-ni, North Korea, was where I was going to die."

Murray issued a simple order to his men: "All hands. Make sure every shot counts."

The Marines made preparations for the worst. Ignoring General Almond's orders for a headlong advance, and anticipating a possible

Chinese counterattack, General Smith attempted to position his forces somewhat proportionally in the three strongpoints to avoid being overrun in any one area. A single road, or MSR, seventy-two miles long, linked these positions. Significant portions of the Chinese Army amassed along the entire length of the Marines' salient, which jutted into the spine of North Korea. Hagaru-ri formed the keystone of the Marines' entire defense, because it contained not only headquarters, but also priceless supply dumps and even an airfield under construction that ultimately could be used to evacuate wounded Marines and bring in reinforcements and supplies. If it fell, most of X Corps would be enveloped and destroyed by the Chinese.

According to the official Marine Corps history:

> Hagaru-ri with its supply dumps, hospital facilities, and partially (constructed) C-47 airstrip, was the one base offering the First Marine Division a reasonable hope of uniting its separated elements. Hagaru-ri had to be held at all costs. Yet only a reinforced infantry battalion, less one rifle company, and a third of its (weapons) company and two batteries of artillery were available for the main burden of the defense.

Hagaru-ri had to be reinforced immediately or else it would be overrun. The outcome of the war hung in the balance.*

With barely enough men to hold their position at Koto-ri, Colonel Puller put together a scratch task force to break through to Hagaru-ri. The transportation problems continued, making it doubtful

---

* On the night of November 28, the Chinese attacked Hagaru-ri in full force. Army engineers, cooks, bakers, anyone that could be assembled, quickly rushed into the perimeter to hold the line. The greatest threat came from a massive Chinese attack on a large hill mass, known as East Hill, on the northeast portion of Hagaru-ri. Whoever held East Hill held the high ground over the Marine Corps headquarters. East Hill also overlooked and touched upon the MSR, which entered Hagaru-ri from the south. As a result, East Hill took on enormous importance. Like Little Round Top in the Civil War's Battle of Gettysburg, it would profoundly affect the entire campaign and war. On this night of November 28, the hand-to-hand fighting turned brutally savage. The Chinese nearly overran Hagaru-ri that night. Marine Corps headquarters desperately needed reinforcements.

that reinforcements could reach Hagaru-ri in time. The day before company-sized elements attempted to break through from Koto-ri to Hagaru-ri but were forced back by the Chinese. The transportation problems that had plagued George Company for the last month ironically left them in a position as one of First Marine Division's last reserves. Now, they became crucial to the defense of Hagaru-ri, but they needed to get there first.

Additional leadership for the task arrived in the form of a seasoned British Commando officer, who smartly addressed elements of George Company command: "I'm Lieutenant Colonel Drysdale, and I'm here to take you to Hagaru-ri."

A Marine who was near the George Company command post at the time recalled Drysdale introducing himself: "They [the British] were spit-and-polish and professional, clean shaven. We were dirty and combat worn."

Lieutenant Colonel Douglas B. Drysdale commanded 41 Independent Royal Marine Commando Group,★ 235 Marine commandos, many with WWII combat experience. He would head up "Task Force Drysdale," a nine hundred-man plus task force, which included 41 Independent Royal Marine Commando, George Company, elements of a tank company, B Company, Thirty-First Infantry, and cats and dogs from various headquarters' units. This was only the second time U.S. and British Marines would campaign together, the first being the Boxer Rebellion. Once assembled and on the road, the column of men, tanks, and trucks stretched for over a mile.

Elements of an entire division of Chinese troops held bunkered positions on the high ground all along the single-lane road that wound between the mountains from Koto-ri to Hagaru-ri. The ice-covered dirt road, which might better be described as an elevated dike, paralleled a narrow-gauge railroad that snaked through the mountains and valleys. It is estimated the task force was outnumbered at least ten to one. Despite the odds, the Brits were confident.

★ To this day, George Company and the British Marines maintain a strong affinity; each often invites the other company to its reunions.

On the ground, the first hurdle the men faced on the eleven-mile route was a pair of hills outside of Koto-ri. Both hills were ingloriously named for their elevation, 1236 and 1182, respectively.

To soften up the Chinese defenses, three Marine Corps Corsairs dropped pods of napalm "danger close," since the Chinese hugged the hills directly in the path of the task force.

"The napalm was awesome. Fireballs destroyed everything. As the planes returned, the heat followed us, and it touched our faces. The explosions were only about 300 yards away," Harrell Roberts recalled. The planes also pounded the hills with rockets and machine gun fire, further softening up the Chinese position, or so many members of the task force thought.

With snow flurries gently lashing their faces, Drysdale's commandos formed skirmish lines for the attack. The commandos surged forward. Harbula recalls Drysdale pointing and saying in his British accent, "Let's give it a bloody go!"

"A sea of green berets bobbed up and down, as the Royal Marines assaulted the hill," recalled Henry.

As the highly trained commandos hit the hill, one British officer stood ramrod straight near Henry, drawing fire and the consternation of the salty sergeant and his fellow Marines.

Boldly, the Brit looked at Henry. "Be calm, my boy."

"Shit was flying all around both of us," recalled Henry.

The commando officer then turned, looking for one of his men and politely shouted in a proper British accent, "Leslie, Leslie, where are you? Leslie, go out and strike out that gun."

"Leslie looked about fifteen years old," to Henry, but the commandos took out the gun, and George Company surged forward.

George Company passed through the line of commandos and charged up Hill 1182, later dubbed "Telegraph Hill" for a telegraph pole that capped its crown. The Marines trudged up the icy, snow-covered hill. Harbula recalled seeing the First Machine Gun Section firing tracer bullets and missing their mark: "We were on the ridgeline going up. There was a bunker halfway up the hill. The bullets were cracking and whizzing around us from all the machine gun fire."

As the men slithered up the crest of the hill, Sergeant Tillman yelled, "Get your asses up!"

Suddenly, "the snow erupted" in front of the Marines as Chinese machine guns peppered First Platoon. A mortar screamed down, and shrapnel from the projectile shattered the hand guard on Roberts's M1.

Several George Company men dropped under the withering fire. Courageously, while several of his men sought cover, Sergeant Tillman stood up and attempted to get a better fix on the enemy machine guns.

"Tillman's down!" Someone yelled.

"I saw his steel helmet tumbling down the hill, and a bullet hole pierced the middle of his forehead. He was still moaning," recalled Roberts.

Bruce Farr was staring directly at Tillman when he was shot: "I was looking straight at his face. There was a hole at least as big as a quarter in his forehead."

The Marines dragged his body back down the hill toward a stretcher team making its way up the hill; "the heels from his double-buckle combat boots made two tracks in the snow."

Halfway up the hill, a chaplain "with a cloth around his neck and the tools for the Last Rites" appeared on the scene. The men were feverishly trying to get Tillman back on a stretcher, slipping and sliding in the snow, to the aid station.

"What's this man's name?" asked the chaplain.

"His name's Jimmy Bones, and he don't need ya," snapped Pendas.

"I'm going to give him his Last Rites," said the Chaplain.

"No you're not," Pendas shot back.

"I tried to keep him away as we sent the litter to the aid station," recalls Pendas.

Sensing the momentum was shifting to the Chinese, Zullo took charge of the situation and barked at a youthful bazooka man, "Fuckin' gimme that!"

He grabbed the bazooka from the eighteen-year-old Marine. Another Marine loaded a rocket, and Zullo carefully aimed the 3.5-inch rocket launcher.

Whoosh! Whoosh!

The rocket screamed forward, slamming into the front of the enemy strongpoint and turning it instantly into splinters and dust. The Marines cheered and yelled. "He hit it!" "He hit it!"

Smoke poured from the wreckage. Next, Zullo calmly ordered the bazooka reloaded. He fired again, destroying another enemy position. Several Chinese soldiers fled the second bunker, providing easy targets for the sharpshooting Marines. After Zullo destroyed the two strongpoints, the Chinese retreated to the reverse slope of the hill.

The official Marine Corps history succinctly records the action: "It was nip and tuck until First Sergeant Rocco A. Zullo fired his 3.5-inch rocket launcher at a range of 200 yards. Several rounds brought the Chinese out of their holes, and the Marines took possession of the hill."

PFC Mert GoodEagle scurried down the hill, looking over his shoulder to see dozens of Chinese soldiers emerge from the reverse slope. At first, the Marines thought that they had run the Chinese off the hill when Zullo had destroyed the two bunkers. In reality, the gnomelike Chinese clad in mustard-colored uniforms emerged from the back side of the hill, hammering the Marines as they pulled back on their way to the convoy below.

"Saddle up!" Zullo bellowed.

Frantically, the Marines barreled into the backs of trucks as the convoy rolled down the MSR toward their next objective, another hill.

George Company attacked and again met a storm of mortar and machine gun fire. Stymied by the fierce resistance, Drysdale ordered George Company to break off the attack on the hill and reform near the trucks. With the Chinese in control of the high ground, every hill became a battle, costing the task force precious time and many casualties. Could the convoy make it to Hagaru-ri before it was overrun? George Company and Task Force Drysdale did not have enough men to take every Chinese strongpoint on the MSR. Time was running out. Every minute counted.

◄ 16 ►

Roadblocks

AFTER THE MEN clambered into the trucks, the convoy inched its way down the icy dike at a clip of five to ten miles per hour. Next, Task Force Drysdale faced roadblocks made of anything the Chinese could get their hands on: logs, destroyed vehicles, rocks, and rubble. At every roadblock, the entire column jammed to a halt. With the task force not moving, the trucks became sitting ducks on the elevated dike. The combination of withering fire from the high ground and the makeshift roadblocks slowed the convoy's advance to a creeping snarl.

Mortars also rained down on the column, causing numerous casualties. One mortar scored a direct hit on a Marine commando truck. "The mortar went through the canvas cover and detonated in the truck bed, killing or wounding everyone in the truck," recalled PFC Steve Olmstead, a member of the second replacement draft Olmstead was a natural leader with a keen mind who rose to the rank of lieutenant general.

Preregistered on the road, the Chinese mortar positions stood ready to fire as soon as the trucks came into view—an ideal kill zone. Another mortar dropped down on a group of army troops that were "grouped together like a football huddle. The mortar came in right in the midst of these guys, and they peeled apart like bananas," recalled Harrell Roberts.

At least two George Company men were injured by the blast—PFC Jim Byrne and PFC Paul Price. A large piece of shrapnel lodged in Byrne's back. Heroically, an Army soldier from Baker Company/31, Corporal John Agostini, drove up in a Jeep and through-out the course of the afternoon, made countless treks up and down the road, retrieving the wounded and transporting them back to Koto-ri. Normally equipped to handle four men, the military ambulance was packed to the gills with nearly eight individuals, including a driver and an observer who rode shotgun on the fender of the vehicle.

"We're going back toward Hungnam," the doctor informed Byrne and the other men. "Aren't those hills full of Chinese?" asked Byrne nervously. "Ah, don't worry about it. The last ambulance got through." "That didn't give me much reassurance," remembered Byrne.

As the ambulance made its way over the Funchilin Pass, Byrne heard the staccato sound of machine gun bullets. A twelve-round burst went right across the bow of the ambulance, nearly hitting the front hood. The driver and the man riding shotgun stopped the vehicle suddenly. Everyone in the back looked at one another. Byrne thought to himself, *This is the end of the road.*

Every man in the back was unarmed because they were non-combatants. *Any second they are going to open the doors, spray the inside with machine-gun bullets, and hurl grenades,* thought Byrne. He prayed over and over. Five seconds. Ten seconds. Time seemed to stand still. But the Chinese machine gun didn't open up again.

The ambulance made its way down toward Hungnam without further incident. The olive-drab ambulance had two bright red crosses painted on its side. "I often think about it, and to this day, I believe that I'm alive because some Chinese had second thoughts about firing on an ambulance," recalled Byrne.*

The convoy of 141 trucks slowly became fragmented. Burned-out GMC trucks began to pile up on the road. George Company took many casualties. They were fired on from both sides of the road. "It was like the old Wild West as the Indians fired on the wagon train," remembered Olmstead.

The men began a deadly routine that would be repeated throughout the journey: encounter Chinese roadblocks, disembark under withering fire, clear the roadblocks, and mount up again.

"We would have to get behind the tires of the truck for cover, and we would have to throw grenades. I remember getting on and off the trucks at least nine times. For thirty or forty minutes, we would have to bail out and wait and hide behind the tires, as more and more men went down," Mert GoodEagle emotionally remembered.

The men had a hard time moving in the arctic weather, but Clark Henry kept the forward observer section together, "almost like a mother hen." He kept his men focused barking, "Shoot your fucking rifles!"

The Chinese bullets hit the slats on the trucks as they "exploded, sending splinters of wood everywhere." The beds of the trucks, with thin canvas tops, provided no cover for the men. Bruce Farr recollected:

> Bullets [were] coming through the canvas covers. While in the truck, the guy on my right had his knee shot. One red-headed Marine we named "Red Ryder" had his rims shot off his glasses from the right side. The bullet whizzed around the inside of his steel pot and cut a streak of hair from his head. Remarkably, it produced one single drop of blood. We were like sitting ducks, and [we just] hoped and prayed.

---

* Later, George Company made Agostini an honorary Marine. When he attended George Company reunions, he would get up and say, "I'm John Agostini." The entire room would give him a standing ovation.

Harbula lost all his earthly belongings in one moment: "When we got on and off the trucks, that's when most of the casualties happened. When my truck started moving, I lost all my gear in my rucksack, including a Japanese sword I found in Seoul and my precious sleeping bag. Without [a sleeping bag], I would freeze to death outside. So I just jumped on the next available truck." Besides losing his belongings, Harbula thought he might lose his life. Turning to his best friend, Joe Rice, he said, "I don't think we are going to make it. This looks like a suicide mission, Joe."

The Chinese goal: split the convoy into smaller parts, then divide and conquer. The Chinese made every attempt to strike an enemy on the move. "A cornered rat will fight fiercely if it is provided a limited avenue of escape. If it is kept on the move, it can gradually be worn down with slight damage to the attacker." Surprisingly, everything worked according to plan. The Chinese plan.

Communication is one of the most important elements of command on any battlefield. With the exception of the radios inside tanks, the sub-zero weather froze radios throughout the convoy. Through one of the working radios, Drysdale received word that fresh armor from Dog Company First Tank Battalion would be coming in around 1300. Drysdale was in a quandary: push ahead and somehow make up the time that was lost taking the two hills, subjecting his column to constant Chinese fire; or wait for armored reinforcements that could punch through the Chinese defenses. The extra tanks could possibly help them break through and also defend Hagaru-ri. Drysdale decided to wait for the reinforcements.

The tanks arrived nearly on schedule shortly after 1300, and the convoy reformed about fifty minutes later. Next, Drysdale requested that the tank commander, Captain Bruce Clark, stagger his two platoons of Pershings and one platoon of Sherman tanks throughout the column. "The opinionated young man," as Drysdale called him, refused the order, stating that the tanks needed to be put up front to break through. Since Puller had not placed Clark under Drysdale's command, the tanker broke rank and would not succumb to Drysdale's direction. That refusal would have an enormous impact on the overall mission.

Because the tanks were clustered at the front of the convoy, Drysdale couldn't communicate with the rest of column. In later years, soldiers and historians would debate whether this decision ultimately saved lives or sent young men to early graves. If the tanks had been staggered, they might have had better communications and better protection throughout the convoy. On the other hand, without the tanks at the front, they might not have had enough firepower to punch through the Chinese roadblocks.

In any case, Drysdale immediately put the newly arrived armor to good use. They quickly blew away several houses under Chinese control and freed George Company and the convoy to move forward. While the tanks took out a Chinese target, it also halted the convoy and made it vulnerable to enemy fire. "Every time the tanks shot, the world fell in around us because it caused the entire column to come to a screeching halt and we became easy targets. There was so much confusion getting back on the trucks," recalled Bob Camarillo. "It was a nine-hour fire fight."

The convoy resumed its fateful journey.

On the afternoon of November 29, Zullo rode with Captain Sitter and was constantly dismounting and firing on the Chinese as the convoy halted each time. As the column rolled forward, he looked back at the convoy and saw that it snaked behind him for over a mile. Shrapnel hit his shoulder blade as he looked back. It felt like a massive bee sting as it burrowed into his torso.

Burning trucks and explosions lit up the skyline as the battered convoy moved forward. Clark's seventeen tanks at the vanguard led the way. What was left of George Company's twenty-two trucks limped behind the tanks as the Royal Marine Commandos followed. Trailing the Brits were the remaining vehicles of Baker Company/31. Trucks from miscellaneous units, including the division's headquarters troops, followed the convoy. Several tanks later attempted to join them, but turned back.

As the newly reinforced convoy resumed the crawl toward Hagaru-ri, progress was painfully slow. Chinese roadblocks continued to impede progress up the MSR and forced the convoy to repeatedly stop and engage. As they had throughout the journey, Chinese mortar rounds continued raining down on the trucks. After one strike, machine gunner Tom Powers recalled seeing a fellow Marine's eyeball grotesquely hanging from the socket by a thread, like a shiny golf ball.

The Marine screamed, "Am I okay?"

Powers pulled gauze from his first-aid kit and gently placed the eye back in his socket. In his Brooklyn accent, he responded, "Ah, it's just a scratch."★

Wham!

Another mortar round screamed down on George Company.

As the men in Task Force Drysdale limped along, several trucks slid off the icy MSR, only to be towed or pushed back onto the winding road. Zullo and Sitter rallied their men. Zullo's "pleasant" voice boomed in the distance:

"Let's get ahead!"

"Move along!"

"Move it."

"Move along!"

"We had to break through to Hagaru-ri at all costs. We had to get through. I knew we were crucial to the defense of Hagaru-ri," Zullo reflected nearly sixty years later. "If we didn't get up there, we would have lost the whole damn army—maybe the whole damn war."

As the convoy moved farther up the road, the Chinese attacks intensified. "Fifteen or twenty yards and they were right up on us. It was a lot like the island fighting in the Pacific," remembered Zullo.

George Company casualties steadily continued to mount.

About four miles outside Koto-ri, at 4:30 p.m., Task Force Drysdale reached a turning point. An immense wall of mortar and

---

★ Fifty years later, that same Marine would recognize Powers at a reunion. "I'd have recognized that booming Brooklyn accent from anywhere; you're the one that told me it was just a scratch." Powers later replied, "What did you want me to say?" The only saving grace about the weather was that the −30 degree temperatures caused blood to freeze and wounds to close up faster. That fact actually saved the lives of several George Company veterans.

small arms fire stopped the column in its tracks. Captain Clark informed Sitter and Drysdale that he doubted anything other than the tanks could break through to Hagaru-ri. The craters in the road, the roadblocks, and above all, Chinese resistance were proving overwhelming. They had to make a decision.

"At All Costs"

CRANING THEIR NECKS to the whirl and crack of the tank's radio, Lieutenant Colonel Drysdale and Captain Sitter heard General Smith's determined voice: "Press on at all costs."

Facing potential defeat and a wall of Chinese resistance, Drysdale had radioed Smith minutes earlier and asked if the convoy should continue north or retreat to Koto-ri. When Smith received Drysdale's message and request for a quick decision, he was visiting casualties at "E Med," one of the two Navy tent hospitals established within the perimeter of Hagaru-ri. Smith quickly weighed the costs. He knew that without reinforcements, Hagaru-ri would fall. Holding this town was key to the entire campaign and reuniting the division.

In the din of battle, amid the crackle of Chinese machine gun fire and the whiz of stray bullets, Sitter soberly nodded to Drysdale. Drysdale responded to Smith in his proper British accent, "Very well, then. We'll give them a show."

Task Force Drysdale resumed the perilous trek north. As they reached the halfway point between Koto-ri and Hagaru-ri, the tanks began running low on fuel. The column halted in a valley that was about a mile long and covered with snow, with sparsely wooded hills rising sharply to the right of the road. Here, a dry stream bed ran parallel to the Changjin River, which was a couple of hundred yards away. A thin crust of snow covered the hills that reminded the men of those around Camp Pendleton. The task force pulled alongside the stream bed and began to refuel. The men dismounted, provided security for the tanks, and returned fire against the Chinese.

After topping off the tanks, Drysdale again ordered the column forward. Less than a half-hour later, the convoy experienced what would prove to be one of the most critical events of the mission. As had happened countless times before, a mortar round turned one of the trucks into a flaming pile of burning rubber, flesh, and metal. This time, however, the results of the blast were far-reaching. Drysdale and Sitter didn't know it at the time, but the column had been split into two parts.

Using the flaming truck as a roadblock, the Chinese poured small arms and mortar fire onto the convoy. Since the tanks weren't staggered and only the front portion of the column had radio contact, Drysdale did not realize that the middle and rear portions of the convoy were not moving forward. They were cut off and surrounded by the Chinese. Unit integrity became nonexistent as "infantry elements mixed with headquarters troops."

Despite the chaos, the tanks, followed by George Company and three-quarters of the commandos, pushed forward. Sixty-one commandos, most of Company B, Thirty-First Infantry, and nearly all the division headquarters and service troops were left behind fighting for their survival. The Chinese cut the middle and rear elements into one large and three smaller groups that they could deal with piecemeal. In remembrance of the ensuing carnage, the entire area was later dubbed "Hell Fire Valley" by Drysdale himself.

While the Chinese mauled the middle and rear elements of the convoy, Sitter, Drysdale, and the tanks pushed forward with the armored

First Dog Company tanks in the vanguard. George Company followed with the commandos. Without communications, they were unaware of the tragedy befalling the rest of the column. However, as dusk fell, George Company faced its own personal hell. The Chinese attacked, blowing whistles and bugles. Flares lit up the early evening sky.

"I was so mad. I was so goddamn mad. I could not stand seeing my Marines being shot. As the First Sergeant, I was supposed to be the first soldier. I needed to do something about it!" Zullo later reflected.

He soon got his chance. After a machine gunner on a .50 caliber machine gun went down, Zullo took over. He pulled back the belt and cleared the jam. Then Zullo barked to Frank Bove, "Get your guinea ass up here, and go find me some ammo!" *Christ, Chinese are all around*, he thought as his eyes scanned the ten or fifteen yards to his left and right.

After receiving several boxes of ammo, the burly Italian pulled back the bolt on the machine gun and threaded the copper and steel belt into the chamber. He adjusted the head space on the weapon and began cutting Chinese down like a scythe.

"It seemed like we hit the entire Chinese army. There was a lot of them," recalled Bob Camarillo. "Zullo was throwing a lot of lead into the masses." The rounds sprayed from the gun at a cyclic rate of over five hundred rounds per minute. The projectiles tore some men in half; body parts flew into the air. For nearly an hour, Zullo administered a steady drumbeat of death as the convoy drove through the Chinese assault.

"Bullets were flying everywhere," remembered Zullo.

Bove heroically continued running up and down the convoy yelling, "Gimme ammo for the .50!"

He was still searching for ammo to feed Zullo's hungry .50 when he went down. "He was a brave man, all over the place looking for ammo," reflected Zullo.

The machine gunners tried to keep their units together. Ammo carriers frantically stayed close to the gunners, feeding them ammo as they maintained a steady hail of bullets. The gunners fired at muzzle flashes, and the men directed the tracers (the fifth round in every ammunition belt), which made a brilliant scene. Tragically, in all the melee and excitement, a Marine fell to his death under the treads of a Dog Company tank.

Suddenly, PFC William Baugh screamed, "Grenade!"

The grenade landed in the back of a truck as the men were dismounting. A bazooka man who was attached to George Company, Baugh faced a split-second decision: either hurl the grenade back out of the truck or dive on it to protect the men in the cab with his own body. Baugh heroically dove on the grenade and cradled it with his hands and chest, absorbing the entire blast. Moments later, the mortally wounded twenty-year-old private from Kentucky died in his comrade's arms. He was posthumously awarded the Medal of Honor for his courage and self-sacrifice.*

Shortly after Baugh sacrificed himself on the grenade, the Chinese shot Captain Sitter's Jeep out from under him and turned it into Swiss cheese. "I really miss that Jeep. It had my green overcoat and a brand new box of cigars. I lost them both. I think I miss the cigars more than the coat," quipped Sitter.

He continued, "As the trucks were going by, my first sergeant, Rocco Zullo, slowed down, and I jumped on the driver's running board. Then we'd go up and get stopped by fire. Up and stop; up and stop." The same monotonous maneuver of stop, dismount, fire, conquer, mount up, and push forward continued.

During one of the many stops, Tom Powers recalled bailing out of the truck and rolling into a ravine next to the road. He remembered looking to his right and telling the men to "mount up." In the corner of his eye, he saw a shadowy figure, not in an American uniform. Comrades up the road yelled, "It's a Chinaman! It's a Chinaman." A hail of bullets cut down the lone Chinese straggler.

"The Chinese were all around us. It was a complete mess as we switched trucks several times," remembered Dick Hock.

---

* In 1984, a Navy cargo ship was named in his honor, the *William B. Baugh*.

As the convoy passed a railroad embankment, "all hell broke loose." Dale McKenna recalled the torrent of fire:

> There was a wall of machine gun fire on either side of us. It was an ambush! It was so heavy, rounds were flying everywhere. The only protection we had was to lie completely prone on the bed of the truck. I was lying down; I could not see where we were going, I could only see where we'd been.

Unflappable, Captain Sitter directed his men during the ambush.★ "Get off the trucks!"

"Everyone face out!" Sitter yelled.

Deploying what seemed like an invisible shield, as bullets passed within a hair of his body, Sitter made his way up to the front of the convoy and found Drysdale. Drysdale, his arm bloodied crimson, looked over to Sitter and said, "I'm hit. You now have command."

Sitter responded, "All right. I'm going to get the tanks and we're going to start moving."

Sitter then ordered everybody back on the trucks. "Dead and wounded too. We weren't going to leave anybody behind," recalled the pear-shaped leader.

Powers remembered a machine gun that was firing directly onto the convoy: "A truck loaded with men got hit with something. It burst into flames. I could see guys standing in the fire. It was horrifying as the truck slid off the road into a ravine."

Orace Edwards bailed out of the tailgate of the burning truck as it slid over the side of the mountain. In almost suspended animation, the fiery, two-and-a-half-ton truck and Edwards tumbled down the cliff together. "I was afraid the truck would roll over on me while it tumbled down the mountainside," said Edwards.

The burning hulk careened into an icy stream. Edwards burst through the ice with the truck. "I had on four layers of clothes, plus a

---

★ Later, he remembered one of his countless brushes with death: "I had left the side of the truck only seconds before. If I had stayed I would have been shot."

parka. I guess that helped me survive all the tumbling." Waterlogged and freezing, the rifleman fought his way out of the stream. "The ice froze on my clothes and all over me. I tried to stand up, but my leg wouldn't hold me up," he said.

Edwards crawled out of the stream and looked around for his rifle, finding it with its stock broken off in two pieces. Tracers arced across the skyline, and the firefight continued on the road above. His boots were filled with water and froze along with his clothes. As Edwards attempted to crawl back to the mountain road alone, "It was pitch dark except for the occasional light from tracers." The burning truck provided illumination, as two silhouettes crunched in the snow toward him.

I'm captured, thought Edwards. Chinese were all around. "Then one of them said, 'Bring a stretcher. Here's another one.' Boy, you can't believe how really relieved I was. They gave me a shot of morphine, then strapped me on a stretcher and took me back up the hill feet first. When we got to the road, the stretcher was fastened onto the hood of a truck. I remember looking up, seeing tracers going over me, and saying to myself, *There is no way I'm going to make it out of this*."*

Without Edwards, George Company progressed in the now-familiar stop-and-start fashion, the column had reached a point several hundred yards from Hagaru-ri when two or three vehicles were blown to pieces. The Chinese hurled a satchel charge under a tank, disabling it. The crew abandoned the vehicle. The snow stopped falling, and an odd downpour hit them. In a lame attempt to stop the armor, the Chinese threw bales of burning hay from rocky outcroppings onto the Pershings. Men riding the tanks brushed off the burning straw with a mere kick of a foot.

By now, it was becoming dark, and the convoy could not utilize its headlights. The slightest wrong turn would send a truck careening over the side. Powers sat on the front fender of the truck and guided the driver: "Let's go, let's go!"

---

* Eventually, Edwards was evacuated to Japan.

George Company pushed through the roadblock and formed up at the head of the column with the tanks.

"After the last roadblock, I saw a tent, and lights for the airfield," recalled Zullo, who still manned the ring-mounted .50.

Harbula added, "The lights for the airfield—they were working. It was one of the most beautiful sights I have ever seen in the world."

Several individuals came out of the tents in Marine uniforms and approached the convoy. Zullo asked Sitter, "Captain, what's our next move?"

At that moment, small arms fire erupted from the tents. A bullet tore through his side, leaving a hole the size of a grapefruit. Blood gushed from his guts like a geyser. "You could put your goddamn fist in here," Zullo recalled almost sixty years later. "How could I have been so goddamn stupid?" Shrapnel had perforated his shoulder and lacerated his wrist; this was his third wound of the day.

After cutting down the Marine impersonators, Zullo's men carefully placed him in the back of a truck headed for Hagaru-ri. To protect the first sergeant from additional small arms fire and mortar rounds, three of the men cradled his badly broken body. As they rolled through the gates of Hagaru-ri, they could not feel Zullo's pulse. He was slipping away.

While George Company, most of the commandos, and the tanks broke through to Hagaru-ri, the rest of Task Force Drysdale faced almost certain destruction. Major John McLaughlin commanded the largest group of the cut-off convoy.* Using weapons no larger than 75 mm recoilless rifles, the men fought on bravely in Alamo fashion, with hope that the tanks and reinforcements from Koto-ri would break through.

Slowly, the Chinese overran portions of McLaughlin's group. Rather than going for the kill, the Chinese first busied themselves

---

* McLaughlin was the Assistant G-3 and Corps liaison officer with First Marine Division.

looting the trucks and probing McLaughlin's border with small groups armed with grenades.

To no avail, McLaughlin sent small teams of runners south to link up with the other perimeters. One of the men assigned as a liaison between McLaughlin's group and George Company was PFC Jimmy Harrison, the young marine who loved to play *Dixie*. Henry emotionally recalled Harrison's death on the exact day and time almost sixty years later: "He was no more than eighteen years old. I didn't know the lieutenant assigned him as a liaison. Had I known of his assignment, I would have found a way to stop it. He was shot between the eyes by the Chinese with a .45. He was the first man I lost in Korea."

Courageously, McLaughlin stood and fought, hoping the Marine Air would come on station in the morning to strafe and bomb the Chinese. As the night wore on, the situation along the road became more and more desperate.

McLaughlin's group successfully repelled several large Chinese attacks, each time losing their man on the 75 mm. Army crews returned fire on numerous enemy mortar positions, driving them backward twice, and cutting off several probing attacks. By 0200, the 75 mm was destroyed.

About an hour before dawn, the Chinese sent captured American prisoners into the pocket and demanded that McLaughlin surrender. Accompanied by a stalwart commando, the American officer attempted to buy time. "Initially, I demanded the CCF [Communist Chinese Forces] surrender," McLaughlin haughtily recalled.

The Chinese weren't amused. They gave McLaughlin ten minutes before launching an all-out assault on his fragile perimeter. The major checked his men; many were unarmed or down to their last eight rounds of ammunition. They had no grenades, no projectiles for the 75 mm, and many were wounded.

Buying time for some of his able-bodied men to slip away from the perimeter, McLaughlin continued negotiations. He finally agreed to surrender with the condition that the Chinese allow them to evacuate the wounded. The Chinese accepted his surrender with those terms.*

After McLaughlin's group laid down their arms, the smaller perimeters followed suit or were overwhelmed. Only a few pockets of daring men slipped back to Koto-ri and lived to tell the tale of the doomed convoy.

---

* Operation Big Switch, where of the forty-four Marines listed as MIA, twenty-five either escaped or were liberated in the operation.

Hagaru

THREE SUBDUED MARINES struggled to control their emotions as they carefully lifted Zullo's broken body into the makeshift morgue. Entering the standard Marine Corps pyramidal tent that served as a house for the dead, the men saw the bodies of other deceased Marines lying stiff, stacked on top of each other like cordwood. Without speaking a word, they agreed that Zullo's body would be treated with more care. The three gently placed Zullo's body outside near a corner, away from the others. Dejected, they left the tent and rejoined their brothers, who were still staggering into Hagaru-ri.

As they wandered deeper into the defenses of Hagaru-ri, George Company first passed 3/1 Weapon Company's roadblock. The Marine strongpoint faced south toward Koto-ri. Ironically, the checkpoint was manned by Steve Olmstead's brother-in-law, Charles Fleig. As Olmstead passed through the roadblock, Fleig immediately recognized the familiar face. Dumbfounded, Fleig said to Olmstead, "Jeez, are we glad to see you!"

Olmstead responded, "Why?"

Charlie said, "Well, we're surrounded."

"No shit. Where the hell do you think we've been?"

With no time for a longer reunion, Olmstead and the rest of George Company moved deeper into Hagaru-ri. The town resembled a "Klondike mining camp" reminiscent of the heady days of the Gold Rush. Scattered houses, buildings, and tents speckled the horizon.

That evening, Captain Sitter and Lieutenant Colonel Drysdale reported to Lieutenant Colonel Ridge, 3/1's CO, who now commanded the defenses of the besieged town. Under the faint glow of a Coleman lantern, with blood dripping from his arm, Drysdale smartly saluted Ridge: "41 Commando present for duty."

Ridge placed the commandos and George Company in perimeter reserve, ordering them to take up positions about 250 meters from East Hill in an open field behind a Marine artillery battery. A Chinese attack on East Hill seemed likely, even imminent, as they moved into position.

Boom! Boom! Boom!

The artillery throbbed steadily, as it lobbed shell after shell into the Chinese lines. George Company moved into the assigned field and began to dig in to get what sleep they could with the sounds of war around them. Those who still had them broke out their sleeping bags and shelter halves, and bedded down in the icy tundra. Unfortunately, during the convoy, many of the men had gotten on and off the wrong trucks, sometimes leaving behind their personal belongings, including the all-important sleeping bag. Without the insulation, men were likely to freeze to death in the −30 degree temperatures. One of the unlucky men was machine gunner Bob Harbula:

> I had jumped into another truck and lost my sleeping bag and personal belongings. It was freezing cold; you could not get warm. To this day, the VA assumes that all "Chosin Few" survivors have frostbite. They don't have to jump through a lot of hoops to prove their medical condition.

Fortunately for Harbula, the high number of causalities sustained by the garrison at Hagaru-ri afforded spares, and he was issued a new bag. Even with a bag, sleeping on the ice-hardened tundra was its own ordeal. "Your back hurt so badly on the frozen ground, you thought it was breaking," remembered Bob Camarillo.

As they settled in for the night, the men of George Company noticed the Marine engineers at work on the airstrip. Floodlights illuminated bulldozers and other excavation equipment that had been working around the clock for the last ten days. Completion of the airfield was crucial to the entire campaign because it would allow evacuation of the wounded and incoming flights of new reinforcements and supplies. George Company would help buy priceless time as the engineers completed the airfield.

"Cough, cough!"

A faint sound from the corner of the morgue tent caught the attention of the corpsman.

"Cough."

Hearing it again, the Marine who had entered the tent bearing the body of yet another casualty, turned toward the startling sound. As he made his way toward the corner of the tent, the medic's hairs stood up on the back of his neck. Noticing that some of the corpses had eyes wide open, he wondered if he might not be alone. He continued moving toward the cough until he came upon Rocco Zullo's body.

My God! He's alive! he thought.

Ironically, a cough saved Zullo's life. The Marine, whose identity is unknown, pulled Zullo from the makeshift morgue, and a stretcher team rushed him to the 3/1's surgical tent. Doctors began doing everything they could to stabilize him. Unbeknown to most of George Company, Zullo underwent hours of surgery to stabilize his perforated belly. Few men, if any, realized Zullo was still alive.

Injured in the hand and shoulder and with a gaping wound in the side of his abdomen, Zullo suffered frostbite on his hands and feet from his time spent in the morgue. The Marine hero, in and out of consciousness, recalled only one incident: "Things became very hazy for me at the time . . . until I got to the Army Hospital 118th."

As members of what amounted to the battalion reserve, the weary men of George Company fought all day up a lonely eleven-mile stretch of road. They originally expected to be used as a fire brigade to plug a hole in the line and fend off Chinese assaults. Had the Chinese assaulted East Hill, they could, in all likelihood, have penetrated Hagaru-ri that night, but the Chinese did not attack.

It wasn't an accident. It could have been Dick Carey. Earlier that day, Lieutenant Carey, now part of battalion intelligence, or S-2, had effectively used several South Korean "line crossers," or spies. After infiltrating the Chinese lines, they had returned to Carey with valuable information regarding Chinese force positions and their attack route. With this priceless information in hand, Carey called in air strikes and artillery on Chinese assembly areas, as they were preparing to assault Hagaru-ri. Air and artillery power pulverized Chinese positions, creating massive casualties in some units.

Most importantly, the advance of Task Force Drysdale discouraged the Chinese from attacking Hagaru-ri from East Hill.★ The MSR passed right by East Hill and near the Chinese assembly areas, thereby effectively spoiling their plans for attack on the night of November 29. Despite their expectations for a short sleep, George Company slept through the night, which passed quietly into the annals of time.

★ O. P. Smith put it best: "The casualties of Task Force Drysdale were heavy, but by its partial success the Task Force made a significant contribution to holding of Hagaru, which was vital to the Division. To the slender infantry garrison of Hargaru were added a tank company of about 100 men and some 300 seasoned infantrymen." See notes for further discussion.

East Hill

AT DAWN, the men emerged from their frozen cocoons and ate a quick breakfast of whatever they could scrounge up. Food was scarce, so the men lived on a diet of Tootsie Rolls and canned fruit cocktail, which often froze solid. The candy was all most of the men had and provided quick energy. "They were so hard you had to leave them in your mouth for an hour before they melted. If you bit down on them right away, they would break your teeth," remembered Tom Powers.

Groggy, Captain Sitter called the company together and said, "Now you see that hill over there." In unison, George Company, dirty and exhausted, turned around and stared at the ominously large hill. Roughly five hundred meters high, East Hill, as it was called by the Marines, was Hagaru-ri's greatest vulnerability.

"That's our next job!" Sitter proclaimed. "We're going to go up that hill and secure it."

How are we going to do that with this shot-up company, and how many of us will die trying to take that mountain? wondered Mert GoodEagle.

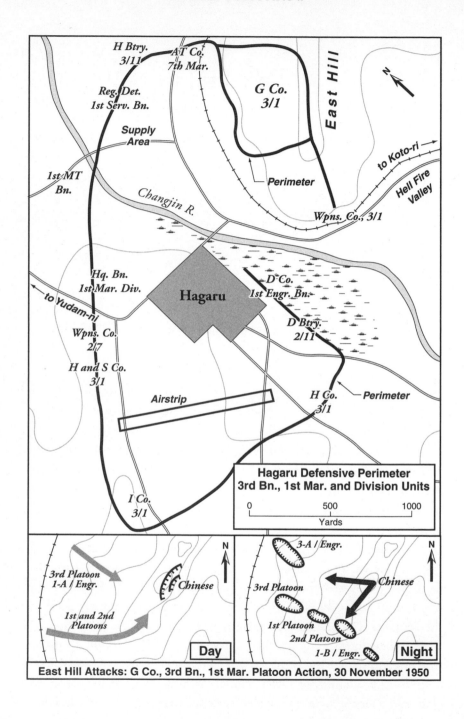

Hagaru Defensive Perimeter
3rd Bn., 1st Mar. and Division Units

East Hill Attacks: G Co., 3rd Bn., 1st Mar. Platoon Action, 30 November 1950

If the Chinese controlled the high ground, they could freely lob artillery shells or mortar rounds into the camp's fragile supply dumps. They could also possibly disrupt the effort to build the airfield. If the Chinese took Hagaru-ri, First Marine Division would never be able to reunite and would almost certainly be destroyed.

The broken and rough terrain around the hill provided Chinese forces excellent concealment and cover from American artillery and air power. Further complicating matters, the hill overshadowed the main supply route, which passed right near it. Vast numbers of American fuel and ammunition dumps lay along that route. The bottom line was that whoever controlled the hill controlled Hagaru-ri.

The plan called for George Company to retake East Hill. If things went south, the Royal Commandos, in reserve, would be placed into the melee. Sitter planned to utilize First and Second Platoons to spearhead the effort. Third Platoon and two platoons of engineers would follow up the planned breakthrough, temporarily remaining in reserve. A smattering of engineers and other service personnel were holding positions near the base of the hill.

One of the service troops barely holding their position on East Hill was Sergeant Joe Leibee, a wireman from the Marine First Signal Battalion. "George Company really saved our asses," recalled Leibee, a WWII veteran who fought on Okinawa and hailed from Huntington, West Virginia. Leibee's role as a rifle platoon sergeant began two nights earlier when they became a fire brigade for How Company near the airfield.

A platoon sergeant demanded that Leibee put together thirty-five men who were cooks, truck drivers, and other wiremen. The small unit fought for several hours, holding off the Chinese at the airfield. "We screamed the rebel yell at the Chinese and fired back at them," recalled Leibee.

After the melee was over, there were bodies "all over the place." Many of them had been killed by How Company's machine gun. As Leibee was leaving the area and his platoon was shifted to another hot spot, one of the bodies, blood-spattered and broken, raised up a rifle and took aim at Leibee. "He was in terrible shape. He had several machine gun bullets that pierced his chest. And there was blood all over his quilted uniform," recalled Leibee. Suddenly, a "kid from How Company" screamed at Leibee, "Shoot that son of a bitch. He killed one of my buddies." Futilely, the Chinaman attempted to pull the trigger on his Mauser. Leibee ripped the rifle right out of his hands. "I think we shot him enough," responded Leibee. After grabbing the rifle, "we looked each other in the eye for a minute or two. I just didn't feel like shooting him." The Chinese soldier slumped over, dead.

The night of November 29, the same evening that George Company was making its way up the MSR with Task Force Drysdale, Leibee's scratch platoon was ordered up East Hill. "We had to lay across the ground. We had no entrenching tools, so there was no way we could dig in," remembered Leibee. Leibee's men were armed with nothing more than carbines. "We didn't have any mortars or machine guns. Finally, they gave me one mortar. They fired two rounds and the third was a dud, which the mortar man threw over the top of the hill by hand. At that point, there was no way we could hold them if they attacked in force," recalled Leibee. At that time, the Chinese near East Hill were heavily engaged fighting the forward elements of Task Force Drysdale.

Off on Leibee's right flank was an engineer unit with a .50 caliber emplacement that was dug into a shell hole. "They had been blown to pieces. One of the men had his bowels sticking out of his dungarees," recalled Leibee. But several of the dead men had their M1 Garands. Leibee ordered his men to remove the weapons from the fallen engineers. That evening, the Chinese shot and sniped at Leibee's position. "I made my peace that night," remembered Leibee. He thought to himself, *There's no way I'm going to get out of this.*

He told his men they would be relieved the next morning, though he had no confirmation of this. "We were sacrificial lambs," recalled Leibee. That morning, George Company did indeed arrive. Somebody from George approached Leibee: "Who's in charge here?" Leibee responded, "I am."

"Then, you're relieved," responded the George Company NCO.

After being harassed all the way down the hill by sniper fire, Leibee's small band made it down to Hagaru-ri. They later plugged other holes in the line and carried ammunition back up to the men of George Company on East Hill.

Leibee was slightly wounded several times, but "I didn't want to turn it in," recalled the sergeant from West Virginia. "If you could walk, you could fight. I'm damn lucky to have survived, but I'd do it all over again."

George Company passed through the remnants of these units and made "a sharp left turn to attack either side of the ridge." Spread out in small groups, George Company was coiled like a spring as it readied to assault the hill. Hot air billowed from their nostrils as they moved across open ground and up East Hill. "My lungs and throat burned from the bone-cold air. It hurt just to breathe. It was so cold, the men moved around like mummies," reflected Powers.

No sooner had the Marines attacked than they were met by a hailstorm of Chinese small arms fire and mortar rounds from the hilltop. Bob Camarillo remembered the maelstrom: "The bullets were like angry hornets hitting the snow. Remarkably, I remember I was not hit; but many of the guys around me were. I marvel making the move under that type of fire and not getting it."

George Company scrambled up the hill, or at least tried to, but hundreds of Chinese and American feet had packed the ground into an icy sheet. The Marines had a hard time staying on their feet. Machine gunner Bob Harbula recalled, "[We] hacked away at the frozen earth with our entrenching tools and bayonets, trying to get the least bit of footing."

GoodEagle remembered many of the men slipping and falling back down the hill: "The hill was a sheet of ice. One step backwards for every one step forward."

Harbula hacked and crawled his way up the hill along with the First Machine Gun Section. The group made its way up toward the first level of the hill, a small knoll that swung around to create a ridge line. As an airburst of shrapnel exploded over the machine gunners, Harbula's assistant and best friend was sitting next to him. Harbula turned to Rice, "Let's go, Joe."

That's when Harbula noticed that Rice was not moving. A gaping wound covered the back of his head.

Meanwhile, as the men were scaling the hill, the Chinese .50 caliber machine guns opened up on the climbing Marines. Harbula lost it. After the death of his best friend, he was overcome by emotion. He set his .30 caliber machine gun down and started firing madly in the direction of the Chinese .50. This brought Harbula's position to the attention of the Chinese. Rounds exploded around him, kicking up dirt and ice. His actions drew the ire of Captain Sitter, who sternly walked over to Harbula and shot him an icy glance: "Take it easy. There is plenty of time to get even."

Harbula ceased fire.

Shortly after it began, the attack broke down. Sensing the assault was faltering, Sitter switched tactics and ordered his reserve, Third Platoon and the engineers, to envelop the Chinese left flank holding a portion of East Hill.

For Powers that day on the hill is seared in his mind:

> Initially, we were held in reserve. We saw dead bodies coming down left and right, a lot of wounded and KIA being brought down the hill. Then we were called upon to attack the Chinese left flank. That hill was a sheet of ice, and I slipped several times. We moved toward a knoll on the top of the hill. We had two guys that were immediately KIA as they went around the knoll. We could not drive the Chinese off the left flank as we took such overwhelming fire.

During the engagement, Powers served as first ammo bearer and later acted as an assistant machine gunner with Fred Hems. After every firefight, Fred would ask, "How's my brother? Have you seen my brother?" Although in separate platoons, he and E.C. were practically inseparable.

With the attacks petering out, several men recalled reaching the top of the hill and even advancing on the reverse slope. Due to the complex nature of the terrain, each platoon had its own vantage point. The multiple rock formations, ridges, saddles, and knolls blurred terms like *topological crest* and *military crest*.

After the Chinese retort, Sitter received permission to set up a defensive position alongside the service and engineer units that George Company had passed through earlier. The platoons formed a reverse *L* like line along the top ridge. Second Platoon was on the top far right; First Platoon, at the elbow of the line; and then Third Platoon, on the left of the line at the bottom of the hill.

The men did the best they could to dig in on the icy rocks. Harrell Roberts swung his entrenching tool into the rock.

Ping!

His hand rang with the vibrations.

Ping!

Again, the tool barely burrowed an inch into the crust of the hill.

Crack!

On his next swing, the wooden handle of the pickax splintered and broke. "That was the only entrenching tool in First Platoon," recalled the burly Georgian.

"We couldn't dig in—we had to scrape in because the ground was so hard," reflected Steve Olmstead.

"We were exhausted and we knew the Chinese counterattack was coming. Since the ground was frozen, most of George Company could not dig foxholes. Either we could lie exposed on the frozen rocks or we could pile up dead Chinese for protection" recalled Harbula. He told one of his men, "Get me a dead body."

He quickly began constructing a bunker with corpses. To avoid accidentally firing into Second Platoon, Harbula placed the dead Chinese soldier to the right of his machine gun. Trying not to think about what he was doing, the Marine mechanically placed another body in front of the machine gun as a crude sandbag.

After digging in, one First Platoon member foolishly took the fight to the Chinese. Climbing a ridgeline located on top of a saddle in the middle of the hill, he stood up near Dick Hock and started picking off Chinese.

"Get your ass down!" barked Hock.

It was too late. "Like in the movies, a round hit him, and he went flying," remembered Hock.

The Marine then said, "I'm hit. I can't move."

Hock went to the Marine. Mortally wounded, he was bleeding out in Hook's arms. Hock and several other members of George Company began to carry him down, refusing to leave a wounded man behind.

Wham!

A mortar slammed down on the men.

"One round hit four of us," remembered Hock. The area became a "hornet's nest" of small arms fire as several razor-sharp pieces of jagged metal from the mortar sliced open Hock's stomach.

Bleeding profusely, the rifleman lay in the snow next to his wounded comrades.

I'm so thirsty, thought Hock as he reached for his canteen.

He placed the canteen to his blistered lips. Luckily, the water in the canteen had frozen solid. "The sip would have killed me," Hock recalled later. Drinking water is usually fatal with a gut shot. A corpsman jammed a morphine syringe into Hock's leg, and he was taken to the bottom of the hill. Nearly a year would pass before he recovered. A doctor later remarked incredulously, "You should have died on that hill."

Meanwhile, Sitter attempted to rally his men. He cut the bullshit and went straight to the chase, barking: "What are you going to do? You're going to fight, damn it! You must fight or you aren't getting out of here. It's that simple."

◄ 20 ►

"We're Going to Fight like Hell!"

THE MEN OF GEORGE COMPANY shivered and their teeth chattered as they struggled to fight off the Siberian weather; the temperature once again plummeted into negative double digits. Stationed in a reverse *L* near the lower portion of East Hill, Third Platoon braced for the counterattack they knew was coming. Fred Hems, Fred Garcia, and Red Nash positioned their machine gun in a rough foxhole facing uphill. Tom Powers started shuttling ammunition to Hems; as he handed a box to the machine gunner, his face became pale: "I'll never forget Powers's face as he brought in the ammo. I remember it like it was yesterday," recalled Hems.

A green Chinese illumination grenade had gone off, dimly lighting the entire contour of the hill. Hems and Powers looked out and saw "the hill literally moving." Like "an army of ants, thousands of them descending upon us," recalled Hems. Suddenly, the piercing sound of enemy bugles and whistles shattered the quiet of the night.

The Chinese attacked in regimental strength: 2,000 to 3,000 men. Bathed in the eerie light of the illumination grenade, Chinese officers screamed at the men, urging them on: Shā! Shā! Shā! [Kill!]

"Holy shit! There are gooks all over the place!" screamed Hems.

Now the shit really hit the fan, thought Powers. He recalled, "In my dreams, I've been fighting on that hill for fifty-nine years. And in my dreams, the Chinese always appear outlined in an eerie green tint." After more than ten minutes of constant fire, Powers looked down at Hems's machine gun. It "glowed like a neon light" from thousands of rounds that passed through its barrel.

Third Platoon's machine gun combined with a nearby tank helped trap hundreds of Chinese in a deadly crossfire in the small depression between two ridges on East Hill. The snow on East Hill turned "crimson" as the bodies stacked up in front of George Company, but waves of Chinese soldiers kept coming.

The main Chinese effort hit First Platoon with full force. Bob Harbula squeezed back the trigger on his .30 caliber machine gun. A single round exited the chamber. Clack! . . . Misfire.

"I survived five campaigns in the Korean War, and I had never been more scared, because there was nothing I could do," he recalled. Angrily, Harbula shucked his helmet and frantically pulled back on the bolt. He did everything he could think of to get the machine gun to fire, including kicking it. It was too late.

"Pull back!" yelled an officer.

"They were all over us," recalled Harbula. "I smashed one of them in the face with my helmet and then I fired my .45. When you hit them with the .45, they stop, period."

Harbula scrambled down the hill, getting off a few rounds from his .45 before stumbling and falling into a crater created by an artillery shell. He landed on flesh and bone. He quickly counted four American bodies lying in the hole: *They're all dead*, he thought.

Another flare illuminated the sky, and Harbula began to climb out of the foxhole. A sputtering voice said, "Bob, don't leave me." Harbula turned around and realized that fellow machine gunner Richard Heller, shot in both legs, was still alive. He yelled to Haller, "We're getting out of here."

Harbula lifted Haller up and half-carried him down the side of East Hill, struggling to get him to the safety of the aid station. As they stumbled and tumbled down the icy slope, Harbula ruptured his Achilles tendon. Both men were evacuated, but Harbula would be back in action a couple of months later.

During the melee, Bruce Farr, an ammo carrier for First Platoon's machine gun section, recalled, "I know three men that predicted their own death within three hours." Like Lieutenant Beeler at Majon-ni, and countless men throughout the history of battle, an ill-omened premonition is almost always fatefully realized. As they worked their way up the slope, Farr remembered fellow ammo carrier Ed Green ominously saying, "I won't live to see the top of the hill." Farr responded, in a reassuring voice, "We are all afraid. If we don't get back to the top with this ammo, none of us will be alive come daylight."

Farr heard E.C. Hems cry out, "More ammo!" Farr scrambled to Hems's machine gun with two boxes of .30 caliber ammo, handing off the ammo to Hems's assistant gunner.

Bobby Hallawell was also attempting to feed First Platoon's hungry guns, when a Chinese bullet penetrated his skull. "Oh, my God!" he yelled. Farr crawled to Hallawell through the blistering fire on his elbows. "When Bobby went down. I passed him and spun around, and grabbed his ankles and dragged him out." Hallawell bled out in Farr's arms.

Fulfilling the promise he had made Hallawell six months earlier, Farr gently removed Hallawell's watch and other personal effects. Farr was thinking, *I have to get them back to his family*. He carefully pocketed the items in his field jacket.

"There is no way to explain how I felt about Bobby or how Bobby felt about me," recalled Farr. "The men of George Company are all that close. I stayed with him until he was dead." Farr angrily yelled out, "Bobby is dead!" Remarkably, in the din of battle, Captain Sitter heard Farr's cry and shouted back, "PFC Farr! Is Hallawell wounded or is he dead?" Farr responded, "He is dead, sir. I'm going to take his body to the foot of the hill."

"You are not," Sitter snapped. "If he is dead, no one can help him. If he is wounded, take him to foot of the hill as quick as you can.

If he is dead, leave him here, and we will take care of it in the morning. We need every man on this hill, period."

During the exchange, Farr's brother-in-arms and foxhole buddy, Mert GoodEagle was fighting his own personal war. While making his way back up the hill with his precious .30 caliber ammo cans, two bayonet-wielding Chinese soldiers confronted the burly Native American. The mustard-clad soldier on his right charged him straight away. GoodEagle pounced first. He threw him down and bashed him in the head with a metal box of ammunition. The second soldier charged him from the left. With one hand, GoodEagle emptied a full fifteen-round clip from his M1 carbine. Then the first soldier started to move. "I jumped on him with my bayonet. I was so scared that I ran the rest of the way up the hill. I got to the top of the hill, and I was shaking like a leaf. It was then that I realized I wet my trousers!" recalled GoodEagle. That night the Pawnee Indian earned his warrior's feather.

Mortar shells dropped from the sky and detonated around Second Platoon. "They came right over top of us," recalled Clarke Henry.

Bob Camarillo remembered firing his weapon into the mass of the oncoming Chinese, killing scores of them: "They were all over the place. They were everywhere. They got close, very close. Then they were up on top of us. I don't understand to this day. Several Chinese were actually so close, they ran right by us, looked at me, and didn't shoot. It's a mystery to me, but I guess God did not want me to die that night."

With his ammunition bearers knocked out of the fight, Camarillo had to go down the hill several times to get his own ammo. Going back up the hill, he recalled, "Chinese were everywhere—it was a free-for-all. If you see someone with a padded uniform, shoot him."

He recalled passing GoodEagle and Green, who, he remembered, had a troubled expression on his face, a look of resignation. Green had told his fellow Marines his premonition that he would die that night. The next morning, corpsmen reported that Green had gone into shock from a compound bone fracture and literally froze to death on East Hill.

Chinese bullets wounded Dalton Hilscher and Stanley Walerski, who was doubled over with his hands cupped to his legs. In pain, Walerski gasped, "I think I'm hit." In a somewhat comical manner, Clark Henry replied, "Well, when you find out, let me know."

Both men slid down the hill and made their way toward the aid station. With officers in short supply, Clark Henry helped keep the men together. "Sitter told him [Henry] he was in charge," Camarillo remembered. He kept the men's spirits up by bringing ammo to their positions and urging them on. "He was all over the place." Camarillo recalled.

On the back side of the *L*, defending the lower part of East Hill, Third Platoon's Fred Hems recalled firing from a prone position. Enemy bullets passed so closely to his head that "they zinged and snapped." Many of the weapons froze. Some of the guys "pissed on their guns to keep them operational and firing," recalled Hems.

Tom Enos, a gunner with First Platoon, recalled that he was "positioned on a slope perpendicular to the crest of the main hill. All of our troops were behind me; I didn't have a foxhole for the gun. They came en masse, human waves, squads of Chinese."

Enos's gun fired into masses of Chinese soldiers, cutting into flesh and muscle. One group came within grenade range and hurled a Chinese stick grenade into Enos's nest. Life passing before his eyes, he reached down, grabbed the grenade, and threw it back into the hordes of oncoming Chinese, hitting several of them.

Despite his best efforts, groups of Chinese overran his position and continued down the hill toward Hagaru-ri. "The combat was so close. I was blasting them with my .45. I could see their split-toed tennis shoes as they were running around us."

Enos recalled Captain Sitter creeping toward his position. Sitter shouted the password, "Lincoln!" Enos replied, "Abraham." Sitter informed Enos that he needed to hold at all costs. The men who had overrun his position were being handled with "bayonets and rifle butts."

"I carried a pistol: that's all I had. I went hand-to-hand with the bayonet, and I threw some grenades. No rifle," recalled Sitter.

Second Platoon, stationed near the crest of the hill, enjoyed relatively open fields of fire. "They were right on top of us as we slaughtered them," recalled machine gunner Jack Daniels. "We opened up with everything we had, and the barrels of our machine guns turned blood red as we fired ten to twelve cans of ammunition." The barrel warped on Daniels's gun, and his assistant gunner had to run down the hill to one of the Marine tanks to borrow a spare barrel.

"It was fun killing 'em until we realized later that they were human beings," a Marine recalled, sobbing, nearly sixty years later. After losing several of his ammo bearers, Daniels remembered the boot camp adage: "Don't make no friends because you'll lose 'em," his drill instructor had said.

The machine gunners were spread out among each platoon. One Marine reflected, "If the machine guns were firing, we knew we could hold." Many of the men fired on the Chinese attackers, only to be frustrated by their own weapons malfunctioning. Blood from their wounds also froze, effectively cauterizing them.

A Chinese .50 caliber machine gun was working over Harrell Roberts's position, green tracer rounds streaking toward him. As he was taking cover, a .50 caliber round caught Roberts through the left wrist. He recalled, "My left glove and gauntlet came clean off my hand. I felt my wrist snap back. It was almost like I put my hand in a 110-volt light socket and was electrocuted. My foxhole buddy then tied a leather tourniquet, which was actually resting on his helmet earlier, onto my arm, and we stopped the bleeding."

As Roberts and his foxhole buddy made their way down to the aid station, Roberts thought, *Oh my God, I committed the cardinal sin. I left old 2447720 out there.*

Trained since boot camp never to leave his weapon behind, Roberts had no choice but to go back for his rifle. However, as Roberts wove his way back toward his foxhole, a bullet drilled a neat hole through his trouser leg. Miraculously, avoiding further injury, he turned around again and scrambled down the hill. *To hell with old 2447720,* he thought.

On the way down, Roberts saw Sergeant James Fry coughing and spitting up blood and cursing. Fry's bloody cheek dangled on the side of his face. Roberts helped him down the hill where he could receive medical treatment. The hill was steep at this point, so Roberts sat down, pulled up his parka, and began sliding down the hill like a child on a sled.

At the bottom of the hill, the convoy of injured men received another addition. "I'm blind, I'm blind," a voice moaned. Roberts recognized the voice as one of his men who was always playing a small musical instrument: "We'd nicknamed him Piccolo."

Roberts called to Piccolo, "Follow my voice and ease your way over to me, using my voice." When the blind man reached the group, Roberts could see the cause of the "blindness." Blood from a head wound had frozen all over Piccolo's eyes, and he couldn't see. Limping and staggering, the men eventually made their way to the aid station in Hagaru-ri.

Back on the hill, the Chinese were overrunning portions of First Platoon. At 0100 hours, they began to pour through a gap between First and Second Platoons. To plug the hole, Lieutenant Carey, now 3/1's intelligence officer, grabbed every available man and surged toward the line. Headquarters personnel, cooks, bakers, and commandos charged forward with all the ammunition they could carry.

When they reached the front lines, Carey reported to Sitter's embattled command post. "Thank God, you made it. Go up and take over the First and Second Platoons," the exhausted captain told Carey.

Carey bolted out of the command post. Carrying cardboard cylinders full of pineapple fragmentation grenades, he moved further up the slippery hill. "Dark shadows of the enemy seemed all around us," he recalled. A bullet passed between Carey's fingers, and another struck his cartridge belt and passed clean through his parka, missing his stomach by a hair. "I was lucky," remembered Carey.*

Carey shot two eight-round clips from his M1 as he ran, "dropping several Chinese." He dived into a foxhole, where he found

---

* Carey would later retire as a Lieutenant General.

Jack Deloach, the platoon sergeant, practically blinded by blood flowing into his eyes from a shrapnel wound. The stalwart NCO refused evacuation and continued to lead his men. Masses of Chinese swarmed their position. Deloach began taking the grenades out of their cylinders and feeding them to Carey, who hurled them at the enemy.

"Keep 'em coming. They are coming fast!" Carey screamed.

"I'm doing the best I can. You just keep 'em as accurate as you can," responded Deloach.

The grenades had four- to five-second fuses. To make sure they exploded on contact with the enemy units, Carey threw them according to a rhythm, yelling "One—Two! One—Two!"

In the din of battle, the men around him thought it was a Chinese curse word, "Wambatu! Wambatu!"

Lying in his makeshift foxhole, Steve Olmstead heard "Wambatu!" and thought, *What the hell does that mean?*

Word then filtered down to the men that *wambatu* was a Chinese obscenity meaning *turtle shit*. In unison, the Marines yelled at the top of their lungs: "Wambatu! Wambatu!"

Following up the verbal insults, the Marines hurled grenades at the mass of Chinese troops.

As the enemy came ever closer, body parts, blood, and bits of uniform began to speckle the Marines' uniforms. "They were mingling all around us. It wasn't a situation of them being twenty or thirty yards away. It was a matter of feet, not yards. Dark shadows were moving all around you. I remember shooting several at point-blank range with my M1 Garand," recalled Carey.

Sometime before the melee began, Steve Olmstead recalled a Marine asking Sitter, "Captain, what happens if we're surrounded?"

"We're going to fight like hell!" said Sitter.

Fight like hell they did, as Carey plugged the hole in the line, thereby saving First Platoon, his old command, from massacre.

But the victory was short lived. As the battle wore on, the Chinese again threatened to overwhelm sections of the line. Seeing that the line was bowing, Lieutenant Colonel Thomas L. Ridge ordered his last reserve, a group of Drysdale's Royal Commandos, to bolster the defenses.

It was enough. Before dawn, the Chinese attack ebbed. Henry and what was left of Second Platoon surveyed the damage. Hundreds of Chinese bodies littered the hill. Henry found PFC Richard Jewel, who said, with tears in his eyes, "Sarge, I killed a lot of people."

"That's the business we are in," Henry responded over the cries of the wounded Chinese. Many were moaning, and several chanted prayers.

Sporadic firing continued from the piles of mangled Chinese bodies. A typical Chinese tactic was to play dead. Several George Company Marines reported that some of the Chinese were attempting to pitch a grenade as their last gasp. The wounded Chinese troops remained a threat.

As the first rays of dawn began to illuminate the hill, Daniels also surveyed the carnage. He saw "a whole lot of dead" out in front of the machine gun, and along the ridge, the snow that had fallen the night before was tinged red with blood.

To E.C. Hems's horror, he watched as one of his comrades "had to be picked up with a shovel." The man's body had been blown to pieces by a mortar round.

Trudging back up the hill, Farr passed two stretcher bearers bringing a body down. An olive-drab blanket covered the face of the dead man. Farr shot the stretcher bearers a cold, icy stare.

"Who is this?" he demanded. They pulled back the blanket to reveal the face of Donald Williams. Like Green, he had predicted his own death on the hill. Stunned, Farr thought to himself, *My God, it's my close friend.*

At 9:00 a.m., Marine Air units arrived on station, blasted away at any surviving Chinese units, and dropped napalm bombs on the hill.

Farr returned to one of the section's abandoned machine guns. Dozens of dead Chinese lay around the gun. A Chinese lieutenant had frozen solid on his hands and knees, almost as if he had been firing the gun. Farr pushed the frozen corpse on its side and searched the officer's pockets for intelligence. What he found haunted him: pictures of the officer's wife and children. He also found a flashlight stamped "Made in China" and a cigarette case.

That morning Farr bumped into GoodEagle, one of the few survivors of the First Platoon's machine gun section. Farr said, "Here's Bobby's watch. You know the promise we made to each other." GoodEagle looked down and carefully took Hallawell's watch and put it in the pocket of his field coat for safekeeping. The two men exchanged glances and went about daily tasks.

Further down at the base of the hill, Third Platoon was facing the same moral dilemma: take care of the Chinese wounded and risk getting killed in the process, finish them off, or just let them die.

"One of our sergeants ordered us to finish off any survivors," recalled Fred Hems. "I refused the order! The sergeant went out and completed the task. I remember the sergeant coming back with pictures of the Chinese. 'Get those away from me. I do not want to see them!'" Hems had snarled.

Almost sixty years later, the memories and emotions of the Battle for East Hill remain vivid. Hems reflected, "War is hell and some things that happen there are unbelievable. Some of these guys enjoyed killing."

◂ 21 ▸

Holding the Line

AMBLING UP the side of East Hill, Fred Hems frantically searched for his twin brother E.C. "Has anybody seen my brother?" he called out to the haggard remains of First Platoon. E.C.'s machine gun position lay in the direct path of the main Chinese assault. Hems feared the worst but hoped his brother had somehow survived the night. As he moved toward the first machine gun position, his fears subsided when his eyes locked with his brother's. "I was really lucky," responded E.C., as he showed his brother his battle-scarred helmet: a Chinese bullet had drilled a hole clear through the crown. The Hems brothers' reunion was short lived. Under constant sniper fire from the Chinese, who still held strong, the men went back to consolidating their positions on the hill, cleaning weapons, and preparing for another assault.

The division hospital nestled within Hagaru-ri consisted of nothing more than a bunch of tents and old broken-down houses. The crude facilities were overwhelmed with casualties. More than six hundred Marines lay dying or wounded inside the makeshift hospital. Over a thousand more patients were expected to overwhelm the facility from Marine units fighting to the north and army units filtering in from east. Something had to give.

Barely alive but stabilized and one of the six hundred, Rocco Zullo clung to life in a cot. Zullo already had had several emergency surgeries to patch up the machine gun wounds piercing the side of his abdomen. Something had to be done with Zullo and the other wounded Americans who flooded Hagaru-ri's field hospitals.

After twelve days of around-the-clock back-breaking work, Lieutenant Colonel John Partridge's First Engineer Battalion had hacked out a semblance of an airfield. Although few people knew it at the time, December 1, 1950, would be a turning point in the fight for the Chosin Reservoir.

For days, the engineers had toiled against the elements and the enemy, often jumping off their equipment to take up arms to fend off the Chinese. George Company's stand on East Hill had played a key role and ultimately a crucial link in Hagaru's defenses, helping allow Partridge's engineers to build the field.

The crude airstrip was wedged at a diagonal inside the Hagaru-ri perimeter. By December 1, it was only 40 percent complete and a mere 50 feet wide and 2,900 feet long. It was considered far too short to meet the official airstrip landing specification for transport aircraft of the time. Nevertheless, General Smith took a gamble and ordered the airfield operational. Casualties like Zullo had to go out, and replacements had to come in.

At 2:30 p.m., the men of George Company looked down East Hill and gave a brief cheer along with the other Marines from the base as they saw the first plane—an olive drab, weather-beaten C-47—touch down on the frozen runway. It took about a half-hour to upload twenty casualties. The C-47 bumped and lurched over the rough strip. The next two planes removed another sixty casualties, while the fourth plane, heavily laden with ammunition, touched down, only to collapse its landing gear on the runway. Fortunately, the cargo was salvaged, but the plane had to be destroyed to keep the airstrip operational.

Zullo was eventually evacuated. After spending years in military hospitals and undergoing countless operations, Zullo lost track of George Company. Nearly every Marine thought he was dead.

While wounded and dying in Task Force Drysdale, Zullo had called out for one of his men. The man, PFC Philip Loughlin, had been wounded and paralyzed from the hip down while attempting to find bandages to dress Zullo's wounds. In honor of that man's sacrifice, Zullo retired from the Marine Corps and dedicated his life to the education of children. He later became a high school principal. While he had been recovering on an operating room table, Zullo had met the love of his life and his future wife, a nurse-officer whom he married during his recovery.

As Zullo was flown out, hundreds of reinforcements flew in. Along with the fresh troops came a gaggle of reporters. Stateside, the press had predicted the demise of the First Marine Division, claiming they could potentially face massacre. The CIA chief, Walter Bedell "Beetle" Smith thought the division would survive the Chinese onslaught only through negotiations. A British reporter called the withdrawal from the Chosin a "retreat." Smith quickly corrected him, pointing out that they were merely attacking in a new direction. The press quickly improved on Smith's initial remark, turning it into "Retreat, hell, we're just attacking in a new direction."

Behind the public bluster and bravado, the First Marine Division was in serious trouble. While the Chinese casualties were staggering, they still had over 40,000 troops between Hagaru-ri and Chinhung-ni. The press reports in the States were all doom and gloom. *Time* described the Eighth Army's rout as "the worst defeat the United States ever suffered." *Newsweek* was worse: "Perhaps it might become the worst military disaster in American history . . ."

At least the Eighth Army had a line of retreat. The Marines were surrounded, and front-page newspapers stated the division was "entrapped." Using the same fundamental tactics as Xenophon in 401 B.C.—the Ten Thousand cut their way through Persian and

Asiatic hordes to the Black Sea—First Marine Division would have to do the same.

For the Marines of the First Marine Division, December 1 turned out to be a momentous day. Not only was the airfield operational, but the Fifth and Seventh Marines planned their breakout to the south, placing their best battalions in the front. The Seventh Marines CO, Colonel Homer Litzenberg—known as "Litz the blitz" for his command of certain forms of the English language, rather than his command style— issued a simple order: "In our order for the march south, there are no intermediate objectives: The attack will start at 0800 on December 1. Objective Hagaru."

Lieutenant Colonel Ray Murray, CO of the Fifth, reflected: "Haguru [is] fourteen miles down the road, and there is a hell of a lot of Chinese between us and them." Inwardly, Murray doubted they would make it. Making matters worse, the Chinese brought up two fresh regiments from Manchuria. The hills swarmed with tens of thousands of Chinese. A breakthrough seemed against all odds.

That morning, the two Marine regiments fought their way down the MSR toward Haguru-ri. The Fifth moved along the axis of the MSR, while the Seventh fought through the Chinese over land, taking the hills overlooking the MSR. Audaciously, Litzenberg covertly pushed one of his battalions over winding mountain paths, through Chinese lines. They intended to link up with the Marines of Fox Company, 2/7, who continued to hold Toktong Pass open against all odds. Fighting all day, the regiments pushed south linking up with Fox Company at the pass.

The nights of December 1 and 2 on East Hill remained much quieter than the previous night for George Company. A blinding snowstorm blanketed the men and coated their positions with a fresh layer of freezing snow. Combined with the storm, the Chinese hit George Company's position with a grenade attack. In the snow, the grenades' explosions looked spectacular as they mixed with the icy crystals. Fortunately, the grenades largely fell short of their target and did not have the intended effect.

The standard Chinese grenade was a typical "potato masher" about eight inches long. It had an iron cylinder and fixed explosives on one end. The other end was a bamboo shaft attached to the iron cylinder. To use the grenade, the Chinese removed a small metal cap at the end of the wooden handle and pulled it. The string then fastened to a match fuse that burned for roughly four seconds. Sparks from the burning fuse trailed the grenades as they were hurled through the air. In a typical Chinese attack, the soldiers took four or five grenades and latched them together with twine, hurling the group through the air. Fortunately for the Leathernecks, many of the grenades didn't detonate. Sergeant Ronald Wyman, a replacement Marine who came in with the second draft* recalled: "Only half of them would land anywhere near a target and the other half failed to go off—duds. We all respected the grenades because every once in a while they would do what was intended, but if they were successful, the charge was so intense that it would vaporize the metal fragmentation sleeve instead of sending fragments over the target area."

Tom Enos recalled the ensuing grenade battle: on the slope perpendicular to the crest of the hill, "I would throw out an illumination grenade about twenty yards in front of us, whenever they would attack. The tanks below would use this as a sign of sorts. They would sweep the hill with .30 and .50 caliber machine gun fire, killing the attackers."

That evening, Clark Henry also actively engaged the Chinese: "I heard voices in the gulch over to our left." The aggressive Irishman then requested that he take a squad from Second Platoon and clean out the Chinese. "Can we go see what is going on?" Henry asked Sitter. Sitter replied, "We don't have enough men."

---

* Wyman later rose to sergeant major in the Marine Corps.

Henry decided to act on his own. Carrying a BAR, he and a commando slithered on their stomachs toward the gulch. They crept into position and began firing in the direction of the voices. "I'm not sure if we hit anything, but the talking stopped and they dispersed," he recalled. Henry and the commando made their way back toward George Company's lines.

On the morning of December 2, Enos and what was left of the First Machine Gun Section—six men—woke up. (They had started with seventeen men.) The machine gunners had somehow survived another night on the hill. There were no more whistles or bugles, just the occasional crack of gunfire from wounded Chinese sniping at them. The Marines took turns going down the hill to get additional ammunition and food.

As Enos made his way downhill, his legs and toes screamed with pain. He remembered that after grabbing several boxes of ammunition, "I started making my way up the hill, but kept falling down." After each fall, he started again. Soon he began crawling up the hill on all fours. Finally as his feet and knees gave out, "I started breaking down. I was lying there in the snow and couldn't get anywhere."

The new NCO found the forlorn machine gunner outstretched in the snow, crying. He tried to help Enos up, but each time, they fell down. The NCO left to get a medic as Enos lay there with fresh flakes of snow hitting his face. Time seemed to fade away as he slipped in and out of consciousness. The medics arrived and placed him on a stretcher. Suddenly, he woke up in a medical tent and realized he was not on the hill. As the doctor cut off his sock, he found that all of Enos's toes were black and green. His toes were pus-filled and eaten with gangrene. Revived from the heat in the tent and a little bit of rest, Enos insisted on receiving a fresh pair of boots and going back up the hill. With a stern look, the doctor said, "No, son, you're in no condition. You're going to be out of here in a few days. You're more of a liability to us walking. You might as well be flown out." Enos was later evacuated and flown to a hospital in Japan.

Over the next several days, George Company continued to be harassed by the Chinese, who probed George's positions on East

Hill. They never mounted an assault on the scale of the night of November 30. Reinforcements continued to filter onto the hill in the form of U.S. Army troops and even "buddies" or ROKs who were paired up with Army personnel.

Wyman recalled several ROKs assigned to his squad: "I put them further to the right because I didn't trust them. I felt that if anything happened during the night, they wouldn't be firing at my squad. When I went over to check on them that night just after dark, they were gone, bugged out."

Staff Sergeant Harold "Speedy" Wilson, an NCO, had arrived as a replacement in November. Wilson's leadership on the hill kept Third Platoon together.★ He recalled that one Army officer asked, "Where's the bug-out route if we get overrun?" Wilson calmly patted the back side of his foxhole as he shot the Army lieutenant a menacing look, saying, "This is as far as we go. I don't get out of my hole at night because these guys [pointed at his Marines] shoot at anything that moves."

Most of the Army troops came to the hill haggard and weapon-less. PFC Steve Olmstead† remembered one of the Army troops who filtered into his position. The replacement turned to Olmstead and said, "I survived the Battle of the Bulge, but this is worse."

What would have made the GI say that? On December 2, the bedraggled survivors of three U.S. Army battalions were beginning to make their way into Hagaru-ri. It is highly probable that the doggie had been part of these doomed units, called Task Force Faith.

Five nights earlier, division-sized elements of the PLA had torn into Task Force Faith, which was holding separate perimeters on the eastern end of the Chosin Reservoir, about fifteen miles from Hagaru-ri. For twenty-four hours, the battalions held their Alamo-like position while being resupplied by air. After the commanding officer died,

---

★ Wilson would earn the Medal of Honor six months later in another epic stand on Hill 902.
† Olmstead later retired as a lieutenant general.

Lieutenant Colonel Don Carlos Faith, a former paratrooper officer who had fought in the Eighty-Second Airborne Division during World War II, took command of the three battalions' fight for their lives.

One battered soldier under Faith's command described their CO: "Here comes Colonel Faith in his shiny helmet and new parka and riding pants. He had a grenade attached to each side of his back-pack harness and was holding a .45 in his hand. Really, I thought he looked too sharp, too West Point, compared to the rest of us."

The Chinese attacks took an enormous toll, hundreds of wounded men flooded makeshift field hospitals inside the perimeter, and dead GIs lay stacked in rows four feet high. Hope of holding the pocket faded when a company-sized relief force was mauled. Thousands of Chinese attacked and nearly overwhelmed Faith's fragile position.

Fearing annihilation, Faith ordered his men to destroy their artillery, form up into a convoy, and attempt to break through west to Hagaru-ri. As the convoy formed up, the Chinese riddled it with small arms fire and descended from the hills, taking up ambush positions along the road west. Under constant attack from Chinese on each side of the narrow road back to Hagaru-ri, the battered convoy pushed on. Drivers became the Chinese target of choice. Wounded men were piled into the trucks alongside dead bodies. As the pounding continued, the wounded were often hit a second and third time, or killed outright.

In an attempt to relieve the relentless PLA attacks, Marine air support strafed and bombed them with napalm, often with deadly effect, yet sometimes tragically killing GIs caught in the crossfire. PFC James Ransone recalled:

> [GIs] were burned to a crisp, their skin peeling back like big potato chips. Still others just blazed away like torches. There I was practically in the middle of them and couldn't do anything to help. Someone hollered, "Keep going. The medics will take care of them." There was nothing the medics could do. The worst thing was when a couple of them begged me to shoot them.

Trucks were blown away. The cries and screams of the wounded overwhelmed even the shrieking of the arctic wind. A massacre had begun. At one point, Faith personally manned a .50 caliber machine gun and fired into the Chinese hordes.

As the convoy rolled forward, control broke down, and men refused to fight. Brandishing his .45, Faith pushed into the mass, attempting to maintain unit cohesion. It was hopeless. Slowly the task force disintegrated before his eyes as companies and platoons morphed into a tattered mob of individuals.

At one point during the doomed death ride, Faith confronted two South Korean soldiers who were attempting to hide under a truck and lash themselves to the vehicle's undercarriage. Faith ordered the men into the open. "Faith extended his right arm toward the cowering man and pulled the trigger, then shifted his aim and shot the other as well."

"Shoot anyone who tries to run away," Faith barked.

As the purple tinge of dusk cascaded over the convoy, a Chinese grenade detonated near Faith, mortally wounding him. With Faith down, nothing remained to hold the convoy together. Scattered and leaderless, small bands pushed west. Wounded and frostbitten, they made their way across the ice of the frozen Chosin Reservoir. All wounded and able-bodied men who remained with the convoy were massacred. Miraculously, hundreds of men found their way through the minefields, wire, and Chinese lines into Hagaru-ri.

Despite the bloodbath taking place on the convoy, some of the Chinese helped the wounded get back to American lines. The official history states: "Far from hindering the escape of the Army wounded, the Chinese actually assisted in some instances, thus adding to the difficulty of understanding the Oriental mentality."

Unlike their Army brethren, the Fifth and Seventh Marines marched into Hagaru-ri in perfect battle order. Like a well-oiled machine, the Commandos seized a nearby hill along the MSR. About five hundred yards from the perimeter of Hagaru-ri, trucks and tanks in the convoy halted. Lieutenant Colonel Raymond Davis barked to his Marines: "You people will shape up and look sharp. We are going in like United States Marines."

With drill instructor cadence harking back to boot camp, the weary Marines of the Fifth and Seventh straightened their backs, and their steps became surer and smarter. To men in Hagaru-ri, the Fifth and Seventh, tattered and dirty, "looked like zombies" as they proudly marched in perfect unison.

From atop East Hill, George Company saw the proud, iconic moment unfold: "It's the Fifth and Seventh coming in," the men heard Marines shout.

"I heard the Marine hymn in the distance," recalled Tom Powers, "and we all started singing it on the hill."

> From the Halls of Montezuma,
> To the shores of Tripoli;
> We fight our country's battles
> In the air, on land, and sea;
> First to fight for right and freedom
> And to keep our honor clean;
> We are proud to claim the title
> Of United States Marine.
>
> Our flag's unfurled to every breeze
> From dawn to setting sun;
> We have fought in every clime and place
> Where we could take a gun;
> In the snow of far-off Northern lands
> And in sunny tropic scenes;
> You will find us always on the job
> The United States Marines.
>
> Here's health to you and to our Corps
> Which we are proud to serve;

In many a strife we've fought for life
And never lost our nerve;
If the Army and the Navy
Ever look on Heaven's scenes;
They will find the streets are guarded
By United States Marines.

Inside Hagaru-ri, Lieutenant Colonel Murray wiped tears from his eyes with the filthy sleeve of his parka. In an interview with *Chicago Tribune* reporter Keys Beach, he said, "I didn't think we could do it."

For the first time in weeks, most of the First Marine Division was reunited at Hagaru-ri. During the afternoon of December 5, elements of the Second Battalion Fifth Marines relieved the haggard remains of George Company. Bruce Farr looked at the three remaining men of the First Machine Gun Section; the other fourteen were either dead or wounded. The men shuffled off to their new position in fighting holes on the western end of the newly completed airstrip. George Company relieved another unit and occupied their fighting holes.

"We were in absolutely terrible shape," recalled Farr. "I grew the first and only mustache in my life." Due to the constant combat, the men had not had a chance to shave. Beads of mucus and sweat froze to their faces. Sickness seemed ubiquitous throughout the unit; many of the men had diarrhea. As Farr vividly related:

> I had about four layers of clothes on and I had to constantly defecate. You know how hard it is to do that? I remember pulling my trousers down and seeing the snow explode around me from Chinese machine gun fire. I raced into a makeshift shelter made of parachute silk, four other guys dove on top of me trying to avoid the fire also.

One Marine remembers trying to urinate and it seemed like his "kidneys froze." Another recalled, "I cried, I've never cried so hard in my life just trying to relieve myself."

First Marine Division and George Company were starved for replacements; they combed the rear areas and even hospitals for fresh men. As Farr recalled, "We received a replacement who had recently come from Japan and still had pneumonia. He was in bad shape, but on the line with us."

"That night a rumor went around the company that we were going to be hit by Mongolian cavalry. What the hell is Mongolian Cavalry?" recalled Powers. Apparently, the company had found a few horses, and rumors abounded that George Company would face a mysterious Chinese cavalry unit. Powers remembered asking, "Do you take out the horse or the rider first?" A few captured horses used as pack mules by the Chinese fueled the initial speculation, but there were reports of mounted Chinese east of East Hill.

As the purple dawn streaked across the airfield, hundreds of Chinese emerged from the shadows and stormed George Company's lines. The previous night, they had silently crept through a gully where there was a low sloping hill and formed up in a ditch about a hundred yards in front of the airfield and George's lines.

"They came charging toward us at dawn, a daytime attack," recalled Farr.

First Machine Gun Section was down to one gun instead of two; the firing mechanism seemed to have frozen solid. Frantically, Farr reached for his carbine and attempted to fire. Clack! The firing pin had frozen. Pulling back the bolt of the machine gun, Farr squeezed off one round at a time at the oncoming Chinese. Another Marine, whose hands were crimson with blood from a shrapnel wound, frantically assisted Farr as he attempted to fire his single-shot machine gun.

Further down the line, Powers brought ammo to Fred Hems and Red Nash's machine gun as they blazed away at the oncoming Chinese. Taking heavy casualties, the Chinese attack halted and retreated toward the ditch. Olmstead recalled an unusual situation:

"There was firing from the Chinese toward their own men who were fleeing through the gully. We weren't firing on them."

The Marines also took twenty or thirty prisoners. "Several of them had feet that were elephantine and deformed since they had been exposed to the frost. They looked like they were blocks of ice," recalled Olmstead. "We were poorly equipped, but they were a hell of a lot worse."

Mao had a policy of using his former adversaries as cannon fodder and eliminating them. In keeping with that policy, many of the officers captured claimed to have fought in Chiang Kai-shek's army. They considered themselves allies of America during WWII. The officers were willing to fight with the Marines again, if they were given food and weapons.

Breakout

ON THE AFTERNOON of December 5, through the din of battle, Lieutenant Colonel Murray delivered a stirring speech to the men of the Fifth Marines:

> We're going to hold our position until the Seventh Marines clear the road to Koto-ri. When the time comes for us to march, we are coming out like Marines, not stragglers. This is not a retreat. There are more Chinese between us and the sea than there are to the north of us. General Smith said it best: "We're attacking in a different direction." Any officer who doubts our ability to break out better catch himself a case of frostbite, and I'll see that he's evacuated. We're coming out like Marines.

The men of George Company heard similar words as they prepared to break through tens of thousands of Chinese holding the road and the high ground from Hagaru-ri to the sea.

The next morning, after holding the airfield that cold December night, George Company and the First Marine Division began the long march south. The first objective for the division was to break out of the Chinese encirclement and head south to link up with Colonel Chesty Puller's forces in Koto-ri. George Company, and the rest of the division, had to fight their way down the MSR to reach the ships waiting in the port of Hungnam. On their way, they once again fought through Hell Fire Valley, where they had taken so many casualties, this time with superior numbers.

Behind the bluster, many in General Smith's command, including Colonel Al Bowser, privately wondered if the First Marine Division would make it:

> For one thing, I kept wondering if Koto-ri would even be there in a few hours. We knew by now that elements of the 76th, 77th, and 78th Chinese Divisions were in position along the eleven-mile stretch between Haguru and Koto-ri. We also knew that elements of the 89th and 60th Chinese divisions were deployed near Koto. And we had the bridge problem to solve, not to mention the trestle below it.

"The bridge problem" he referred to was the bridge that spanned the Funchilin Pass. It was the only way in and out of the reservoir. To the Marines, it appeared that the Chinese would make their most determined stand at this chokepoint. Worse, the bridge had been blown to bits.

Near the crucial bridge, water from the Chosin flowed through large pipes or penstocks that carried it to a power plant in the valley hundreds of feet below. Earlier, the Chinese had detonated the one-way concrete bridge that crossed over a gatehouse containing valves for the penstocks. The bridge spanned a 2,900-foot-deep abyss that George Company had crossed before entering Koto-ri back on November 28. The detonation had created a twenty-four-foot gap over the yawning chasm that had to be traversed before the Marines could bring out their heavy equipment. Off the gorge, to block road traffic, the Chinese had dynamited supports from a massive concrete trestle. This roadblock would have to be removed so the division could make the trip south.

"The enemy could not have picked a better spot to give us trouble," remarked Smith. There simply was no other way out.

The Marines could not construct a bypass due to the mountainous terrain. The engineer who masterfully completed the Hagaru-ri airfield took on the Herculean feat of getting the division past the blown bridge. "It was a damn serious situation," recalled Lieutenant Colonel Partridge. Because the division had no prefabricated sections of bridge, they had to be air-dropped. The lives of every Marine in the division depended on the successful drop of the spans, at the right time and in the right place.

"To your knowledge, have bridge sections ever been dropped by parachute?" General Smith asked Partridge. "Never heard of it, General."

In fact, the air drop would be a historic first. To prepare, Smith ordered a test drop.

Miraculously, the Army's Fifty-Eighth Treadway Bridge Company had somehow made its way to Koto-ri before the Chinese cut off the MSR in late November. While the unit did not have bridge sections, it did have the knowledge and know-how to build the Treadway.

On December 6, an Air Force C-119 dropped a section at Yonpo. The 2,500-pound section smashed to pieces. There was no time for a redo. Partridge ordered eight sections of Treadway bridge to be parachuted into Koto-ri at 0930 on December 7. He needed at least four sections of bridge to span the gap, but ordered extras in case they smashed or fell into enemy hands. In the end, six sections landed inside the village, while another parachuted into Chinese lines, and the eighth section smashed to bits on impact.

A large mountain dominated the area near the bridge. Heavily defended by the Chinese, the Marines had to take the mountain out at all costs. Smith therefore ordered Lieutenant Colonel Donald Schmuck of the First Battalion, First Marines, at Chinhung-ni to advance three miles up the MSR and capture the hill. Fortuitously, a blinding snowstorm pelted the reservoir as Schmuck and his men pushed forward, masking any movement. They surprised the Chinese and took the hill.

George Company began to "lighten up" for the long fight toward Hungnam. Many Marines dumped their worthless carbines and grabbed some spare, reliable M1 Garands that had greater stopping power. To deny the Chinese use of the discarded weapons, they quickly field-stripped them, scattering the parts and breaking the wooden stocks over a wall or a post. Engineers destroyed everything in sight that the division couldn't move.

"There were fires going off and explosions everywhere," Ron Wyman recalled. "As we sat in company formation in the middle of Hagaru-ri, a tremendous explosion went off. It seemed to be on the far end of the village, but debris, rocks, dirt, and wood rained down on us for several minutes. No one seemed to be too concerned, and everyone took it in stride."

The company snagged red silk lying about the perimeter from parachutes that had been used to supply the division. Using their trench knives, the men cut the silk into small pieces that they tied around their necks to identify themselves as friendlies. Otherwise, Marine airmen might strafe them. Seeing the crimson scarves, someone dubbed the unit "Bloody George." The motto stuck, and the unit became the infamous "Bloody George."

That afternoon, George Company moved out. Frostbitten, cold, sick, and tired, the men passed by East Hill. Over 1,000 Chinese bodies littered the rocky jagged slopes, most of them the result of George Company's stand. PFC Steve Olmstead recalled, "As I looked up at the hill, I remembered the five-day struggle to hold it. That made one hell of an impact on me. It has been with me for sixty years."

Remarkably, George Company had held the hill, though many of the Marines were replacements from the First and Second drafts. Leadership from NCOs and officers proved pivotal as they kept the men fighting against overwhelming odds. "To this day, I don't know how we did it. So many of the guys hardly even knew each other or even went to boot camp," remembered Bob Harbula. It was a testament to the leadership and fortitude of the men.★

Thanks to their sheer numbers, elements of the Fifth Marines had later retaken East Hill, somewhat anticlimactically. Nevertheless, the Fifth took numerous casualties. One Fifth Marine remembered a mortally wounded comrade: "I recall lifting the helmet off a wounded Marine and seeing his brains pour out like a stew from a pot, while his heart continued to beat."

During the long march to the south, the Chinese peppered the Marines with small arms fire. George Company and the last of the First Marine Division took heavy fire from both sides of the road. It was a repeat of what had happened to Task Force Drysdale on a much grander scale, with real firepower and the ability to take the high ground surrounding the road.

As the Marines fought their way south, artillery units fired on the surrounding hills at the Chinese. "I admired those artillerymen. Normally the 105s had to be sandbagged so they wouldn't scoot across the road. The men used their body weight to hold the 105s in place," recalled Farr.

Haggard and tired, the men of George Company fought their way down the MSR, passing the wreckage and debris of Task Force Drysdale that littered the road. Tom Powers' eyes focused on dozens of laceless and bloody hobnail boots that littered the area. The footwear had belonged to the dead members of the 41 Commando. Remembering the Chinese prisoners that George Company had captured near the airfield, whose feet were grotesquely frostbitten "blocks of ice," Powers wondered to himself, *Why didn't they take the boots?*

★ As Colonel Willie Buhl, 3/1's commanding officer in Fallujah and later CO of the Fifth Marines, would comment, "The men of 1950 were of the finest stock."

In addition, the remains of care packages, which the Chinese had rummaged through, lay scattered about. Powers quipped, "Those sons of bitches probably got my Jamison." (Since Inchon, Powers had been receiving a monthly supply of Jamison whiskey from his grandmother.)

By the night of December 7, the Fifth, Seventh, and 3/1 had fought their way back to Koto-ri. Chesty Puller had warming tents and hot chow ready for the men. George Company was told to find whatever sleeping accommodations they could. Powers and Red Nash found shelter—a metal truck. It was their first night's sleep under shelter in over two months. They slept inside the cab. "It was really uncomfortable, two guys that were six feet tall in the tiny cab, but at least we were out of the elements. I bullshitted with Nash that night, and we talked about home," recalled Powers.

As the men poured in, the garrison swelled to over 14,000 troops. This number included about 2,300 GIs and 125 Royal Marine Commandos. The bloated town became a prime target for the Chinese. Therefore, the breakout toward the sea had to be carefully orchestrated. Each unit was given a specific objective and task, which fit into the overall drive south. The Seventh Marines spearheaded the charge, while the Fifth Marines passed through the Seventh to take and hold high ground in a leapfrog manner. Third Battalion First Marines defended Koto-ri as the Fifth and Seventh pushed forward.

The Marines seized the key hills near the destroyed bridge, fighting through thousands of Chinese troops in the process and killing hundreds that were defending the crucial chokepoint. The priceless bridge sections traveled with the Seventh Marines in Lieutenant Charles Ward's Brockway trucks.

The most harrowing part of the campaign took place when the trucks attempted to position the bridge sections into the breach. "We took some incoming mortar rounds near the Brockways. The trucks, with their hydraulic operating systems, were vulnerable items of essential equipment. We had to get them out of there," remembered Partridge.

With mortar rounds raining down on the trucks, a more disturbing problem surfaced. The engineers found the gap in the blown bridge measured twenty-nine feet long. At only twenty-two feet long, the bridge sections were seven feet short. The gap had to be filled.

Thinking fast and under fire, the engineers came up with a novel solution. They built a crib of railroad ties that extended out over a ledge eight feet below the bridge where it had been destroyed. Using Chinese prisoners to move the ties, they built the crib and solved the problem. When the ties ran out, frozen corpses of Chinese soldiers were placed in the crib by the POWs.

Next, they laid the two parallel spans on the Treadway bridges. The men would gingerly cross the 2,900-foot-deep chasm balanced on the narrow plates of a single Treadway. Tanks would carefully place one tread on each span.

After bridging the gap, the engineers then had to deal with the massive concrete trestle that had been blown by Chinese sappers and lay directly across the road, blocking all movement. Initially, they thought the only way to get over the trestle was to blow it apart piece by piece, which would take an enormous amount of time. One of Partridge's engineers suggested, however, that he could take the butt of his bulldozer blade and push against the massive trestle: "It was like opening a farm gate: the whole structure just swung aside, and he skated this huge object right off the road [into the chasm]."

With the gap spanned by a bridge and the trestle removed, the Marines had a clear path toward the ports.

The Living Walked. The Dead Rode

THE LIVING MARCHED down the MSR, while George Company's dead rode on the trucks. The cadavers' feet and legs dangled over the sides of the olive-drab 6x6s, their faces frozen stiff and etched in time. By the morning of December 9, George Company and the rest of the First Marines were heading south toward the port of Hungnam. In order to get there, the miles-long convoy would have to blast its way through several Chinese divisions.

Suddenly, a figure snapping pictures startled the long haggard line of George Company Marines. In unison, First and Second Platoons barked, "Don't take our pictures! Don't take our pictures!"

The Third Platoon, not so camera shy, said, "Take ours!"

David Douglas Duncan was a Marine officer in WWII and is an American photojournalist among the most influential photographers of the twentieth century. Douglas is renowned for his dramatic combat photos during WWII, Korea, and Vietnam, and for his famous photos of Pablo Picasso. Duncan's still pictures captured an iconic shot of machine gunners Red Nash, Tom Powers, Fred Hems, and Sergeant Fred Garcia. The photographer later approached a haggard George Company Marine near him: a "quiet Marine who never said anything, but did his duty."

In Duncan's words:

> Dawn was just over the horizon. A Marine ... kept prodding with his spoon, trying to break loose a single, frost-coated bean from the others in his can. He could neither move it nor long continue holding the spoon between his gloved but almost rigid fingers. He found one, and slowly raised it to his mouth. He stood unmoving, waiting for it to thaw.

"What would you want if you could have any wish?" Duncan asked.

The Marine "continued to stand motionless, with empty eyes. Then his lips began to open ... [and] his eyes went up into the graying sky.

'Give me tomorrow.'"★

After the brief, but historic encounter, Duncan's photo, one of the war's most famous, captured the feelings and grit of combat in the reservoir. Duncan summed up the picture this way: "That photo represents all of us who were there."

Late on the afternoon of December 9, George Company marched down the MSR and pushed up a hill labeled Objective A. The hill, roughly a thousand meters high and white with a fresh coat of snow, lay astride the MSR and had to be held at all costs. Once atop the rocky mount, George Company quickly occupied frozen foxholes that had been scraped and dug out by the Chinese weeks earlier and more recently occupied by the Seventh Marines.

That night, the temperature plummeted to its lowest levels of the entire campaign. According to the meteorological officer assigned to the First Marine Division, the mercury dropped to −60 with a

---

★ [Korea, December 1950.] This Is War!, p. 144.

sixty-five knot wind. The combination created a windchill factor of −125.

"It was the one time Captain Sitter actually gave us orders to stand up in our sleeping bags," recalled Bruce Farr. "I remember standing up in my bag with my M1 Garand in my hand. We needed the bags just to stay alive."

The Siberian wind howled as the icy snowflakes blew sideways, pelting the men's faces. Clark Henry's most vivid memory of the experience involved squeezing into a tiny one-man foxhole with Carlos Banks. Banks's shoes were "threadbare," and he looked sickly.

"I'll never forget the expression on Carlos's face as we tried in vain to stay warm," recalled Henry. In desperation, Henry placed a poncho over the hole and lit a cardboard ration box on fire to gain a few fleeting minutes of warmth.

Earlier in the day, Fred Hems and Red Nash had cleared out a foxhole and set up their machine gun. Sleep-deprived for days, the two were as exhausted as the rest of George Company. In the driving snowstorm, Nash turned to Hems and said, "Fred, I just can't stay awake."

Meekly, Hems responded, "Nash, I know. I will try to keep my eyes open. But we're in the forward-most position. If they come, they will kill us in our bags."

Despite Hems's dire warning, both men fell asleep. Nash slept like a log.

At about 0400, a startled Hems heard voices and the tramping of hundreds of marching feet.

"I immediately woke up. We were surrounded by hundreds of Chinese," remembered Hems.

He quickly woke up Nash, yelling, "Wake the fuck up! We're about to be overrun."

Exhausted and practically in a semi-coma, Nash eventually came to, as Hems frantically depressed the trigger of his .30 caliber machine gun, firing into the mass of assaulting Chinese. Within minutes, fifty or so dead Chinese lay within the first five to fifteen yards in front of their position.

"Where are the grenades?" Nash screamed.

"I've got two," Hems said.

Nash threw both into the horde.

"Give me your carbine!" Nash snapped.

It would be the last time the friends spoke.

An illumination flare lit up the area and revealed scores of dead Chinese, as well as twenty or more Chinese who were attempting to take any cover they could from Hems's deadly crossfire.

"How far can you fire to your right?" Hems barked to Nash.

Nash was bent over. *Damn it, falling asleep again*, thought Hems.

From the corner of his eye, Hems spotted a shadowy figure. He quickly fired at the apparition and then turned to give Nash hell for falling asleep: "As soon as I touched him, I knew he was dead." Nash fought till he fired the last rounds in Hems's carbine. Only two bullets remained in the 30-round clip.

As a flare went up, Hems glanced at his watch. It was 4:20 a.m. Shouts went up that the enemy was attempting to overrun Third Platoon's position. Hems's machine gun lay at the eye of the storm. He cried out to Sergeant Garcia, "Nash is dead! Send me another assistant!"

PFC Harry Hobbs arrived several minutes later with no gloves. Hems looked at Hobbs's icy, frostbitten hands. Incredulous, Hems asked, "Where the hell are your gloves?"

Over the din of battle, Hobbs stammered, "I took them off and can't find them."

Quickly, Hems pried the frozen gloves off of Nash's hands. They resisted, but finally broke free. Hems tossed them to Hobbs.

During the course of events, the Chinese threw a grenade into their position. Hobbs scrambled for it heroically to toss it back at the Chinese. It exploded in his hands, turning them into a dangling mass of crimson and flesh. A corpsman stopped the bleeding and brought Hobbs to the rear.

Hems cried out for another gunner. The six-foot Irishman who dove into the hole was Tom Powers. Hems turned to Powers, saying, "I killed Red Nash. You're going to have to work the gun; I can't do it." In the confusing melee, Hems incorrectly took on the burden of guilt for Nash's death. Based on the position of the gun it was impossible for Hems to have fired on Nash, Powers recalled fifty-nine years later.

The Chinese continued to swarm their position, coming close enough that the men could have reached out and touched them. As the horde charged forward, "Give me tomorrow," looked seriously in doubt.

"I remember the whistles and yelling, and bugles," recalled fire-team leader Joe Sagan. Drowned out by gunfire, the howling wind, and Chinese bugles, Sagan kept screaming, "Here they come!" to warn the rest of George Company.

Clack!

Sagan squeezed the trigger on his M1. Completely frozen, the useless gun refused to fire. Feverishly, Sagan took off a glove and pulled out the only weapon at his disposal, a lone Mark II Fragmentation Grenade. To get a better grip on the metal pineapple, he tore off his mittens and pulled the pin. As he hurled it, the skin came off his hands.

Thud!

The grenade hit one of the advancing Chinese squarely in the chest and then bounced down to the ground and detonated. "I'll never forget thinking to myself, *God, here I come.* It was the longest seven seconds in my life," mused Sagan.

The explosion took out several enemy fighters, but despite the detonation, the Chinese kept coming. One advanced until he stood directly over Sagan's position. Unarmed, Sagan played dead as the Chinese soldier attempted to rip the prone Leatherneck's M1 from his clenched hands.

Fortuitously, George Company's 60 mm mortars then erupted in front of Sagan's foxhole. Next began the slow chatter of a machine gun, manned by Jack Daniels, located behind Sagan. In almost slow motion, the .30 caliber bullets spun through the gun's barrel.

Ping!

A Chinese round glanced off the tripod on Daniels's M1919A4 light machine gun as he touched the gun's trigger. Another pierced the olive-drab box of ammunition lying next to his heart on top of the foxhole. "I was sure I was hit," he recalled. But three rounds of belted ammunition coiled in the ammo box stopped the Chinese projectile from hitting Daniels's chest. His right index finger pulled back on the trigger of the machine gun, letting loose a another deadly volley of lead and cutting down dozens of Chinese soldiers, including the man in front of Sagan.

Suddenly, a Chinese soldier appeared directly in front of Daniels's gun, poised to hurl a grenade. As the soldier raised up, Daniels looked down the barrel of the gun and "cut loose" another burst. Daniels's bullets blew a hole "about the size of my fist" into the Communist trooper's torso, "blowing out the Chinaman's backbone." In his last gasp for life, the Chinese soldier crumpled down on his knees and tried to pull the string on the potato-masher grenade clenched in his hand.

By dawn, the attack was over. Caught by surprise as they were moving from one position to another, the Chinese assault had focused on Third Platoon. Later, after-action reports estimated that George Company had beat off an attack of over 350.

The next day, the company was ordered off the hill. George Company then became part of the rear guard for the push south toward Hungnam. Their job was to protect several tanks that were part of the rear guard. The tanks rumbled forward, but their turrets and 90 mm guns spun around toward the rear. They faced north to blast any Chinese that menaced the column. Additionally, the tanks destroyed any equipment and vehicles that couldn't make their way south, denying their use to the Chinese. Behind the miles-long convoy trailed a mob of Korean civilians. They were retreating from the Chinese Army with the forlorn hope of somehow evacuating with the Marines. "There were thousands of them," recalled Powers.

Suddenly, the mob charged the tanks and George Company. "It was wild. People were shooting everywhere; refugees and Chinese soldiers were everywhere."

"Don't come near the tanks, or we'll shoot!" some of the men in George Company shouted.

The Korean civilians then screamed, "The Chinese are amongst us!"

Powerfully and in a calculated fashion, the Chinese used their allies, the innocent North Korean civilians, as human shields to screen their movements as they positioned to attack the tanks.* The Chinese completely disregarded the laws of war. With no choice, the M26's 90 mm fired into the crowd.

"It was like a fucking bowling alley. Bodies, limbs, and heads were flying everywhere!"

The Chinese in civilian clothes continued driving the civilian mob into George Company and the tanks.

"They were swarming all over us, and we were fighting them off hand to hand."

One Chinese soldier jumped on a tank right in front of Powers. "I shot him in the face with my .45, and the bullet split apart his nose," remembered Powers. Another Chinese soldier jumped on Powers's back: "I wrestled him to the ground and had him by the throat. His eyeballs were popping out."

Someone screamed at Powers, "We're pulling out. Get on the tank!"

Powers jumped up, put his hands around the Pershing 90 mm gun and attempted to pull himself up onto the tank's engine compartment.

Boom!

The tank's 90 mm fired back into the gaggle of civilians and Chinese troops. The blast blew Powers off the gun and knocked him out. Luckily, someone from Third Platoon grabbed the burly Irishman and hurled him onto the engine compartment of the tank.

For several seconds, "everything turned white," and Powers slipped into unconsciousness. When he came to inside the tank, he was temporarily blinded. Several hours later, his sight returned, but the memory is forever sealed in his mind's eye as a phantasmal killer, a dream.

---

* Despite the loss of civilian life the U.S. forces evacuated a staggering 91,000 of these civilians from the port of Hungnam.

"For the rest of my days, I see that Chinese soldier I shot in the face. He has appeared in my dreams practically every night for over fifty years. Each time he tries to strangle me," recalled Powers.

The Final Push

GEORGE COMPANY remained part of the rear guard for the First Marines as they pushed down the Funchilin Pass, an abyss that dropped over 2,000 feet into blackness. The purple haze of dusk settled over the mountains and bathed Power Plant 1 and the large intake tubes that fed the power station from the Chosin Reservoir. Lieutenant Colonel John Partridge's jerry-rigged Treadway bridge had been placed over the road that lay directly in front of the gatehouse.

"It was like a sheet of ice going down an incline toward the bridge. A tank lost traction on the road and slid down the icy thoroughfare and tumbled into the abyss," recalled Bruce Farr.

George Company approached the yawning chasm. The metal Treadway consisted of just four indented metal struts that allowed the wheels of a truck or tank to cross the crevasse. In the middle of the bridge was nothing but air.

"Don't look down!" somebody yelled.

"It was absolutely breathtaking looking down into the chasm," Steve Olmstead reflected.

"I tried not to look down, but it was absolutely frightening," recalled another Marine.

After the final elements of the convoy crossed, engineers placed charges on the Treadway and neatly severed the struts, which plunged into the abyss.

As the men made their way down the MSR, the red and yellow streaks of dawn illuminated the area.

Bedraggled, dirty, bearded, frostbitten, and hungry, George pushed south toward the friendly port of Hungnam and the waiting ships in the Sea of Japan. Standing alongside the MSR, alone and "bullet-proof," the men noticed a familiar figure: their regimental commander, Colonel Chesty Puller.

As the men passed by Puller, their spirits soared. Their backs straightened. They continued to march forward. Powers remembered, "Our steps got smarter. Puller made us feel great. Only in the movies? No, sir! We were Marines!"

Eventually, George Company marched into an assembly area at Chinhung-ni. Engineers were busy wiring everything for detonation. Starving and cold, the famished men foraged for food to fill their empty stomachs. There were piles of rations scattered around the base camp. The hungry men pounced onto the crates. Someone barked, "Sorry you can't have those. They're wired to be blown."

Menacingly, the Leathernecks turned around and drew their weapons on the engineer: "We fuckin' want 'em."

Sheepishly, the engineer backed down, saying, "Take all you want."

The Marines tore into boxes of fresh apples, gorging on the goodies. "In twenty minutes, we were all sick as dogs," recalled Olmstead.

George Company boarded flat cars on the narrow-gauge railroad headed for the port of Hungnam. "It was orderly chaos, but as PFCs, we had blind faith in our NCOs and officers. We knew they could get us out," recalled Olmstead.

Thousands of Marine and Army troops piled into the ships like sardines, stretching them way over capacity. Miraculously, over 250,000 Marines, Army troops, civilians, and equipment were safely evacuated from the port.

"The nicest thing in my life was being on that ship."

"It was finally warm," recalled another Marine.

On board, the dirty and bloody Marines of George Company were met with scores of random acts of kindness. One of the ship's crew asked Olmstead, "You men are Marines right? Come with me. Take my bunk."

Although they had not bathed for over three months, they discovered that warm water was nonexistent on the ships. Their only option was to take a freezing cold shower. Most of the men avoided it, but not Farr. "I decided to take an icy cold saltwater shower," remembered Farr. "Months of dirt, blood, and grime just washed away." Memories would be harder to wash away.

Colonel Wong Lichan's command car pulled up alongside the white face of a hill near the Chosin Reservoir. Snow covered the hills. The liaison from the People's Republic of China to the North Korean Front Headquarters in Pyongyang spotted several mounds on the side of the road. Then he passed several more. They appeared to be snowmen. The sight brought him back to his childhood in Manchuria where he had made similar snowmen himself.

He thought to himself, *Who could be making snowmen in these empty mountains? It's been two days since I've seen a child.*

Worried about the threat of being strafed by U.S. aircraft, Lichan's driver stopped the car, and the Chinese colonel got out. He emerged in the midst of a cluster of the figures. With a sickening shock, he realized he was surrounded by the dead; the snowmen were the corpses of his fallen comrades. He was ringed by a frozen army of the fallen— like the ancient terra-cotta armies of China's great emperors—that filled the icy hills and valleys of the reservoir.

"There's hundreds like this, maybe thousands," his Korean driver said tersely. "Some of them coolies, most of them soldiers." He added, "There'll be a dreadful stink round here next spring."

Epilogue

ON A BEAUTIFUL June day in 2004, a seventy-year-old man quietly shut the door on an amber, weather-beaten cab. A soft breeze swept over the neat lines of white headstones in Golden Gate Cemetery. The sun shone brightly and gently warmed his face as he walked between the stark rows of rectangular headstones, looking for a specific marker, his past. His eyes quickly scanned the area and fell upon the graying, etched stone of Robert H. Hallawell, killed in action, November 30, 1950, U.S. Marine Corps. The stone was weather beaten. The crumpled remains of a few leaves lay scattered around its edges. He was probably the grave's first visitor in many years.

Bobby, I'm here, Bruce Farr thought to himself. *Bobby, it's been a long time, but I'm finally here. I know you would have done this if I were in your place.*

The senior Marine then pulled out a camera from his bag and snapped a picture. He stood over the headstone for several minutes, gazing upon the cemetery and reflecting back fifty years to a war "that just won't go away." He remembered the bloody fight on East Hill.

Along with Hallawell, part of Farr has remained on the hill and will always stay there. The invisible scars of war, rather than fading, have grown deeper, and the memories more vivid.

Farr's circuitous journey by car, plane, and cab to visit Bobby Hallawell took four days. Months earlier, he had visited Hallawell's brother and returned Bobby's gold watch, which Mert GoodEagle had worn through the Vietnam War.

Farr's return by Greyhound bus was even more arduous. His wife and friends didn't understand. "Why would you travel four days just to get to California, take a picture for two minutes, and then leave?" they asked.

"It was just something I felt like I had to do. If you weren't there, you couldn't understand. There's no way you could understand war unless you were there. They were all my friends," he replied.

Exactly twenty-nine steps away in the same row, Farr visited another friend who died the same night, in the same battle: Ralph Whitney. Over the years, Farr and the other men of George Company have visited their friends. On November 10, 2010, the 235th birthday of the Marine Corps, the members of George Company will dedicate a monument in Quantico, Virginia, listing the 149 names of those forever-young members of George Company.★

Farr summed up his travels in a single sentence: "I went to tell them good-bye."

★ See Appendix E for a complete list of the fallen members of George Company.

AFTER CHOSIN

FOLLOWING the Chosin Reservoir campaign, George Company fought through the remainder of the Korean War and made several more epic stands. Although the war became increasingly unpopular with the American public, George Company's battle record throughout the balance of the war deserved recognition then and now. From 1951 to 1953, George Company fought in important battles with heroic tenacity, yet their story is more untold and unsung than their prior battles chronicled in this book. These stories deserve a separate treatment in their own volume. Nevertheless, this appendix attempts briefly to chronicle these heroic actions.

From Hungnam, George Company along with the First Marine Division sailed back to the port of Pusan. George Company and 3/1 headed to the strategic town of Masan for refitting, with orders to hold the town in the event of a Chinese breakthrough. The breakthrough never materialized, and George Company was sent north.

In January 1951, the Chinese launched their Third Phase Offensive, also known as the Chinese Winter Offensive. Overwhelmingly successful, the operation forced the Eighth Army to withdraw south. Seoul once again fell into North Korean hands.

During the fighting, Walton Walker, Commanding General of the Eighth Army, was killed in an automobile accident on December 23, 1950. The Army assigned airborne legend Lieutenant General Matthew Ridgeway to replace Walker, and Ridgeway's presence had an immediate, positive effect on the esprit de corps of the Eighth Army, stiffening their resolve.

The Chinese and North Korean offensive petered out near the strategic South Korean town of Wonju. The armies had overrun their supply lines, which stretched all the way back to the Manchurian border. After holding at the centrally located town of Wonju, Ridgeway counterattacked in a series of operations and also halted another Chinese offensive.

After initially hunting guerrillas for the first two months of 1951, George Company took part in Ridgeway's counteroffensive, including Operation Killer. The company traveled by truck to Wonju. Tom Powers recalled the arduous journey:

> On February 21, 1951, we jumped off on Operation Killer. It was raining very hard, so hard that many of the trucks and tanks that would be used in the assault were bogged down in the mud. In the tradition of the Corps, the troops were served steak and eggs before jumping off. It was raining so hard my steak and eggs were floating around in my mess kit.

The men of George Company fought on several hills, including Hill 303, and suffered numerous casualties. The First Marine Division pushed north toward the 38th Parallel. Operation Killer reoccupied territory south of the Han River and also the strategic town of

Hoengseong. The living conditions for the men of George Company were miserable, as Powers explained:

> Operation Killer ended in March, but from February to March, it was wet and cold—bone-chilling wet and cold. One night when George Company was in reserve, we holed up in a barn. Well, the roof leaked, and I was right under one of those leaks. During the night, the leak got so bad I was in water up to my waist, my teeth were chattering, and it was so miserable, I started to cry. The next day, not one man in the area who heard me said a word to embarrass me. I know they all knew how I felt that night. We all knew what the next guy's misery was because it was ours.

On March 7, the Eighth Army attacked in Operation Ripper, clearing Seoul for the fourth time.

On April 11, 1951, President Truman relieved General MacArthur as the Supreme Commander in Korea for a variety of reasons. MacArthur's dismissal became the subject of Congressional hearings, generating a political firestorm at home.

With 700,000 troops, the Chinese once again counterattacked in April 1951 with the Fifth Phase Offensive (also known as the Chinese Spring Offensive). Their goal was to drive UN forces into the sea. Initially in a reserve position, the First Marines rushed forward to plug holes in the front lines.

With the Chinese offensive in full swing, the Sixth ROK Division collapsed on the left flank of the Marines around midnight on April 22. George Company received orders to take and hold Hill 902, which guarded the approaches to the strategic Mojin Bridge. Machine gunner Bob Harbula recalled how elements of the South Korean Army retreated in chaos: "We had a rough time getting through the ROK Army as they were hightailing it, trying to get away from the Chinese that attacked their positions. This left the First Division's left flank wide open. We threatened to shoot them if they didn't get out of our way."

The hill had to be held at all costs to block the offensive and allow friendly forces, including the Fifth and Seventh Marines, to withdraw across the bridge. George Company was involved in a footrace to beat the Chinese to the top of the strategically important Hill 902. Harbula remembered:

> The climb to the top of 902 was a steep several miles, and we were loaded down with extra ammo. It was a grueling climb. Most of the men had emptied their canteens on the way up. Officers and NCOs prodded their men to keep moving. Many had started to fall out. We were told that resupply of ammo and water would be a big problem.

George Company's Third Platoon was in the eye of the storm. Gunnery Sergeant Harold "Speedy" Wilson held his platoon together through the massive oncoming Chinese assault. His actions helped blunt the Chinese attack on the hill.

For his stand on Hill 902, Harold "Speedy" Wilson was awarded the Medal of Honor (see appendix C).

Harbula reflected on the flow of the battle:

> I wasn't on the top when the Chinese first attacked. All the action was on the crest and a saddle that connected it to another hill to the north. I pulled one of my machine gun squads from a quiet area and reinforced the crest where the action was. When I got to the top, it was a madhouse of activity. Corpsmen were helping the wounded, and riflemen from other quiet areas were being fed into position. We knew the Chinese would be back. When the Chinese attacked again, I was amazed at the firepower we hit them with. Four machine guns, mortars, and artillery were really pouring it on. Dead Chinese were all over the hill. We stopped them cold in the saddle. After the second attack, we were told to break

off action and get back across the river with the rest of the division. We were all dying of thirst, and seeing the river down below only made us thirstier.

Withdrawing from the hill became almost as difficult as fighting on top of it. As Powers remembered:

We saw three [U.S.] Corsairs coming right at us. They shot their 20 mm cannon. The man in front of me was killed. Smoke was coming out of his chest from the round. The planes began to then turn. Everyone shouted "Napalm!" We knew what was next—they were going to spray us with napalm. We shouted for the guy in front of us to pull out his marker panels from one of the back-packs. He did just in the nick of time as the planes began making their napalm run.

By the end of May, the Chinese had suffered a decisive defeat in their Spring Offensive. With their offensive in ruins and North Korea once again in jeopardy, on June 23, 1951, the Soviet Union proposed peace talks. It was largely a ruse to buy time for the badly mauled Communist forces to consolidate their position. Nevertheless, the Chinese also used the peace talks as a propaganda victory.

Sometime around September 1951, after the peace talks had stalled and the Communist forces had strengthened their lines, PFC (who was in fact an acting corporal and fire team leader) Richard Williams recalls seizing a long-forgotten objective known as Hill 751.

We had just taken the objective. My fire team was the lookout. We were up front making sure they wouldn't surprise us with a counterattack. Some Marines as they passed by us yelled, 'Lieutenant wants to see you.' So I took my fire team and moved toward the lieutenant. As he started talking to me, I was watching the scout. All of the sudden, they opened up with machine guns and rifle fire. As I was getting back to our positions for cover, we were moving up a 75 mm recoilless rifle. Mortars screamed in and destroyed the 75. There were a lot of us bunched up in one spot. As the lieutenant walked over, I remember looking up at him. I think he was about to say, 'You're all bunched up.' Another mortar came down. As I came to, he was dead, along with another man. I was knocked silly, and my head was ringing. I was crawling on my hands and knees and found other wounded men. Me and several of the other men brought the wounded back down the hill. We made two or three trips.

The Eighth Army once again launched a counterattack, driving deeper north. They pushed past the 38th Parallel and established Line Kansas. Along this line, George Company would man strategic outposts along with other UN forces. Little territory would be exchanged in a stalemate that would last until 1953. The line was known as the MLR or "Main Line of Resistance."

Rifleman Peter A. Beauchamp recalled a raid along the MLR during a period known as the "Outpost War":

One evening, the squad I was in was told to go out to no-man's-land in front of the lines, to meet up and support another platoon to carry out a raid on a North Korean position. Prior to reaching the platoon, we decided to leave our parkas in a pass in no-man's-land, although the snow was about knee deep, because the parkas were cumbersome. We would pick them up on our way back to our positions after the raid.

When we reached the platoon we were to support, the Platoon Leader was on the radio, asking permission to abort the mission, as they had gone up the wrong hill, and now the North Koreans were on the alert. Permission was denied, and we were to carry out the mission. Our squad was at the rear of the column as we proceeded up the hill. As we advanced, the North Koreans opened up with machine guns, mortars, and grenades. The word came down to return to our own lines. I don't know if there were any casualties. The mission was aborted.

When our squad reached the pass where we had left our parkas, North Koreans opened up with burp gun fire. Since we couldn't see where they were firing from, we couldn't return fire. We decided to leave the parkas where they lay, and return to our lines. A head count was made as we went through the gate in the barbed wire fence. Behind us were some North Korean soldiers spraying our lines with burp gun fire. Luckily no one was hit.

They retrieved the parkas without incident the next day.

Throughout this period of countless raids, men and officers shipped in and out of George Company. One such officer was Second Lieutenant Bing Bingham, who would later rise to the rank of colonel. When asked his most vivid memory of the time, Bingham said, "I was a green second lieutenant, brand new, and placed in command of a rifle platoon. Men who had survived Hill 902 and other operations accepted me." Bingham successfully led his platoon through several months of combat on the MLR.

The war dragged on in stalemated positions for over a year and a half. Men continued to die on both sides. By June 1953, the Chinese were once again ready to accept the terms of an armistice proposed by the UN. Nevertheless, they were determined to gain several key strategic positions that would give them greater negotiating power at the peace table and further provide easy access across the Imjin River and a thoroughfare to Seoul. Known as Boulder City, this key terrain became the focus of the Chinese Army and would be the last battle on the last day of the Korean War. Once again, George Company would be vastly outnumbered, perhaps ten to one, and once again would make an epic, unsung stand.

For weeks there had been talk of an armistice. Unlike during World War I, when the German army gave ground days before the armistice and even the day of the armistice, the Marines of First Division and George Company wouldn't yield. On the night of July 24, the Chinese hit Boulder City and Hill 111 with one of the largest artillery bombardments of the war. Tens of thousands of shells hit George Company, and thousands of Chinese soldiers assaulted the company, as Corporal Harvey Dethloff, who was manning a .50 caliber machine gun in the apex of the attack, remembered:

> The big stuff came in. A rocket round hit the corner of my .50, bending it and making it useless. They started coming over the wall from all directions. There's quite a difference between a company and a regiment, like 20 to 1 odds. They came right in under their own artillery fire. As we scrambled out of the bunker, I remember there was a flamethrower left there from a previous outfit. I picked it up. I couldn't get the striker to work. I aimed the flamethrower down the trench, and the whole trench lit up. The trench was loaded with concertina wire, and the Chinese were climbing through it. As I was about to fire another jet of flame, a concussion grenade exploded, rendering my right arm useless and blowing the hose off the flamethrower tank. Luckily, the flamethrower didn't explode on my back.
>
> It was completely dark as I scrambled down the trench. There were boxes of grenades embedded in the trench wall. After groping around for a few minutes, my hand found a box. As I was stumbling backwards down the trench, I was throwing grenades with my left arm and pulling the pin out with my teeth. Your teeth aren't meant to pull grenade pins out; they're not made

that way. I later lost all my teeth after the war because they became so loosened. As I stumbled down the trench, I kept throwing grenades at the Chinese with my left arm as they fired at me. I emptied the entire box and somehow found a second box. I heard a mortar come flying in right over my head. It detonated on top of me and blew me backward down the trench line. I don't know how I survived, but it broke my leg. I was dragging one leg and crawling down the trench on one elbow.

After throwing more grenades at targets and over the side of the cliff, all I had left was a .45 with five rounds of ammunition. There was a left turn or intersection in the trench line. I crawled down it. I found a first aid bunker that had two rooms filled. I couldn't get into the back room because it was so filled with dying men. The corpsmen were so busy tending to the wounded that I didn't bother them. I could hear the Chinese climbing over the top of the bunker, but for some reason they never threw in grenades, which they normally did. I used a belt and my bayonet as a tourniquet, and I kept my .45 at the ready in the event the Chinese hit the bunker.

On July 27, 1953, the armistice was signed, and Corporal Dethloff would be transported to the United States, on his back, all the way to Great Lakes Naval Training Center. He was awarded the Silver Star for his actions.

George Company had made the last great stand in the last battle of the Korean War. If the Korean War is a forgotten war, Boulder City is its forgotten battle. When the war ended on July 27, 1953, only 25 percent of George Company would make the muster call. That day marked the single greatest loss of life of any battle for the company. Twenty-four men, roughly every ninth man in the company, were killed. Thousands of Chinese bodies covered the ground around Boulder City and 3/1's position.

During the Korean War George Company took on the brunt of elements of an enemy regiment (Seoul, Task Force Drysdale, East Hill, Hill 902, and Boulder City). They stood tall on each occasion. The North Koreans and their allies would never have come to the peace table if it had not been for the forgotten stands of men from George Company and thousands of other Americans and Koreans.

The war consumed over a million North Koreans and their Chinese allies and left over 36,000 Americans dead. The war would end not with a peace treaty but with an armistice. On March 27, 2009, North Korea officially withdrew from the armistice and continues to pose a threat to the world.

THEN AND NOW

James Beeler—leader of Second Platoon. Beeler, a charismatic and athletic former all-American football standout, was killed in action.

Jim Byrne—rifleman, First Platoon; member of the second replacement draft. Bryne started a family and became a successful high school teacher and historian who painstakingly preserved George Company's history over the years.

Jesus Roberto "Bob" Camarillo—After serving in Vietnam, Camarillo later became a Los Angles County Deputy Sheriff and continued his education. He earned a PhD in criminal justice, a subject that he then taught. He has since retired.

Richard Carey—commanding officer of First Platoon. Now a retired lieutenant general of the Marine Corps, Carey currently teaches Sunday School and has a family. He is actively involved in helping veterans returning from Afghanistan and Iraq deal with post-traumatic stress disorder and other issues.

Jack Daniels—ammo bearer and later machine gunner, Third Platoon. After the war, Daniels started a family and currently resides near his ancestral home in South Carolina.

Douglas Drysdale—colonel and intrepid commander of 41 Commando, which led Task Force Drysdale. Under his daring and heroic leadership, the operation of Task Force Drysdale was a remarkable success.

Orace Edwards—rifleman, First Platoon. Edwards first worked at the Lone Star Arsenal after returning from Korea. He later earned his mechanical engineering degree and worked for a number of different companies as an engineer. He raised a family, sang with a gospel quartet, and continues to be active in his church.

Tom Enos—machine gunner, Second Platoon, later moved to First Platoon. Enos started a family and a successful engineering business after the war.

Bruce Farr—ammo bearer and later machine gunner, First Platoon. After being wounded in 1951, Farr returned to Tennessee, where he started a family, worked for the state, and later became an independent contractor. He spent many years reuniting the members of George Company and honoring the fallen. He also maintains contact with current members of 3/1, believing firmly, as he so perfectly expressed it, that their experiences are "interconnected."

Sergeant Garcia—third machine gun section, Third Platoon.

Mert GoodEagle—ammo bearer, First Platoon. GoodEagle remained in the Marine Corps, retiring as sergeant major. He fought in Vietnam and carried Bobby Hallowell's watch through that war. He later started a family in Oklahoma; he was the only member of George Company to actively seek his "warrior's feather." He died in 2008.

Ed Green—ammo bearer in the machine gun section attached to First Platoon.

Bob Harbula—ammo bearer and later machine gunner, First Platoon. Harbula honorably served in the Marine Corps in several of George Company's major actions, including 902. After the war, he returned to Pittsburgh, had a family, briefly worked for the railroad, and later founded a highly successful business in which he helped change countless lives.

Jimmy Harrison—member of the forward observer team. Harrison, the most "southern" member of his unit, was killed in action.

Fred and E. C. Hems—Fred retired from the Marine Corps, had a successful career, and started a family in Bristol, Pennsylvania. His twin brother, E. C., stayed in the military.

Clark Henry—sergeant, forward observer team. Henry retired as a colonel of the U.S. Marine Corps. He started a family in the San Francisco area. He is actively involved in the lives of 3/1's modern Marines who have gone to Afghanistan and Iraq. He is also writing mystery and adventure novels.

Dick Hock—rifleman, First Platoon. Following months of agonizing surgeries, Hock recovered from his wounds and resettled in Milwaukee, Wisconsin, where he started a family and his own plumbing contracting business. He's currently battling cancer and winning. "I've seen much worse," he says.

Spencer Jarrnigan—leader of Third Platoon. Red-headed Jarrnigan was killed in action.

Douglas MacArthur—general and commander of UN and American forces during 1950 and the early part of 1951. He was relieved of command by President Harry Truman on April 11, 1951. MacArthur arrived home to a hero's welcome, and his dismissal led to a Congressional investigation spearheaded by the Republican Party. He died in 1964.

John N. McLaughlin—colonel. McLaughlin survived Chinese captivity and retired as a lieutenant general. He later inspired his nephew Colonel Preston McLaughlin to become a Marine. Preston now serves as chief of staff of a Marine brigade in Afghanistan.

Frank McNeive—assistant squad leader, First Platoon. A private first-class, McNeive became assistant squad leader. He later served as a first sergeant during the Battle of Khe Sanh in the Vietnam War. He retired as a sergeant major and raised a family.

Mao Tse-tung—ruthless leader of Communist China until his death in 1976. His revolutionary ideas forever changed China and modern warfare. He was responsible for the suffering and death of millions of Chinese citizens.

Red Nash—assistant machine gunner, third machine gun section, Third Platoon.

Steve Olmstead—rifleman, First Platoon. Olmstead rose through the ranks from private and retired from the Corps as a lieutenant general. Currently, he's actively involved with various nonprofit organizations.

John Partridge—lieutenant colonel and legendary Marine engineer. Partridge worked miracles at Hagaru's airfield and later bridged the Funchilin Pass. He retired from the Corps as a colonel in 1965 and died in 1987. Remarkably, he was awarded only the Bronze Star for his extraordinary efforts.

Peng Dehuai—leader of all Chinese forces in Korea. He fell out of favor with Mao after criticizing his policies. He was publicly humiliated and brutally tortured on Mao Tse-tung's orders during the Cultural Revolution. He was nearly killed, but ultimately survived. He died of cancer in 1974. In 1978, four years after his death and Mao's, the Chinese communist government finally cleared Peng and exonerated him of all wrongdoing.

Tom Powers—ammo bearer and later machine gunner, Third Platoon. Powers remained one of the lowest-ranking members of Third Platoon because his rap sheet was "longer than Jesse James's." A retired police officer, Powers later became an active member of the George Company Association. He is actively pursuing the matter of Zullo's Medal of Honor. After writing a letter recommending Zullo for the Medal of Honor and reading it to other members of George Company, Powers was so moved that he openly wept.

Chesty Puller—First Marine commanding officer. Puller later became the assistant commander of First Marine division. He rose to the rank of lieutenant general and received an astounding total of five Navy Crosses. He died in 1971.

Harrell Roberts—reservist from Savannah, Georgia; rifleman, First Platoon. Roberts started a family in his home state of Georgia. He worked for the state of Georgia and was responsible for the design of various roads, bridges, and other infrastructure projects. He is currently president of the George Company Association.

Carl Sitter—George Company's second commanding officer, who led them to victory. Sitter retired from the Marine Corps as a colonel. He was awarded the Medal of Honor for his actions with Task Force Drysdale and on East Hill. He eventually became an ordained minister. He died in 2000.

Oliver P. Smith—commanding general of First Marine division. Smith was promoted to lieutenant general in 1953 and retired in 1955 at the honorary grade of four-star general. He died in 1977.

Gerald Tillman—sergeant, First Platoon. Known as the "ultimate Confederate warrior" and Lieutenant Carey's right-hand man, Tillman was killed in action.

George Westover—captain, the original commander of George Company. Westover later retired from the Marine Corps and started a family. He happily remarried at the tender age of 90.

Harold "Speedy" Wilson—legendary non-commissioned officer in Third Platoon. Wilson later received the Medal of Honor for his heroic actions on Hill 902 in the spring of 1951.

Ron Wyman—Wyman started a family and retired from the Marine Corps as a sergeant major.

Rocco Zullo—first sergeant and the heart and soul of George Company. After spending years in military hospitals and undergoing countless operations, Zullo lost track of George Company. Nearly every Marine thought he was dead. While recovering on an operating room table, Zullo met the love of his life and his future wife, whom he married during his recovery. Zullo retired from the Marine Corps and dedicated his life to the education of children. He dedicated his work to the man who was wounded and paralyzed from the waist down while administering first aid to Zullo during Taskforce Drysdale. Zullo later became a high school principal. During the Cuban Missile Crisis, Zullo sent a letter to the commandant of the Marine Corps and requested reinstatement. He did the same during the Vietnam War. At the age of 92 years young, Zullo still loves the men of George Company and the Marine Corps. And the men of George Company, as well as the author, firmly believe he deserves the Medal of Honor for his actions at the Chosin Reservoir.

Appendix C

CITATIONS

The President of the United States takes pleasure in presenting the
MEDAL OF HONOR to

CAPTAIN CARL L. SITTER
UNITED STATES MARINE CORPS

For service as set forth in the following CITATION:

For conspicuous gallantry and intrepidity at the risk of his life above and beyond the call of duty as Commanding Officer of Company G, Third Battalion, First Marines, First Marine Division (Reinforced), in action against enemy aggressor forces at Hagaru-ri, Korea, on 29 and November 30, 1950. Ordered to break through enemy-infested territory to reinforce his Battalion the early morning of November 29, Captain Sitter continuously exposed himself to enemy fire as he led his company forward and, despite twenty-five percent casualties suffered in the furious action, succeeded in driving through to his objective. Assuming the responsibility of attempting to seize and occupy a strategic area occupied by a hostile force of regiment strength deeply entrenched on a snow-covered hill commanding the entire valley southeast of the town, as well as the line of march of friendly troops withdrawing to the south, he reorganized his depleted units the following morning and boldly led them up the steep, frozen hillside under blistering fire, encouraging and redeploying his troops as casualties occurred and directing forward platoons as they continued the drive to the top of the ridge. During the night when a vastly outnumbering enemy launched a sudden, vicious counterattack, setting the hill ablaze with mortar, machine-gun, and automatic weapons fire and taking a heavy toll in troops, Captain Sitter visited each foxhole and gun position, coolly deploying and integrating reinforcing units consisting of service personnel unfamiliar with infantry tactics into a coordinated combat team and instilling in every man the will and determination to hold his position at all costs. With the enemy penetrating his lines in repeated counterattacks which often required hand-to-hand combat and, on one occasion infiltrating to the command post with hand grenades, he fought gallantly with his men in repulsing and killing the fanatic attackers in each encounter. Painfully wounded in the face, arms and chest by bursting grenades, he staunchly refused to be evacuated and continued to fight on until a successful defense of the area was assured with a loss to the enemy of more than fifty percent dead, wounded and captured. His valiant leadership, superb tactics and great personal valor throughout thirty-six hours of bitter combat reflect the highest credit upon Captain Sitter, and the United States Naval Service.

/S/ HARRY S TRUMAN

The President of the United States takes pleasure in presenting the
MEDAL OF HONOR *to*

PRIVATE FIRST CLASS WILLIAM B. BAUGH
UNITED STATES MARINE CORPS

For service as set forth in the following CITATION:

For conspicuous gallantry and intrepidity at the risk of his life above and beyond the call of duty while serving as a member of an Anti-Tank Assault Squad attached to Company G, Third Battalion, First Marines, First Marine Division (Reinforced), during a nighttime enemy attack against a motorized column en route from Koto-Ri to Hagaru-ri, Korea, on November 29, 1950. Acting instantly when a hostile grenade landed in his truck as he and his squad prepared to alight and assist in the repulse of an enemy force delivering intense automatic-weapons and grenade fire from deeply entrenched and well-concealed roadside positions, Private First Class Baugh quickly shouted a warning to the other men in the vehicle and, unmindful of his own personal safety, hurled himself upon the deadly missile, thereby saving his comrades from serious injury or possible death. Sustaining severe wounds from which he died a short time afterward, Private First Class Baugh, by his superb courage and valiant spirit of self-sacrifice, upheld the highest traditions of the United States Naval Service. He gallantly gave his life for his country.

/S/ HARRY S TRUMAN

The President of the United States takes pleasure in presenting the
MEDAL OF HONOR to

TECHNICAL SERGEANT HAROLD E. WILSON
UNITED STATES MARINE CORPS

For service as set forth in the following CITATION:

For conspicuous gallantry and intrepidity at the risk of his life above and beyond the call of duty while serving as Platoon Sergeant of a Rifle Platoon attached to Company G, Third Battalion, First Marines, First Marine Division (Reinforced), in action against enemy aggressor forces in Korea on the night of 23–24 April 1951. When the company outpost was overrun by the enemy while his platoon, firing from hastily-constructed foxholes, was engaged in resisting the brunt of a fierce mortar, machine-gun, grenade and small-arms attack launched by hostile forces from high ground under cover of darkness, Technical Sergeant Wilson braved intense fire to assist the survivors back into the line and to direct the treatment of casualties. Although twice wounded by gunfire, in the right arm and the left leg, he refused medical aid for himself and continued to move about among his men, shouting words of encouragement. After receiving further wounds in the head and shoulder as the attack increased in intensity, he again insisted upon remaining with his unit. Unable to use either arm to fire, and with mounting casualties among our forces, he resupplied his men with rifles and ammunition taken from the wounded. Personally reporting to his company commander on several occasions, he requested and received additional assistance when the enemy attack became even more fierce and, after placing the reinforcements in strategic positions in the line, directed effective fire until blown off his feet by the bursting of a hostile mortar round in his face. Dazed and suffering from concussion, he still refused medical aid and, despite weakness from loss of blood, moved from foxhole to foxhole, directing fire, resupplying ammunition, rendering first aid and encouraging his men. By his heroic actions in the face of almost certain death, when the unit's ability to hold the disadvantageous position was doubtful, he instilled confidence in his troops, inspiring them to rally repeatedly and turn back the furious assaults. At dawn, after the final attack had been repulsed, he personally accounted for each man in his platoon before walking unassisted one-half mile to the aid station where he submitted to treatment. His outstanding courage, initiative and skilled leadership in the face of overwhelming odds were contributing factors in the success of his company's mission and reflect the highest credit upon Technical Sergeant Wilson and the United States Naval Service.

/S/ HARRY S TRUMAN

Appendix D

LETTER TO
DAVID DOUGLAS DUNCAN

✦

Thomas J. Powers

June 15, 1987

Mr. David Douglas Duncan
France

Dear Mr. Duncan:
The enclosed picture taken in Korea, Chosin Res. Area in 1950, is a picture of my Machine Gun Squad. The first man is my Sqd. Leader Sgt. Garcia, the second is me Pfc Thomas J. Powers, the third is Cpl. Fred Hems. The rest of the men are unknown to me.

If possible, send me a copy of the picture and the date it was taken. I think it was Dec. 10 or 11, 1950.

I was a machine gunner in G/3/1 from August, 1950 to May, 1951. You took a lot of pictures of my company, one of a guy eating a can of beans which was on the cover of "Life". My Company Commander, Capt. (Col.) Carl Sitter got the Medal of Honor.

I don't know if you are aware of an Organization now called the "Chosin Few", but I am sure they would like to be able to get in touch with you.

If there is any cost for the pictures please let me know and I will send it to you right away. Also, if I could get a copy of the Life Magazine from the time of the Chosin Res., please let me know who to contact.

Respectfully yours,
Thomas J. Powers

Appendix E

THE FALLEN MEMBERS OF
GEORGE COMPANY, 1950–1953

Cpl Edward C. Anderson   07-25-53
Sgt Homer V. H. Anderson   04-17-53
Pfc Milton A. Anderson   07-26-53
Pfc Joaquin A. Armenta   07-26-53
Pfc James L. Ashbrook   07-24-53
Pfc Ralph E. Ball   11-02-50
Pfc Robert C. Barnhart   07-25-53
Cpl Albert P. Barnes, Jr.   09-15-50
Pfc William C. Barr   09-25-50
Pfc Thomas G. Barrett   07-25-53
Pfc William B. Baugh, Moh   11-29-50
Pvt Herbert L. Bazley   07-25-53
Pfc Donald Beam   07-25-53
2ndLt James D. Beeler   11-02-50
Pfc Ralph L. Bernhardt   07-25-53
Pfc Leo E. Bever   07-25-53
Sgt William Binaxas   09-21-50

Pfc Theodore F. Binette   07-25-53
Pvt Paul Blevins   09-25-50
Pfc Edward J. Boglin   07-25-53
T/Sgt Walter C. Borawski   01-13-53
Cpl Raymond T. Bowers   11-29-50
Pvt Warren Bowling   11-30-50
Cpl Kenneth E. Brady   09-25-50
Cpl Oscar M. Brown   07-25-53
Pfc Jerry R. Bryant   04-05-52
Pfc Glenn H. Byrd   03-11-51
Pfc Froilan Cabrera-Gonzalez   04-17-53
Pfc Joseph E. Caruso   04-24-51
Pfc Gerald E. Charlesworth   07-25-53
Pfc Robinson Chase   07-25-53
Pfc Stanley J. Checki   03-07-51
Pfc Terrill O. Coats   07-25-53
Pfc Harlan R. Cockerman   07-25-53
Pfc Donald R. Comtois   07-25-53
Pfc James L. Cook   07-25-53
Pfc John E. Corbett   05-03-53
Pfc Victor Cordes, III   03-18-53
Pfc Clifton C. Cotton   03-21-53
Pfc John W. Cron   03-11-51
Pfc John Cupryna   07-25-53
Pfc Daniel J. Dalier   11-29-50
Pfc Arthur L. Danzer   04-24-51
Pfc John R. Davis   04-24-51
Pfc Robert T. Davis   09-25-50
Cpl George Debaun, Jr.   07-25-53
Pfc James J. Devlin   03-29-53
Pfc Paul N. Devries 04-24-51
Cpl Paul A. Dixon   07-25-53
Pfc Eugene E. Dodge   07-25-53
Pfc Ray E. Dowler   12-16-52
Pfc John M. Drake, Jr.   07-15-53

Pfc William C. Driskill   11-29-50
Pfc Thomas J. Dunne   04-24-51
Sgt Donel F. Earnest   03-25-53
Pfc Edward E. Eccleston   09-15-51
Pfc Patrick J. Edmunds   07-24-53
Pfc Frank Emanuel, Jr.   09-15-50
Cpl Donald R. Fahrenholz   03-19-53
Pfc Erich R. Fichter   07-26-53
T/Sgt Christian P. Gaaei, Jr.   03-02-51
Pfc Francis C. Gall   11-02-50
Pfc James C. Gilchrist   07-25-53
Pfc Timothy J. Gilmore   07-23-53
Cpl Ignacio S. Gonzalez   07-03-51
Pfc William J. Greene, Jr.   11-30-50
Cpl Orville R. Haber   09-21-50
Pfc Howard J. Hahn   03-19-53
Pfc Robert H. Hallawell   11-30-50
Pfc Willie Hamilton   07-26-53
Pfc Hugo Hammond   11-02-50
Pfc Lloyd W. Hamon   09-21-50
S/Sgt Cornelius F. Harney   09-01-52
Sgt Frank L. Harris   08-31-52
Pfc Jimmie H. Harrison   11-29-50
Cpl Donald J. Henderson   03-03-51
Pfc Lawrence J. Hengy   09-15-51
2ndLt Robert G. Herlihy   07-26-53
Cpl Wayne R. Hill   07-24-53
Cpl Paul J. Himmels   07-25-53
Cpl Allan B. Hoagland   11-29-50
Pfc Charles E. Horn   11-19-52
Pfc Robert J. Hunt   06-06-51
Pfc Kenneth R. Ingman   06-06-51
Pfc Jackie D. Jackman   07-25-53
Pfc William R. James   04-24-51
Sgt Otto C. Jannusch   09-21-50

2ndLt Spencer H. Jarnagin   09-21-50
Cpl Charles B. Johnson   07-25-53
Pfc Robert W. Johnson   09-15-51
Pfc Marvin H. Joliff   07-25-53
Pfc Joseph H.H. Jones   07-25-53
Pfc Roland T. Keesee   09-26-50
Pfc James E. Kimball   03-25-53
Cpl Donald F. Kolb   06-06-51
Pfc Fabian T. Kotara   11-29-50
2ndLt Jered Krohn   09-15-51
2ndLt John J. Leonhard   07-24-53
Pfc John A. Lewchuck   09-15-51
Sgt Gene F. Lilly   09-25-50
2ndLt John E. Lindseth   06-06-51
Pfc James L. Mandrean, Jr.   09-25-50
Pfc William R. Manning   11-30-50
Pfc Amar D. Marks   03-05-51
Pfc Richard W. Marson   09-15-51
Pfc Ray A. McClaskey   09-11-52
2ndLt John J. McCoy, Jr.   04-17-53
Sgt Richard E. McCune   10-23-51
Sgt Dale A. McGregor   11-29-50
Pfc Merlin F. McKeever   08-31-52
Pfc Cecil G. Mellinger   03-19-53
Pfc Jose H. Mercado   03-19-53
Pfc Harry R. Miles   09-18-50
Pfc Ralph J. Murphy   09-15-50
Pfc Tom W. Naney   03-11-51
Pfc William E. Nash, III   12-11-50
Pfc Charles R. Norment   06-13-51
Pfc Walter M. Norris, Jr.   04-24-51
Pfc Norman P. North   09-23-50
Pfc James T. Pickett   11-30-50
Pfc Keith M. Porter   10-03-51
Pfc James R. Quillen   10-23-51

Pfc Lindy J. Raphiel   03-02-51
Pfc Allen E. Rasmussen   11-29-50
Pfc Hugh I. Redmon   11-02-50
Pfc Joseph J. Rice   11-30-50
Pfc Victor M. Rivera Diaz   11-24-52
Pfc Ralph V. Rodgers   11-02-50
Pfc Samuel S. Sage   11-29-50
Sgt Walter L. Seivers, Jr.   09-13-51
Pfc Clayton D. Sepulvado   03-03-51
Pfc Roy E. Shirey, Jr.   11-02-50
Pfc Jack H. Shramek   09-21-50
Cpl Thomas C. Silva   01-29-52
Pfc David F. P. Stapleton   09-15-51
Pfc Leroy G. Storey   11-30-50
Pfc Byron C. Teel   09-21-50
S/Sgt Gerald D. Tillman   11-29-50
Cpl Leroy Waskiewicz   09-25-50
Pfc Paul Weber, Jr.   04-24-51
Cpl Melvin Weiss   08-18-52
Sgt Leslie W. Westberry   06-02-51
Pfc Ralph H. Whitney, Jr.   11-29-50
Sgt Edward H. Whittaker   09-25-50
Pfc Donald R. Williams   11-29-50
T/Sgt Isaac C. Williams, Jr.   06-06-51
Sgt Tommie J. Williams   11-30-50
Pfc Thomas Woolcocks   11-30-50
Pfc Lawrence J. Zinner   09-25-50

ACKNOWLEDGMENTS

I'D LIKE TO THANK my agent and friend Andrew Zack for standing by me and also for his countless editorial suggestions and ideas—everything from the subtitle to rewriting the flap copy on the jacket. To my friends: Ben Ibach, for his numerous ideas and keen eye as well as creative mind; Madison Parker, for her editorial comments and spending hours of her free time helping me with this project, and for her unconditional generosity and friendship; David Mindock, for his keen mind and encouragement; Charles "DeGaulle" Severance, for always checking in on me and just plain old caring; and Michael Heffner for his historian's mind and keen eye. To Theana Kastens for reading and making suggestions to the manuscript, and my friends Chris Butsavage and Brian Fitzpatrick. To Cyndy Harvey for her editorial comments, advice, and other input on the manuscript.

To the staff at Da Capo Press, including the best publicist any author could have, Lissa Warren.

To the men of George Company who opened up their hearts to me and their memories, many of them painful and never told until now. In particular, I'd like to thank Clark Henry, Tom Powers, Bob Harbula, Dick Hock, Bruce Farr, Rocco Zullo, Lieutenant General Richard Carey, Fred Hems, Harrell Roberts, Lieutenant General Steve Olmsted, and Bob Camarillo. Thanks also to the commanding officer of the Fifth Marines, Colonel Willard Buhl, former commander of 3/1, a fellow historian who had recognized and respected the heroic men of George Company and always treasured their participation with the current members of the Thundering Third and Fifth Marines. In addition, thanks to Colonel William Preston McLaughlin for his insight on Task Force Drysdale and his uncle's contribution.

Most importantly, I'd like to thank my editor and friend Robert Pigeon for the ability to capture the otherwise forgotten pieces of history and allowing us to honor the men of George Company. Bob's vision and guidance shaped this book from the beginning, and his peerless editorial skills and support brought this chapter of the forgotten war to life.

NOTES

ORAL HISTORIES

Shortly after I returned from Iraq in 2005, the men of George Company approached me and kindly invited me to their reunions. The heart of this book is based on over a hundred oral history interviews with the men of George Company. I attended their reunions, went to their homes, and interviewed them on the phone over a five-year period. I interviewed many of the men multiple times to establish the veracity of their accounts, and they were corroborated by the accounts of their fellow George Company Marines as well as the unit histories, command chronologies, other after-action reports, and other primary source materials.

The book initially focused on the machine gunners and on Rocco Zullo. It grew from there to include several key riflemen and other individuals. It is impossible to capture all the stories of this unit. Many of the unit's legendary figures have passed away, so through the eyes of these key people I hope to tell George Company's epic story.

Oral history is designated (**OH**).

PROLOGUE

2   "It was like heaven," . . . the war." (OH); Roberts

"Have you talked to Rocco Zullo . . . dead!" (OH); Quotes come from an interview with Zullo and numerous other veterans of George Company who believed Zullo was killed during the war. Some members of the panel who organized the reunion knew he was alive, but most members of George Company did not know he had survived the war.

3 "Get your fucking guinea ass up here . . . ammo!" (OH); Zullo and about a dozen George Company men who remember Zullo's bravery under fire. His bravery, in my opinion, and in the opinions of those I've interviewed who witnessed his actions, merits the Congressional Medal of Honor.

Christ! Chinese are all around, (OH)

4 We made it, he thought. (OH)

"Captain, what's our next move?" (OH)

"I can't find a pulse," (OH)

CHAPTER 1: THE "MINUTEMEN OF 1950"

5 "Minutemen of 1950." (Lynn Montross and Nicholas Canzona, *U.S. Marine Operations in Korea 1950–1953, Vol. II, The Inchon-Seoul Operation*, 25 (Washington, DC: Headquarters Marine Corps, 1955). This is the official Marine Corps History of the war and will be referred to as (Vol. II) or (Vol. III)).

"I don't give a shit . . . line!" (OH)

"You're next." (OH); I interviewed Tom Powers, Bruce Farr, and Bob Harbula over a period of many years. They all "fondly" recall their first encounter with the First Sergeant.

6 This guy is absolutely terrifying, (OH)

"MOS?" (OH)

"Wireman gunner." Zullo shot . . . now." (OH)

"I have three." . . . me." (OH)

". . . talk your ear off," . . . guns." (OH)

North Korean People's Army (NKPA) rumbled across . . . in three days. (Roy Appleman, *South to Naktong, North to the Yalu* 15 (College Station, TX: Texas A&M Press, 1990))

7 "Perhaps we could do something about a couple of tanks." (Joseph C. Goulden, *Korea: The Untold Story of the War*, 148 (New York: New York Times Books))

8 "making heads roll." (OH); (President Harry Truman, *Memoirs, Vol. II: Years of Trial and Hope, 1946–1952* (New York: Smithmark Publishers, 1996)

"dumb, spendthrift" brass in the military. (David McCullough, *Truman* (New York, Simon & Schuster, 1992)

"a police force for the Navy." (OH)

9 . . . Marine Corps General Lemuel Shepherd, "If I had the First Marine Division . . . the war." (OH); Shepherd; U.S. Marine Corps History and Museums Division.

Four hundred civilians immediately . . . tractors. (Vol. II, 31)

"We'll be used to plug holes . . . precedent," (Bill Sloan, *The Darkest Summer*, 92 (New York: Simon & Schuster, 2009); material is quoted from Craig's original hand-written notes.)

10 "We waited till he said 'go.' . . . Marine. McKenna (OH); nearly to a man, practically all the veterans I interviewed echoed the same opinion as McKenna; Zullo possessed unparalleled leadership skills and was one of the "greatest Marines" they had ever met.

"We all worked as youngsters," (Quotes and memories come primarily from my November 2007 interviews with Zullo and will be designated (OH) from here forward.)

"I love the Marine Corps . . . Marine," (OH)

11 "Roc, we need a heavyweight in the fight." (OH)

"How am I going to make weight?" . . . care of it." (OH)

"knocked the hell out of the heavyweight," (OH)

"Colonel, I heard the USS West Virginia . . . understand," (OH)

"the old man." (OH)

"We thought the Japanese were supermen . . . surrender." (OH)

12 'For God's sakes, be careful.'" (OH)

"Gunnery Sergeant, the lieutenant is dead." . . . Machine-gun fire," (OH)

"Every man for himself." . . . a unit." (OH)

"Remember, if you are the first sergeant . . . company." (OH)

"All the men were very sickly . . . friends." (OH)

13 "Every aperture on the cliff in front of us . . . "Follow me!" (OH)

"Stay right here," (OH)

"I put my large index finger in the wound . . . relieved." (OH)

In 1950, the regular Marine Corps, including George Company, was made up of a special breed of men, America's elite. (I have interviewed 3,000 veterans and written five books on the OSS airborne, Rangers, and special operations troops of WWII: *Beyond Valor; Into the Rising Sun; Operatives, Spies and Saboteurs; The Brenner Assignment;* and *They Dared Return*.)

14 "a summer camp." . . . all about," (OH)

"We found out real quickly . . . Marine," (OH)

"These guys don't know shit from Shinola," (OH)

"he would always spit out the right answer" . . . Marine at camp. (OH); Farr

15 I need a war. (OH)

16 "always together." (OH); nearly the entire group of men I interviewed recalled the Hems's unbreakable bond of brotherhood.

"I had been in and out of more brigs . . . devil within ya, boy." (OH)

"he was a great older brother," . . . to tease." (Red Nash's sister sent e-history to me.)

17 "Who do you want?" (OH); McNeive

"ultimate Confederate Warrior," . . . this guy." (OH); Carey

"We were all standing in a line . . . First Marines, 3/1.'" (OH)

18 "the worst training class . . . his words. (OH)

19 "people from all over the country," remembered one Marine, (OH)

"There was a little bit of rifle range training, but it was mostly just climbing hills." . . . rattlesnakes," (OH)

"Throughout this period, . . . United States," (OH)

"adjust their MOS" (OH)

Rap! Rap! (OH)

20 "suspended from his arms, almost holding them there," (OH)

"Tell the captain what you . . . policies." (OH); Westover fondly recalled the incident.

CHAPTER 2: THE GREAT GAMBLE

21 "deep resonance." (Vol. II, 46)

23 "The best that I can say is that Inchon is not impossible." (Max Hastings, *The Korean War*, 101 (New York: Simon & Schuster, 1987))

"Admiral, in all my years of military service . . . in its operations." MacArthur's remarks are largely drawn from his autobiography (Douglas A. MacArthur, *Reminiscences*, 347–351 (New York: McGraw-Hill, 1964) and Robert Debs Heinl, *Victory at High Tide: The Inchon-Seoul Campaign*, 40–43 (New York: J.B. Lippincott, 1968)). See also (Goulden, 195)

"It is plenty apparent that here in Asia . . . in Korea." (MacArthur, 350)

24 "The very arguments you have made . . . attempt." (Goulden, 195)

Pulling his corncob pipe out of his mouth . . . crush them." (Vol. II, 46)

"General, the Navy will get you to Inchon." (Hastings, 102)

CHAPTER 3: VOYAGE

25 "You know, Dick, I'm not gonna make it home." (OH); Carey

"Oh, come on. You're going to . . . come home," (OH)

26 "sickly looking" (OH); Several men, Hems in particular, recalled the automobile accident, which was confirmed by other men.

"I don't care what you say . . . trouble." (OH)

The men flocked around the seasoned NCOs. (OH)

"Being a machine gunner is yours to lose." (OH)

"Training was rigorous . . . the dark," (OH)

27 "Sometimes, they would throw . . . off," (OH)

The men learned every aspect of the light . . . GoodEagle. (OH); I spent several evenings interviewing Mert GoodEagle and some of the other machine gunners at the 2007 George Company Reunion at Quantico. The book has a heavy focus on the gunners as a result of the friendships I formed with those men. Sadly, Mr. Good-Eagle passed away a year after the reunion.

"Don't make any friends, because you're going to lose them." (OH)

28 "I tried to get the men in as good physical conditioning as possible," (OH)

"Many of the men picked on him," . . . Pyle," (OH); Farr

Sheets, blankets, soap . . . take." (OH)

"rice paddy liberty," (OH)

"We found a woman who was married . . . drinking." (OH)

29 Miraculously, every morning at reveille . . . hangover," (OH)

The forward observer team, recently detached from the Eleventh Marines, was an artillery unit organic to the First Marines. I have interviewed every surviving member of the forward observer team assigned to George Company. While memories fade with time, the men corroborated each other's stories. They all praised Clark Henry for his leadership and friendship, which has lasted over sixty years. *Give Me Tomorrow* is not so much a history of George Company as a unit, but a history of the friendships of the men of George Company and their exploits. These men tell the larger story of the company. I initially started with the machine gun section, which was also attached to George, and the story of Rocco Zullo. The story grew from the machine gun section and Zullo to riflemen and includes the forward observer team listed in the 3/1's task organization as "Ln Team & FO Party, 2dBn, 11th Marines" in (*3/1 Special Action Report*, November 22, 1950, Lt Col. Thomas L. Ridge, U.S. National Archives; hereafter SAR I).

Starting at the Solomon Islands, Henry fought . . . observer. (OH); I have a copy of his Purple Heart citation.

30 "You're not welcome in this bar." (OH)

"Where have you been?" (OH)

"These men were in a brawl with us," (OH)

31 The captain of the Japanese crew . . . radioman. (OH); Westover

The "brief for the Inchon landing was . . . one," (OH)

32 "completely lost it." (OH)

"Joe, you're the BAR-man now." (OH)

CHAPTER 4: INCHON

33 Smoke combined with . . . landing area. (OH); I interviewed scores of the men, and "manmade darkness" caused by the smoke came up several times. The epic nature of the panorama is seared in their minds and became the most vivid memory and opening scene for this chapter.

"Hey, they're shooting at us!" (OH)

"Keep your fucking head down!" (OH)

Tick! Tick! Tick! Tick! (OH)

A machine gun zeroed in on the LVT . . . recalled. (OH)

"How do I load my M1?" (OH); Powers recalled the scene.

34 "like a sphinx" (OH); McNeive

"Ready the ladders!" (OH)

"Bring up the cutters!" (OH)

Thud! A sniper round struck Barnes . . . (OH)

35 "This was a wake-up call," (OH)

"We were in a dangerous place . . . life." (OH)

Without hesitating, Lieutenant Carey . . . with the sergeant," (OH)

"The sniper's up in the stack!" (OH)

"They had us zero in . . . recalled Enos. (OH)

36 "Keep your head down! Keep your head down!" (OH)

"He [Garcia] was around . . . mother," (OH)

"well lubricated" . . . Jamison," (OH)

37 "spotted movement on top of Radio Hill." (OH)

"You sons-of-bitches, stop firing! . . . wounded," (OH)

After the friendly fire incident . . . First Platoon," (OH)

That night, George Company . . . in pain." (OH)

38 "everyone liked" (OH)

"I left one squad as a base of fire . . . to the right." (OH)

"The North Korean made a sudden move . . . Carey. (OH); I conducted dozens of oral history interviews with General Carey.

I just killed a man who was surrendering. (OH)

"The round I fired hit his pistol belt buckle . . . prisoners. (OH)

CHAPTER 5: TANK!

40 "I smelled the dead burning . . . forgetting." (OH)

41 "That Corsair never came out of . . . destroyed." (OH); Hock

The pilot of the plane, Captain William F. Simpson . . . the day. (Vol. II, 134)

"There were burnt bodies everywhere . . . burning," (OH)

The Marine tank column passed . . . bodies" (OH)

42 "Our M26 fired at point-blank . . . ear," (OH); Hock

"Why didn't he fire? I will never know . . . of us." (OH)

"The entire column fired, riddling . . . ditch. (OH)

"dirty look." (OH)

43 "Things were getting really hairy . . . beer can," (OH)

"Are those your short rounds?" . . . Korean rounds." (OH); Westover also remembers seeing Clark Henry, as does Fred Hems.

"They dropped a mortar between . . . bleeding. (OH); Hock

"Throw a grenade!" (OH)

44 "The man was absolutely fearless . . . mad at me," (OH)

"You better go over there . . . Sergeant." Powers (OH)

"He came over to the First Sergeant . . . kill me!" (OH)

"I don't mean to get vulgar . . . Zullo was there." (OH)

"Look who's coming up the road!" Dick Carey (OH)

"bullets flying around him." (OH)

"The general fell over" and . . . Lieutenant?" (OH)

"I'm just trying to keep you from . . . kill me." (OH)

CHAPTER 6: YONGDUNGPO

46 "Blood was all over the place . . . fifty years." (OH); confirmed by Banks.

"Our corpsman cut off her arm . . . tiny arm," (OH)

47 "If Yongdungpo is lost, Seoul will fall," (Vol. II, 205)

"The men didn't look menacing . . . ROKs." (OH)

"Go get Sergeant Binaxis!" . . . your rifles!" (OH)

48 Suddenly, with a flick of a wrist . . . seconds." (OH)

"Binaxis is KIA." Hock reflected . . . colorful." (OH)

"There was a dike on either side . . . attack," (OH)

49 "I saw the bullet take off half his face," (OH)

"mission, but what were we going to do? . . . to die." (OH); Hems

"Corpsman up!" (OH); Interviews with several men.

"Blood spots from the powder burns covered my face," (OH)

"I remember seeing the sticky, searing gas-jelly . . . bones." (OH)

50 "I couldn't raise George Westover [on the radio], and . . . no cover." (OH)

"I planned to make the attack with two squads forward . . . third squad," (OH)

"Fix bayonets!" Sergeant Tillman yelled . . . forever?" (OH); Hock

We're in serious trouble, (OH)

"I knew if we didn't move forward . . . the left," (OH)

"Move it! Move it" (OH)

"It could have been from the covering . . . sure." (OH)

Nevertheless, Tillman remained cool . . . been there." (OH)

51 "It was covered with maggots . . . again," recalled Hock. (OH)

The North Koreans were only yards away . . . enemy," (OH)

"Skipper, we found a brewery," . . . "Let's go." (OH)

"the clear measurement tubes on the side of the tanks." (OH); Westover

52 "It was warm and green," (OH)

"We wanted it. Warm, green beer—there was nothin' like it," (OH)

"we found a dead North Korean in one of the large vats," (OH)

"It seemed like we had shits for a week," (OH)

CHAPTER 7: SEOUL

53 Boom! Splash! (OH)

"Our DUKW operator moved the rudder back and forth to zigzag the vehicle, making . . ." (I interviewed Orace Edwards, who gave me his e-history. Portions of this quote and others in the book are derived from that e-mail, along with the oral history interview I conducted.)

54 After Inchon, Kim Il Song had heavily . . . Mao's army. (Vol. II, 233)

55 "As we were going up the rise in the field . . . lot of casualties. (OH)

56 "New was choking on his own blood . . . fire hydrant." (OH)

CHAPTER 8: URBAN HOLOCAUST

57 "Corpsman up! Corpsman up!" (OH)

"I couldn't save him! . . . "his best friend" (OH); several men recall this scene.

"a North Korean woman armed with a rifle . . . house," (OH)

58 "The medic just cracked up . . . hanging out," (OH)

"so thick you could see the bullets." (OH)

"As we were going up Ma Po Boulevard . . . name (OH)

He's a World War II vet . . . us. (OH)

"He had just saved my life . . . painful," (OH)

59 "Are you hit?" Westover asked . . . first time. (OH)

"We gotta move!" (OH)

"Mother of God,". . . "He's dead." (OH)

"When the tank's 90 fired . . . buildings," (OH)

60 "Just nerves," he said. Lilly's dead." (OH)

"cut a Marine in half" (OH)

"I remember the after-effects . . . the war." (OH)

"With the curve in the road, there was such heavy fire," (OH); the George Company men came up with several novel solutions.

61 "Someone threw out the grenades . . . withdrawal." (OH)

"First Sergeant, how about taking . . . McKenna.) (OH)

"Don't fire until I tell you too." (OH)

"I made it clear if the enemy fired . . . recalled. (OH)

62 "someone got trigger happy and fired into the tunnel," recalled Hems. (OH)

"Now they're not going to come . . . 'em all." (OH)

"You stupid son of a bitch. Do you want to die?" (OH)

"I felt bad about it . . . teenager." (OH)

"Later, Hems would recap . . . the fuck up!" (OH)

"My boondockers were coated . . . stench," (OH)

"I wanted to take them prisoner . . . win wars." (OH); I will never forget Rocco telling me this in the living room of his home.

CHAPTER 9: NORTH KOREAN COUNTERATTACK

63 "Tanks! Tanks! Tanks!" (OH)

"The fire team began to call in mortar . . . Banks. (OH)

"You will push your attack *now* . . . forces." (Vol. II, 262)

"The order went out exactly as General Almond . . . delay." (Vol. II, 262)

64 "Son." Known for his aggressive . . . the Dread," Appleman refers to his "power, brusque manner, and sometimes arbitrary actions." (Roy Appleman, *Escaping the*

Trap: The U.S. Army X Corps in Northwest Korea (College Station, TX: Texas A&M Press, 2000))

"He [Almond] and O.P. [Smith] just didn't get . . . division should." (Edwin Simons, *Frozen Chosin: U.S. Marines at the Changjin Reservoir*, 4 (Washington, DC: U.S. Marine Corps Historical Division, 200))

"I want you to coordinate your attack . . . jump off." (Heinl, 233)

65 "inadequate." (Heinl, 233)

"You could hear the clanking of the T-34's . . . street," (OH)

"landed unexploded on a Marine's shelter . . . post." (OH); Walerski, Sagan

"Friendlies coming in! (OH)

"I could hear a tank coming up closer . . . run faster." (OH); Edward's e-history.

"All of the sudden, Edwards . . . my head," (OH)

66 "Does anybody have any M1 ammo?" (OH)

"I never wanted to be caught unprepared . . . the barrier," (OH)

"As I was reaching for the extra bandolier, the T-34 fired another round," (OH)

"I reached for him, but I knew he was . . . July." (OH)

"Son, if you load, I'll fire." (OH)

67 "It backed up in an arc and . . . wall," (OH)

"to stop it from firing and . . . firing." (OH)

"We were on the phone all night," (OH)

In the maelstrom, a small George Company . . . Platoon (I interviewed surviving members of the Collin's patrol and Mr. Collin's wife. Collins passed away several years ago.)

68 "his brains slid out," (OH)

"He changed positions with me and saved my life." (OH)

CHAPTER 10: RETROGRADE

69 "fearless" and "liked to get into trouble," (OH)

"I remember looking inside of the hatches . . . seats." (OH)

70 "Our objective was to cross over . . . side of it," (OH)

"We had a stumbled upon the royal palace . . . inside." (OH)

71 "There was blood all over the place. . . . arms and legs." (OH)

"We didn't know who they really were. . . . the story. (OH)

"They took him around a corner, and the shot rang out," (OH)

"security service" . . . "butt-stroked" (OH)

72 "Drive over that SOB if he doesn't move." (Sloan, 300).

"Three months to the day after the North Koreans . . . were broken." X Corps Communiqué 5, number 1445, Sept. 26, 1950, *New York Times* during that time period.

Mr. President, by the grace of a merciful Providence . . . your constitutional responsibilities. (Heinl, 254–255)

73 Several shards of broken glass hit . . . ceremony. (Vol. II, 284)

"We love you as the savior of our race . . . Korean people?" (MacArthur, 356)

Mr. President, by the grace of a merciful Providence . . . your constitutional responsibilities. (Heinl, 254–255)

On September 27, President Truman authorized MacArthur . . . territories. (JCS 92801, National Archives)

74 "I found a barbershop," recalled Hock . . . cover me." (OH)

"Where are you from?" Hock . . . the cheese?" (OH)

"I still have one of them, which has burn marks on its edges," (OH)

"Everyone had a sword . . . pretty cocky," (OH); it seemed that nearly everyone found a sword, including the FO team; see photo of Clark Henry in the photo section.

75 "Bellhops!" The army belted back . . . chicken shit." (OH); nearly a dozen men I interviewed fondly remember this scene.

"Who's in charge of this outfit?" . . . grenade?" (OH)

CHAPTER 11: WONSAN

76 "Get the men into formation," (OH); several members of G Company recall Hallawell's watch being the only working watch in First Platoon.

"I had a great affinity for these men," (OH)

77 This dumpy, pear-shaped guy from H and S Company is going to lead us? (OH)

"We didn't think much of him . . . Company." (OH)

This isn't the typical spit-and-polish officer. This guy looks frumpy. (OH)

"began having weight problems" (Tom Barlett, "It Might Have Been Different if Col. Lewis B. Puller Said 'No!'" *Leatherneck Magazine*, 46, November 1986)

"I want to go over. I want to fight," . . . a captain?" (Leatherneck)

78 "Sir, we have no more special services gear." . . . not play." (Leatherneck)

"Would history have been altered if Col. Louis B. Puller had answered 'No'?" (Leatherneck); The *Leatherneck* article asks a compelling question. But the reader might ask, after reading *Give Me Tomorrow*, what if Task Force Drysdale failed to break through the Chinese and George Company and the other elements of the task force were not able to reinforce East Hill? Several historians have ignored O. P.

Smith's own words, which stated that while the cost was significant, the elements of Task Force Drysdale that did break through played a "significant role" in the defense of Hagaru. This also provides the seed for the nature of this untold story.

79 "I got the impression initially . . . requested to do." (Simons, 70 and also OH)

80 "We were just anxious. . . get on land." (OH)

"big deal," (OH)

81 "Ha! We got here before the Marines this time!" (OH)

"That pig would sure be good after . . . part do we take?" (OH)

"We'll give you all that food for the pig." (OH)

82 "He wanted the pig's head," recalled Harbula. (OH)

"It was really good food; everyone had a pork chop . . . the tankers." (OH)

CHAPTER 12: MAJON-NI: LUCK OF THE DRAW

83 "We need a platoon to take prisoners . . . other supplies," (OH)

"The charismatic platoon leader accepted . . . shirking." (OH)

84 "defensive position at Majon-ni . . . , this road-net." CG 1st MarDiv message to CO 1st Marine Division. 3/1 Action Report, 1 Jan 1951, Ridge, 3–5. The report is located at the National Archives and hereafter referred to as (*3/1 Special Action Report,* January 1951, Ridge. Hereafter SAR II.).

"control roads to the north, south, . . . and Wonsan." (SAR II)

85 "ambush alley." (OH)

86 "I'm really not quite sure why we were chosen. But our part of the perimeter wasn't seeing any action, so we were asked to join Second Platoon that day," (OH)

Please try something, go ahead, so I can shoot ya, he thought. (OH)

"We hated the North Koreans; . . . around Seoul," (OH)

"scared" (OH)

87 "widow makers." The Marines called them "burp guns," (OH); I am a gun collector.

88 "with their eyes open, in the middle of the road." (OH)

"I hit several of them, I know it . . . machine gun? (OH)

"Let's get out of here!" (OH); confirmed by several George veterans.

"I was in the back of the truck when two guys . . . burp guns." (OH)

89 Hock "cut loose" (OH)

"Brooks, the man next to me, was hit," (OH)

"shaking like a leaf." (OH)

"We gotta get the hell out of here . . . on the back!" (OH)

"I can sure try." (OH)

"Don't move until I tap on the cab of the truck" [indicating he was ready with the machine gun]. (OH)

90 "We kept up a steady stream of fire . . . a lot of fire," (OH)

"unconscious," (OH)

"We're going to get our boys out of there." (OH)

"Don't worry about your buddy; he'll be okay," (OH)

91 "You ain't getting out of here that easy." (OH)

"reducing visibility to almost zero" . . . several mines," (OH); (SAR, 6)

92 "The prisoners caused no trouble and . . . as prisoners." (SAR II, 9)

George Company, took a total of 1,395 prisoners. (SAR II, 9)

CHAPTER 13: GOLDBRICKING IT

93 As the men made their way through the courtyard . . . 1938 Nash automobile. (The church scene comes from the oral histories of multiple George Company veterans including Roberts, who vividly recalls the ruined house of worship.)

94 "Put all of your gear in front of you." (OH)

"Listen up, people, open up your mess kits . . . any extra noise," (OH); Roberts

"whose voice you could hear over a mile away," (OH)

"I was still in a state of shock from what happened at Majon-ni . . . a machine gun," (OH)

95 At this point, 70 percent of George Company . . . and NCOs alike. (OH)

These men don't know shit from Shinola, (OH)

"Sarge, this guy came all the way from division . . . the service," (OH)

"Are you sure these guys are all Jewish?" (OH)

"Yes, they are, Rabbi," Smokey shot back . . . their hats on." (OH)

"Bob" Camarillo walked into camp . . . staff sergeant," (OH); the two men have been friends for sixty years and confirmed each other's recollection of the preceding account.

96 "Don't let it happen again." (OH)

"We were very nervous sitting on gasoline barrels all day," (OH)

"Do you want to survey your weapons?" . . . Marine lingo. (OH)

97 "Everything that came from the Army . . . commandeer it!" (OH)

"If you do, take off your leather sling . . . with theirs." (OH)

"like starving locusts" (OH)

"Jewel was an expert scrounger, and a real piece of work," (OH)

"Apparently, Jewel being the piece he was . . . rail yard." (OH)

"Take it back!" (OH); confirmed by Banks and Camarillo

"The two looked like movie stars," (OH)

"When we heard the firing . . . and rolled," (OH)

98 "All the old souls from Inchon and Seoul bailed off the train in a heartbeat," (OH)

"the attack." (OH)

"Nobody quite knew what they were firing . . . civilians," (OH)

"Cease fire!" "Cease fire!" (OH)

The firing stopped . . . captured enemy weapon (OH)

"Lieutenant, what are you doing here?" (OH)

"I would have followed that man anywhere," (OH)

"Next, the Congresh." (OH)

99 "Dick, you've seen enough." (OH)

"made everything slimy." (OH)

"He turned and looked at us, and . . . ominous look," (OH)

"That ominous look was all that . . . the enemy!" (OH)

"That man ruled the roost, even our officers were afraid of him." (OH)

"When I heard that China had entered . . . the changed." (OH)

I knew it was possible that we might make . . . Christmas," (OH)

100 As is so often the case in American military history . . . new war." (OH)

"Quite often they waved flags, or handkerchiefs. . . to see us," (OH)

"I will get us some more gas," volunteered one of the men at the table. (OH)

The man returned with a full jerry can . . . in here," (OH)

101 "Evacuated to the rear, he returned to active duty several months later. (I interviewed Jim Byrne, who provided the details on this George Company warrior's tragic death.)

CHAPTER 14: THE ROAD NORTH

102 "Saddle up!" (OH)

"Most of my time from Majon-ni . . . was surreal," (OH)

103 "I remember seeing the remains of a damaged helicopter . . . make it." (OH)

"Was this the dog that had not yet barked?" . . . on the other side? (David Halberstam, *The Coldest Winter*, 435 (New York: Hyperion, 2007)

"Victory was won in Korea." (OH)

104 However, the Chinese had clearly signaled their intention . . . of self-defense." (Jung Chang and Jon Halliday, *Mao: The Unknown Story*, 378 (London: Jonathan Cape, 2005))

MacArthur's staff and the general himself failed to connect the dots . . . in great strength. According to notes from the JCS compiled by General Omar Bradley, submitted to Senate Committees in 1951, MacArthur informed the president that "only 50,000 to 60,000 could have gotten across the Yalu River."

A small CIA station located in Japan . . . People's Liberation Army (PLA). [According to OSS interviews I conducted and also mentioned in (Halberstam). See also (Goulden).]

"They have no Air Force. Now that we have bases . . . the greatest slaughter." Notes from the JCS compiled by General Omar Bradley, submitted to Senate Committees in 1951.

105 Another 125,000 or more cleverly positioned themselves around the First Marine Division and X Corps. (Figures vary on the actual number of troops; on the low end, it is 125,000. Other sources state, however, that it was approximately 150,000.)

The Communists constructed a massive trap to "consume" UN troops. (Chang–Halliday) While some critics consider this book "biased" against a dictator who murdered millions of his own citizens, it nevertheless has published several cables between Stalin, Mao, and Kim. The cables are revealing and speak for themselves.

107 "It is snowing thicker than cow shit on the reservoir," [This section and scene is quoted from Russell Spurr, *Enter the Dragon: China's Undeclared War Against the U.S. in Korea 1950–1951*, 168–170 (New York: New Market Press, 1988.) Spurr's outstanding book provides the often ignored Chinese perspective on the war and stems from scores of interviews with Chinese commanders and his "20 visits to China."]

"grind down" the Americans. (Chang-Halliday, 382)

He later told Stalin that after losing 100,000 Chinese soldiers . . . will back down." (Chang-Halliday, 383)

108 Mao planned for the long war . . . great masses." (Chang-Halliday, 383)

"The Chinese soldiers may be considered as volunteers and . . . the Chinese," (Chang-Halliday, 379)

Mao officially authorized a name change for the PLA . . . to help you." (Chang-Halliday, 379)

109 Mao had a lot of people he wanted to "get rid of." (Change-Halliday, 379) This statement is based on oral histories in this book from several Marines who encountered POWs who were former Nationalist Chinese soldiers. It is also confirmed in additional sources, including Change and Halliday's.

"the perfect chance to consign former Nationalist troops to . . . hanging back." (Chang-Halliday, 382–383)

Attacking in wave after wave, the first two waves of men . . . fallen comrades. (OH)

Battalion and regiment forces linked to the same ethnic and . . . 30,000 troops. (Vol. III, 86)

111 "In those days, it was like complete insanity in the Command," (Halberstam, 438)

"he was facing two entire Chinese Divisions." (Halberstam, 439)

Almond flatly stated, "That's impossible . . . North Korea!" (Halberstam, 439)

"We are still attacking and going all . . . stop you." (Halberstam, 439)

"Soon we will meet the American Marines . . . snakes in your homes." (Andrew Greer, *The New Breed: The Story of the U.S. Marines in Korea*, 234 (New York: Harper & Brothers, 1952))

"It looked like a giant circus . . . Koto-ri." (OH)

CHAPTER 15: THE ROAD TO HELL

112 "so each of us had one eye out watching for the enemy on either side." (OH)

"Get your asses up!" (OH)

113 "At 20 below zero . . . touching it," (OH)

a massive Chinese army of twelve infantry divisions . . . destroy them. (Various sources peg it between 120,000 and 150,000.) (Spurr, 167); (Vol. III)

"Once I learned we were being hit from . . . to die." (Russ Clay Blair, *The Forgotten War: America in Korea, 1950–1953* (New York: Times Books, 1987)); Martin Russ, *Breakout: The Chosin Reservoir Campaign, Korea 1950*, 270 (New York: Fromm International, 1999))

Murray issued a simple order to his men: "All hands. Make sure every shot counts." (Russ)

114 Hagaru-ri with its supply dumps . . . at all costs. (Vol. III, 197)

Hagaru-ri had to be reinforced immediately . . . infantrymen." (Vol. III, 235)

115 "I'm Lieutenant Colonel Drysdale, and I'm here to take you to Hagaru-ri." (OH)

A Marine who was near the George Company command post at the time, recalled Drysdale introducing himself: "They [the British] were spit-and-polish and professional, clean shaven. We were dirty and combat worn." (OH)

"Task Force Drysdale," a 900-man plus task force, which included 41 Independent Royal Marine Commando, George Company (Vol. III, 228). Task Force Drysdale consisted of an estimated strength of 922 men and 141 vehicles. The task force lost 75 vehicles to the Chinese and had approximately 321 battle casualties including 162 KIA.

"A task is all we ask," (OH)

116 "danger close," (A term describe to describe when fire is too close to friendly units.)

"The napalm was awesome. Fireballs . . . 300 yards away," (OH)

"Let's give it a bloody go!"(OH)

"A sea of green berets bobbed up and down, as the Royal Marines assaulted the hill," (OH)

"Be calm, my boy." "Shit was flying all around both of us," (OH)

"Leslie, Leslie, where are you? Leslie, go out and strike out that gun." (OH)

"Leslie looked about fifteen years old," (OH)

"We were on the ridgeline going up. . . machine gun fire." (OH)

117   "Get your asses up!" (OH)

"the snow erupted" (OH)

"Tillman's down!" (OH)

"I saw his steel helmet tumbling . . . moaning;" (OH)

"I was looking straight at his face. . . in the snow." (OH)

"Fuckin' gimme me that!" (OH)

118   "He hit it!" "He hit it!" (OH)

"It was nip and tuck until First Sergeant Rocco . . . of the hill." (OH) (Vol. III, 226)

"Saddle up!" (OH)

CHAPTER 16: ROADBLOCKS

119   "The mortar went through the canvas cover . . . the truck," (OH)

120   "grouped together like a football huddle . . . bananas," (OH)

"We're going back toward Hungnam," . . . reassurance," (OH)

This is the end of the road. (OH)

Any second they are going to open the doors, spray the inside with machine-gun bullets, and hurl grenades, (OH)

"I often think about it, and to this day . . . ambulance," (OH)

121   "It was like the old Wild West as the Indians fired on the wagon train," (OH)

"We would have to get behind the tires of the truck . . . went down," (OH)

"almost like a mother hen." . . . fucking rifles!" (OH)

"exploded, sending splinters of wood everywhere." (OH)

Bullets [were] coming through the canvas covers . . . and prayed. (OH)

122   "When we got on and off the trucks, that's when . . . available truck." (OH)

"I don't think we are going to make it . . . Joe." (OH)

"A cornered rat will fight fiercely if it is . . . the attacker." (Greer, 96)

"The opinionated young man," (Simons, 61)

123   "Every time the tanks shot, the world fell . . . it was a nine-hour fire fight." (OH)

124 "Am I okay?" Powers pulled gauze from his . . . a scratch." (OH)

"Let's get ahead!" . . . "along!" (OH)

"We had to break through to Hagaru-ri . . . damn war." (OH)

"Fifteen or twenty yards and they . . . the Pacific," (OH)

CHAPTER 17: "AT ALL COSTS"

126 "Press on at all costs." (OH and Vol. III, 231)

"Very well, then. We'll give them a show." (Russ, 234)

127 "infantry elements mixed with headquarters troops." (OH)

"Hell Fire Valley" (OH)

128 "I was so mad. I was so goddamn mad . . . something about it!" (OH)

"Get your guinea ass up here, and go . . . around, (OH)

"It seemed like we hit the entire Chinese army . . . the masses." (OH)

"Bullets were flying everywhere," (OH)

Bove heroically continued running up and . . . for ammo" (OH)

Suddenly, PFC William Baugh screamed, "Grenade!" (OH)

129 "I really miss that Jeep. It had my . . . the coat," (Leatherneck, 47–48)

"As the trucks were going by, my first sergeant . . . and stop." (Leatherneck, 48)

"mount up." In the corner of his eye . . . a Chinaman." (OH)

"The Chinese were all around us. . . . several times," (OH)

130 "all hell broke loose." OH

There was a wall of machine gun fire . . . where we'd been. (OH)

Unflappable, Captain Sitter directed his men . . . face out!" (OH); (Leatherneck, 49)

"I'm hit. You now have command." (OH)

Sitter responded, "All right. I'm going to get the tanks . . . anybody behind" (Leatherneck, 50–51)

"A truck loaded with men got hit with . . . a ravine." (OH)

"I was afraid the truck would roll over on me . . . mountainside," (Edward's e-history; my oral history with him.)

"I had on four layers of clothes, plus a parka . . . hold me up," (Edward's e-history; my oral history with him.)

131 "It was pitch dark except for the occasional light from tracers." (Edward's e-history; my oral history with him.)

I'm captured, thought Edwards. Chinese were . . . make it out of this." (Edward's e-history; my oral history with him.)

"Let's go, let's go!" (OH)

132 "After the last roadblock, I saw a tent, and lights for the airfield," (OH)

"The lights for the airfield—they were . . . the world." (OH)

"You could put your goddamn fist . . . stupid?" (OH)

Using weapons no larger than 75 mm recoilless rifles . . . break through. (Vol. III, 232–233)

133 "He was no more than eighteen years old . . . lost in Korea." (OH)

"Initially, I demanded the CCF [Communist Chinese Forces] surrender," (OH); I also had a fine interview with Col. Preston McLaughlin, who added to the narrative. John was his uncle and the man who inspired him to join the Corps. (OH and Vol. III, 233)

134 The Chinese accepted his surrender with those terms. (Vol. III, 233)

CHAPTER 18: HAGARU

135 "Jeez, are we glad to see you!" (OH)

Olmstead responded, "Why?" . . . we've been?" (OH)

136 "Klondike mining camp" (OH)

"41 Commando present for duty." (Simons, 70)

Boom! Boom! Boom! (OH)

I had jumped into another truck and . . . medical condition. (OH)

137 "Your back hurt so badly on the frozen ground . . . Camarillo. (OH)

"Cough, cough!" A faint sound from the . . . "Cough." (OH)

My God! He's alive! he thought. (OH)

138 "Things became very hazy for me. . . 118th." (OH); Zullo letter to Powers.

Air and artillery power pulverized Chinese . . . some units. (Vol. II, 236); (SAR II)

"O. P. Smith . . . 300 seasoned infantrymen." (Vol. III, 235) Remarkably, numerous authors fail to appreciate the significance of Task Force Drysdale. Their words confound the veterans of George Company. "Attempting to reinforce Hagaru, Task Force Drysdale has been massacred." (Blair, 509) "In view of the disaster which had befallen Task Force Drysdale the day before." (Blair, 511) "With the demise of Task Force Drysdale." (Hammel 353) "The road to the north of Koto-ri had been closed by the destruction of Task Force Drysdale." (Hammel 357) All of these misstatements contribute to the untold story of George Company.

CHAPTER 19: EAST HILL

139 "They were so hard you had to leave them in your mouth . . . your teeth," (OH)

"Now you see that hill over there." (OH)

"That's our next job!" Sitter proclaimed . . . secure it." (OH)

How are we going to do that with this shot-up company . . . mountain? (OH)

141 "George Company really saved our asses," (OH)

"We screamed the rebel yell at the Chinese and fired back at them," (OH)

"all over the place." (OH)

142 "He was in terrible shape. . . quilted uniform," (OH)

"kid from Howe Company" (OH)

"Shoot that son of a bitch. He killed one of my buddies." (OH)

"I think we shot him enough," (OH)

"we looked each other in the eye for . . . shooting him." (OH)

"We had to lay across the ground . . . dig in," (OH)

"We didn't have any mortars or machine guns . . . attacked in force," (OH)

"They had been blown to pieces . . . out of his dungarees," (OH)

"I made my peace that night," . . . get out of this. (OH)

"We were sacrificial lambs," recalled Leibee . . . "I am." (OH)

"Then, you're relieved," (OH)

143 "I didn't want to turn it in," recalled the sergeant . . . all over again." (OH)

"a sharp left turn to attack either side of the ridge." (OH)

"My lungs and throat burned from the bone-cold . . . mummies," (OH)

"The bullets were like angry hornets hitting . . . getting it." (OH)

"[We] hacked away at the frozen earth with . . . step forward." (OH)

144 "Let's go, Joe." (OH)

"Take it easy. There is plenty of time to get even." (OH)

Initially, we were held in reserve . . . overwhelming fire. (OH)

145 The platoons formed a reverse L like line along the top ridge. (Vol. III, 238)

"That was the only entrenching tool in First Platoon," . . . was so hard," (OH)

"We were exhausted and we knew the Chinese . . . for protection" (OH)

"Get me a dead body." (OH)

146 "Get your ass down!" barked Hock . . . went flying," (OH)

"I'm hit. I can't move." (OH)

Wham! (OH)

"One round hit four of us," (OH)

I'm so thirsty, (OH)

"The sip would have killed me," (OH)

"You should have died on that hill." (OH)

"What are you going to do? You're going . . . that simple." (OH)

CHAPTER 20: "WE'RE GOING TO FIGHT LIKE HELL!"

147 "I'll never forget Powers's face as he . . . was yesterday," (OH)

"the hill literally moving." Like "an army . . . upon us," (OH)

Sha! Sha! Sha! [Kill!] (OH)

148 "Holy shit! There are gooks all over the place!" (OH)

"In my dreams, I've been fighting on that hill . . . green tint." (OH)

"glowed like a neon light" from thousands . . . barrel." (OH)

"crimson" (OH)

Clack! . . . Misfire. (OH)

"I survived five campaigns in the Korean War . . . I could do," (OH)

"Pull back!" yelled an officer. (OH)

"They were all over us," recalled Harbula . . . "they stop, period." (OH)

They're all dead, (OH)

"Bob, don't leave me." Harbula turned . . . out of here." (OH)

149 "I know three men that predicted their own death within three hours." (OH)

"I won't live to see the top of the hill." . . . come daylight." (OH)

"More ammo!" (OH)

"Oh, my God!" (OH)

"When Bobby went down. I passed him . . . him out." (OH)

I have to get them back to his family. (OH)

"There is no way to explain how I felt about . . . "Bobby is dead!" (OH)

"PFC Farr! Is Hallawell wounded . . . the hill." (OH)

"You are not," Sitter snapped. "If he is dead . . . hill, period." (OH)

150 "I jumped on him with my bayonet . . . trousers!" (OH)

Mortar shells dropped from the sky and detonated . . . top of us," (OH); Henry's account is confirmed by the surviving members of the FO team.

"They were all over the place. They were . . . that night." (OH)

"Chinese were everywhere—it was a . . . shoot him." (OH)

151 "I think I'm hit." In a somewhat comical . . . me know." (OH); I have Walerski's official Purple Heart documentation confirming the event took place on East Hill on the night on November 30–December 1.

"Sitter told him [Henry] he was in charge," . . . over the place." (OH); I have Henry's original Bronze Star documentation confirming his leadership on East Hill.

On the back side of the *L,* defending the lower . . . and firing," (OH)

"positioned on a slope perpendicular to the crest . . . Chinese." (OH)

"The combat was so close. I was blasting . . . around us." (OH)

"Lincoln!" Enos replied, "Abraham." . . . "bayonets and rifle butts." (OH); (Leatherneck, 49–50)

"I carried a pistol: that's all I had . . . rifle," (Leatherneck, 49–50)

152 "They were right on top of us as we slaughtered . . . ammunition." (OH)

"It was fun killing 'em until we realized later . . . you'll lose 'em," (OH)

"If the machine guns were firing, we knew we could hold." (OH)

"My left glove and gauntlet came clean off . . . bleeding." (OH)

As Roberts and his foxhole buddy made their way . . . 2447720 out there. To hell with old 2447720, (OH)

153 Roberts called to Piccolo, "Follow my voice and . . . my voice." (OH)

"Thank God, you made it. Go up and take over the First and Second Platoons," (OH)

"Dark shadows of the enemy seemed all . . . remembered Carey. (OH)

"dropping between ten and twelve Chinese." (OH)

154 "Keep 'em coming. They are coming fast!" (OH)

"I'm doing the best I can. You just keep 'em as accurate as you can," (OH)

"One—Two! One—Two!" (OH)

"Wambatu!" "Wambatu!" (OH)

"They were mingling all around us . . . my M1 Garand," (OH)

"Captain, what happens if we're surrounded?" (OH)

"We're going to fight like hell!" (OH)

155 "Sarge, I killed a lot of people." (OH)

"That's the business we are in," (OH)

"a whole lot of dead" (OH)

"had to be picked up with a shovel." The man's . . . mortar round." (Video tape from Fred Hems in which he and his brother were interviewed by a family member); (OH)

"Who is this?" (OH)

My God, it's my close friend. (OH)

156 "Made in China" and a cigarette case. (OH)

"Here's Bobby's watch. You know the promise we made to each other." (OH)

"One of our sergeants ordered us to finish off any survivors," (OH)

"I refused the order! The sergeant went . . . see them!'" (OH)

"War is hell and some things that happen . . . killing." (OH)

CHAPTER 21: HOLDING THE LINE

157 "Has anybody seen my brother?" (OH)

"I was really lucky," (OH)

158 By December 1, it was only 40 percent complete . . . feet long. (Vol. III, 245–246)

159 He later became a high school principal. (OH)

"Retreat, hell, we're just attacking in a new direction." (Vol. III, 334)

Time described the Eighth Army's rout . . . American history . . ." (Vol. III, 334); *Time,* December 11, 1950; *Newsweek,* December 11, 1950.

160 "Litz the blitz" (OH)

"In our order for the march south, there are . . . Hagaru." (Russ, 305); Russ, a Marine, spent years interviewing many of the key commanders who are now deceased.

Lieutenant Colonel Ray Murray, CO of . . . us and them." (Russ, 304)

161 "Only half of them would land anywhere . . . the target area." (Ron Wyman e-history and unpublished memoir. I also extensively interviewed the retired sergeant major at the 2008 George Company reunion and via telephone.)

"I would throw out an illumination grenade about twenty yards . . . the attackers." (OH)

"I heard voices in the gulch over to our left." (OH); confirmed by Camerillo

"Can we go see what is going on?" Henry asked . . . men." (OH)

162 "I'm not sure if we hit anything, but the talking stopped and they dispersed" (OH)

"I started making my way up the hill, but . . . get anywhere." (OH)

"No, son, you're in no condition. . . flown out." (OH)

163 "I put them further to the right because I didn't . . . gone, bugged out." (OH); (Ron Wyman e-history and unpublished memoir)

"Where's the bug-out route if we get overrun?" . . . that moves." (OH); Powers

"I survived the Battle of the Bulge, but this is worse." (Interview with General Olmsted, January 2010)

164 "Here comes Colonel Faith in his shiny helmet . . . the rest of us." (Russ, 275)

[GIs] were burned to a crisp, their skin . . . shoot them. (Russ, 275)

165 "Faith extended his right arm toward the . . . as well." (Russ, 277)

"Shoot anyone who tries to run away," Faith barked. (Russ, 277)

"Far from hindering the escape of the Army . . . Oriental mentality." (Vol. III, 244)

166 "You people will shape up and look sharp. We are going in like United States Marines." (Russ 277)

"looked like zombies" (OH)

"It's the Fifth and Seventh coming in," (OH)

"I heard the Marine hymn in the distance . . . on the hill." (OH)

167 Inside Hagaru-ri, Lieutenant Colonel Murray . . . could do it." (Russ, 361)

For the first time in weeks, most of the First Marine Division . . . mustache in my life." (OH)

I had about four layers of clothes on . . . fire also. (OH)

168 "kidneys froze." (OH)

"I cried, I've never cried so hard in my life just trying to relieve myself," (OH)

"We received a replacement who had . . . the line with us." (OH)

"That night a rumor went around the company . . . Mongolian Calvary?" (OH)

"Do you take out the horse or the rider first?" (OH)

"They came charging toward us at dawn, a daytime attack," (OH)

169 "There was firing from the Chinese . . . on them." (OH)

"Several of them had feet that were elephantine . . . a lot worse." (OH)

CHAPTER 22: BREAKOUT

170 We're going to hold our position until the Seventh Marines . . . like Marines. (Russ, 361)

171 For one thing, I kept wondering if Koto-ri . . . the trestle below it. (Russ, 278)

172 "The enemy could not have picked a better spot . . . other way out. (Russ, 277)

"It was a damn serious situation," recalled Lieutenant Colonel Partridge . . . "Never heard of it, General." (Russ, 357)

173 "There were fires going off and explosions everywhere," (OH)

"As we sat in company formation in the middle of Hagaru-ri . . . it in stride." (OH); Ron Wyman e-history

"As I looked up at the hill, I remembered the five-day . . . for sixty years." (OH)

174 "To this day, I don't know how we did it . . . to boot camp," (OH)

"I recall lifting the helmet off a wounded Marine and . . . to beat." (OH)

"I admired those artillerymen. Normally the 105s . . . in place," (OH)

Why didn't they take the boots? (OH)

175 "Those sons of bitches probably got my Jamison." . . . grandmother.) (OH)

"It was really uncomfortable, two guys that were six feet tall . . . about home," (OH)

As the men poured in, the garrison swelled . . . Commandos. (Vol. III, 307)

"We took some incoming mortar rounds near the Brockways . . . out of there," (Russ, 414)

176 Using Chinese prisoners to move the ties . . . problem. When the ties ran out, frozen corpses of Chinese soldiers were placed in the crib by the POWs. (Eric Hammel, *Chosin, Heroic Ordeal of the Korean War*, 391 (New York: Vanguard Press, 1981))

"It was like opening a farm gate . . . chasm]." (Russ, 416)

CHAPTER 23: THE LIVING WALKED. THE DEAD RODE

177 "Don't take our pictures! Don't take our pictures!" (OH); Powers and Hems

The Third Platoon, not so camera shy, said, "Take ours!" (OH)

178 "quiet Marine who never said anything, but did his duty." (OH)

In Duncan's words: Dawn was just over the horizon. A Marine . . . to thaw. (David Douglas Duncan, *This is War!*, 144, New York: Harper Brothers, 1951)

"What would you want if you could have any wish?" (Duncan)

"That photo represents all of us who were there." (OH) I had the privilege of interviewing Mr. Duncan; he is a living legend. I'm extremely grateful that he generously allowed my publisher to use the photo for the cover of this book.

179 "It was the one time Captain Sitter actually . . . sleeping bags," (OH)

"I remember standing up in my bag with my M1 Garand in my hand. We needed the bags just to stay alive." (OH)

"threadbare," (OH)

"I'll never forget the expression on Carlos's face as we tried in vain to stay warm," (OH)

"Fred, I just can't stay awake." (OH); letter written by Fred Hems to Carl Sitter.

Meekly, Hems responded, "Nash, I know . . . our bags." (OH)

"surrounded by hundreds of Chinese soldiers," remembered Hems. . . overrun." (OH)

180 "Where are the grenades?" (OH)

"Give me your carbine!" (OH)

"How far can you fire to your right?" Hems barked . . . was dead." (OH)

As a flare went up, Hems glanced at his watch . . . assistant!" (OH)

"Where the hell are your gloves?" (OH)

"I took them off and can't find them." (OH)

"I killed Red Nash. You're going to have to work the gun; I can't do it." (OH)

181 "Give me tomorrow," (OH)

"Here they come!" (OH)

Clack! . . . Thud! (OH)

I'll never forget thinking to myself, God . . . my life," (OH)

Ping! (OH)

182 "I was sure I was hit," (OH)

"cut loose" another burst. Daniels's bullets blew a hole "about the size of my fist" (OH)

"blowing out the Chinaman's backbone." (OH)

By dawn, the attack was over . . . over 350 Chinese. (Vol. III, 324)

"There were thousands of them," recalled Powers. (OH)

"It was wild. People were shooting . . . we'll shoot!" (OH)

183 "The Chinese are amongst us!" (OH)

"It was like a fucking bowling alley. Bodies, limbs, and heads were flying everywhere!" (OH); despite the fact the Chinese used the civilians as human shields and civilian deaths occurred, the U.S. Navy evacuated tens of thousands of civilians, a remarkable achievement given the nature of the battle.

"They were swarming all over us, and we were fighting them off hand to hand." (OH)

"I shot him in the face with my .45, and the bullet split apart his nose," (OH)

"I wrestled him to the ground and . . . popping out."(OH)

"We're pulling out. Get on the tank!" (OH)

Boom! (OH)

"everything turned white," (OH)

184 "For the rest of my days, I see that Chinese soldier . . . strangle me," (OH)

CHAPTER 24: THE FINAL PUSH

185 "It was like a sheet of ice going down . . . the abyss," (OH)

"Don't look down!" somebody yelled . . . chasm," (OH)

186 "I tried not to look down, but it was absolutely frightening," (OH)

After the final elements of the convoy . . . "bulletproof."(OH) Hems

"Our steps got smarter. Puller made . . . Marines!" (OH)

"Sorry you can't have those. They're wired to be blown." (OH)

"We fuckin' want 'em." . . . want." (OH)

"In twenty minutes, we were all sick as dogs," (OH)

"It was orderly chaos, but as PFCs . . . get us out," (OH)

187 "The nicest thing in my life was being on that ship." (OH)

"It was finally warm," (OH)

"You men are Marines right? Come with me. Take my bunk." (OH)

"I decided to take an icy cold saltwater . . . washed away." (OH)

Who could be making snowmen . . . next spring." (Spurr, 265)

EPILOGUE

189 Bobby, I'm here, Bruce Farr thought . . . your place. (OH) Farr

190 "I went to tell them good-bye." (OH)

INDEX